The Active Reader

Course work for English

Mike Davis and Alan Pound

to Frances
to Mum and Dad

Text © Mike Davis and Alan Pound 1992
Design and artwork © Simon and Schuster Education 1992
Photographs © The sources credited

First published in 1992 in Great Britain by
Simon & Schuster Education
Campus 400, Maylands Avenue
Hemel Hempstead, Herts HP2 7EZ

British Library Cataloguing in Publication Data
Davis, Michael *1925*−
  The active reader.
  1. English literature
  I. Title II. Pound, Alan
  828

ISBN 0−7501−0183−0

Typeset in Sabon
by Colset Pte Ltd, Singapore
Printed in Singapore by Kin Keong Printing Co. Pte. Ltd.

Contents

Acknowledgements

Preface

Acknowledgments

A number of people were very generous with their time and their ideas and we would like to thank: the English Department at Queen's Park High School, Blackburn, especially to Bob Levey, Head of Communications, for initiating the project through the development of *Love and Hate*, and Janis Livesey and Sandra Pledger for trialling and feedback; the Headteacher, Alan Sharples, for agreeing so readily to a term of professional updating for Alan; the English Department at St Martin's College, Lancaster, especially Hugh Roberts in charge of the English PGCE course, and David Webb for assistance with the *Glossary of literary terms*; John Crewdson, Vice-Principal of St Martin's College; the Library staff at both institutions; Val Randall from Mansfield High School, Brierfield, for the *Wider reading list*; Raw Cotton Theatre Company, Blackburn (Elisabeth Bond and Peter Warde) for *On writing a play*; Chris Morley and Phil Nicholson, (Creative Director and Managing Director) of Quad Advertising, Preston, for a candid interview and the creative brief; Bill Deller, Advisor for English for Lancashire LEA for resolving the problems of copyright ownership. Sarah Blood and Susan Randall of Stoke-on-Trent were appreciative readers and Louise Tipping and Tim Long made useful comments and trialled some of the units. Tina Foster from Chipping Jacqueline Harris of Lancaster and Stephanie Davis from Blackburn were patient and meticulous proof-readers and we are grateful to them for the time they gave up. Finally, without the co-operation of Lancashire LEA this project would not have got off the ground: to the officers responsible, many thanks.

The authors and publishers would like to thank the following for permission to use copyright material:

extract from 'We Have Waited too Long for our Freedom' reproduced by permission of the African National Congress; extract from *Who's Afraid of Virginia Woolf* by Edward Albee (Jonathon Cape) reproduced by permission of the author and the Random Century Group; extract from *The Monocled Mutineer* by William Allison and John Fairley reproduced by permission of Quartet Books Ltd; 'The Responsibility' by Peter Appleton reproduced by permission of *New Statesman*; 'The Unknown Citizen' reproduced by permission of Faber and Faber Ltd from *Collected Poems* by W H Auden; 'Death on a Live Wire' by Michael Baldwin reproduced by permission of the author and A M Heath & Co Ltd from *Death on a Live Wire and Stepping from a Sixth Storey Window*; 'Mohammed Ibrahim Speaks' by Martha Beidler reproduced by permission of McGrawHill Book Company (UK) Ltd from *The Honey and the Gall: Poems of Married Life*; extract from *The Resistible Rise of Arturo Ui* by Bertholt Brecht (trs by Ralph Manheim) reproduced by permission of Methuen; 'Communique to a Child' by Jim Burns reproduced by permission of Salamander Books Ltd from *The Goldfish Speaks from Beyond the Grave*; 'A Happening' and 'Forgive me for Making you Weep' by Nina Cassian reproduced by permission of Forest Books from *Call Yourself Alive?•Love Poems*; 'Lonely Hearts' and 'At 3am' reproduced by permission of Faber and Faber Ltd from *Making Cocoa for Kingsley Amis* by Wendy Cope; extract from *The English Language* by David Crystal reproduced by permission of Penguin Books Ltd; 'Come to Mecca' by Farukh Dhondy reproduced by permission of Macmillan Education; 'Pictures in the Paper' from *The Sad Mountain* by Tom Earley (Chatto and Windus) reproduced by permission of the Random Century Group; extract from *Murder in the Cathedral* by T S Eliot reproduced by permission of Faber and Faber Ltd; 'New Bible Aims at Man in the Pew' (*The Guardian* 9/9/89) by John Ezard reproduced by permission of the author; 'When is a Freedom Fighter just another Terrorist' (*The Guardian* 15/11/89) by Nigel Fountain reproduced by permission of the author; 'Geography Lesson' by Zulfikar Ghose reproduced by permission of Macmillan London from *Jets in Orange*; 'The Destructors' by Graham Greene reproduced by permission of William Heinemann Ltd & The Bodley Head Ltd from *Twenty-one Stories*; *Against all Odds* (Greenpeace leaflet) reproduced by permission of Greenpeace Ltd; 'In the Midnight Hour' and 'What Shall we do with the Drunken Poet' by Adrian Henri reproduced by permission of Allison and Busby from *Collected Poems 1967–85*; 'The Centre of Attention' by Daniel Hoffman reproduced by permission of Robson Books from *Poe, Poe, Poe, Poe, Poe, Poe*; extract from *Out of the Doll's House* by Angela Holdsworth reproduced by permission of BBC Enterprises Ltd; 'Hillstone was Content' by Ted Hughes reproduced by permission of Faber and Faber Ltd from *Remains of Elmet*; 'Sonny's Lettah' by Linton Kwesi Johnson reproduced by permission of Race Today from *News from Babylon: The Chatto Book of Westindian-British Poetry*; 'High Wood' by Philip Johnstone reproduced by permission of *New Statesman*; 'Gotcha' from *Gimme Shelter* by Barrie Keefe reproduced by permission of Methuen Drama; extract from *South Africa* by Graham Leach reproduced by permission of Methuen; 'We will all go together when we go' by Tom Lehrer reproduced by permission of Eyre Methuen from *Too Many Songs*; extract from *The Grass is Singing* by Doris Lessing reproduced by permission of Grafton Books/Collins; extract from *No Easy Walk to Freedom* by Nelson Mandela reproduced by permission of International Defence & Aid Fund for Southern Africa Publications Ltd, 64 Essex Road, London N1 8LR; 'Catching up on Sleep' by Roger McGough reproduced by permission of Jonathon Cape Ltd from *In the Glassroom*; extract from *Coming of Age in Samoa* by Margaret Mead reproduced by permission of William Morrow & Co Inc; 'Appendix IV – Requirements in the Shelter' by Adrian Mitchell (Allison and Busby) reproduced by permission of The Peters Fraser & Dunlop Group Ltd from *On the Beach at Cambridge* (neither this nor any other of Adrian Mitchell's poems is to be used in connection with any examination whatsoever); 'The Combat' by Edwin Muir reproduced by permission of Faber and Faber Ltd from *Collected Poems*;

extract from *The Memoirs of Richard Nixon* by Richard Nixon reproduced by permission of Warner Books Inc; 'My Oedipus Complex' from *My Oedipus Complex and Other Stories* by Frank O'Connor reproduced by permission of Hamish Hamilton Ltd; extract from *1984* by George Orwell reproduced by permission of A M Heath and Co Ltd, the estate of the late Sonia Brownell Orwell and Martin Secker & Warburg Ltd; 'Daedalus and Icarus' from *Metamorphoses* by Ovid reproduced by permission of Penguin Books Ltd; extract from *The Revised English Bible* reproduced by permission of Oxford and Cambridge University Presses; 'Simple Lyric' by Brian Patten reproduced by permission of HarperCollins Publishers from *Storm Dance*; extract from *Understanding Parenthood and Child Care* by Margaret Picton reproduced by permission of Blackie & Son Ltd; 'Night Patrol' by Alan Ross reproduced by permission of the poet from *The War Decade: An Anthology of the 1940s*; letters to *The Guardian* reproduced by permission of the authors (Mike Hampson, Rebecca Bunting, Anne Serraillieu); 'White Hot' from *Forties' Child* by Tom Wakefield reproduced by permission of the author; 'The Heroines' by Penny Windsor reproduced by permission of The Women's Press from *No Holds Barred: The Raving Beauties Choose New Poems by Women*; extract from *The Final Days* by Bob Woodward and Carl Bernstein reproduced by permission of Hodder & Stoughton.

Every effort has been made to trace all the copyright holders, but if any have been inadvertently overlooked the publishers will be pleased to make the necessary arrangement at the first opportunity.

The quotations and definitions in the introductions to all the sections (apart from *Love and Hate*) are based on material in the *Concise Oxford English Dictionary*.

Photographs

Associated Press 88; BFI Stills, Posters and Designs 52, 124, 172; Fay Godwin/Network 115; Greenpeace 150; Hulton Picture Company 27, 38, 44, 49, 108, 121, 133, 135, 175, 179; IDAF Publications Ltd 91, 92, 95; Imperial War Museum 14, 130, 131; Irish Times 15; National Portrait Gallery 106; Nottinghamshire County Library Service 113; Photostage/Donald Cooper 200; Popperfoto 201; Quad Advertising and Marketing 141; Serpents Tail 193

Manchester by William Wylde is reproduced on page 111 by kind permission of Her Majesty the Queen (photograph: Royal Library, Windsor Castle)

Line illustrations pages 20, 65, 70, 154 and 212 by Jane Bottomley

Preface

This collection is aimed primarily at pupils following a course leading to qualification in English and English Literature at GCSE, and for Key Stage 4 of the National Curriculum in English.

The book aims to introduce pupils to a wide variety of literary and non-literary materials; to develop a range of skills which foreground the reader's need to engage actively with text; to encourage pupils to negotiate with text in order to allow them to respond fully to the range of meanings within the text. These aims are in line with the National Curriculum requirements which, among other things, emphasise learners' responsibility for responding appropriately to different kinds of discourse. As the Statements of Attainment for reading at Level 7 (the median level for 16-year-old pupils) say, pupils should be able to:

> 'a) read a range of fiction, poetry, literary non-fiction and drama, including pre-20th century literature, explaining their preferences through talking and writing, with reference to detail.
>
> b) talk and write about Literature and other texts giving evidence of personal response and showing an understanding of the author's approach.
>
> c) show in discussion that they can recognise features of presentation which are used to inform, to regulate, to reassure or to persuade, in non-literary and media texts.
>
> d) show in discussion or in writing an awareness of writers' use of sound patterns and some other literary devices and the effect upon the reader.'

The link made between reading and talk in pairs and groups in the Statements of Attainment is something we would wish to endorse and this is the underlying principle for the way in which the units were assembled and structured.

Much of the material in this collection is demanding, and, without opportunities to explore the texts collaboratively, they would only be accessible to the more proficient reader. The activities are designed to encourage this collaboration. From preparing to read (*Approaching the text*), to responding to detail (*Into the text*), the expectation is that pupils will work together in pairs or small groups, exploring and recording their ideas in a variety of ways. As the English Non-Statutory Guidance says: 'The key to developing (reading skills) is time for reflection. This may take place through talk in small groups . . .' . Only after this active and shared exploration can pupils respond independently through the more structured writing activities (*Beyond the text*). These will allow for a range of levels to be achieved.

Each unit explores, through a selection of related and complementary texts, central areas of human experience which, by their very nature, manifest tensions, contradictions and paradoxes. The active reader is one who can not only identify these tensions but is alert to the potential in the text.

The titles and sub-titles underline this and emphasise that the units are not simply thematic: the materials are inter-related and are selected to provoke discussion about language and the ways in which it reveals and conceals meanings.

The units are self-contained and coherent, and within each one there is a progression and development. They need not be used in the order in which they appear although when used together, in Key Stage 4, they are mutually illuminating.

In meeting the needs of the revised GCSE National Criteria and the requirements of Key Stage 4 of the National Curriculum, each unit concludes with a set of assignments which draws on the experiences gained in working through the texts and the activities. These assignments can either form the basis of coursework or practice for external assessment.

Love and hate: Myth and reality of family life

Contents

Introduction

This unit, as the title tells you, looks at families and the relationships within them, as described by novelists, playwrights, poets and other writers.

It begins with childhood and progresses through adolescence, falling in (and out) of love, to marriage and parenthood.

The unit is called *Love and hate* because while family relationships provide much tenderness, concern and love, they can also generate conflict, anger and bitterness.

These contradictory emotions are often different sides of the same coin: they cannot exist without each other. In many of the extracts you are going to read, that contradiction becomes clear.

The sub-title, *Myth and reality of family life*, contrasts the idealistic view that some people have of family life with the experiences that people actually have. We are bombarded with images of 'successful' families – in advertisements, in some magazines, and on television – and we may feel that our experiences fall short of these ideals.

This is not to say that 'love' is the 'myth' and 'hate' the 'reality', but rather that all human relationships are extremely complex and cannot be presented in simplistic terms.

Before you read some of the literature about family life, write five sentences to illustrate what you believe family life to be. What, for you, are the good points, the bad points, things you would keep, and things you would like to change. Keep these notes. You will need them when you get to page 58 of this unit.

Some definitions

We all assume that we know what is meant by the family, but here are some definitions that may add to your ideas about it.

Shorter Oxford English Dictionary
Family (fae'mili), sb. M.E. [ad. L. familia household, f. famulus servant] 1. The servants of a house (. . .) 2. The body of persons who live in one house or under one head, including parents, children, servants etc. 3. The group consisting of parents and their children, whether living together or not; in wider sense, all those who are nearly connected by blood or affinity. A person's children regarded collectively.

The Synonym Finder, JI Rodale
family, n. 1. parents and children, household, menage; children inf. kids, brood, generation; relatives, relations, Inf. folks, people, kin, kinsmen, kinfolk, next of kin, kith and kin; descendants, offspring, offshoot, progeny, issue, seed, posterity, scions.

Communities in Britain, Ronald Frankenberg
Most people in any society are born into a family. Each has a mother and father, who themselves have mothers and fathers. Mothers and fathers have brothers and sisters. Children have children. Brothers and sisters have children. So each individual has a set of people, different from any other individual who is related to him or her by 'blood'.

Talking about the family, Russell Ash

Many critics (of the family) say that children are forced too rigidly into their parents' mould, rather than finding real identities of their own. Mothers, too, can feel they are household drudges, never realising their creative potential. And fathers can be forced into years of frustration by the ceaseless burden of family responsibilities. Indeed, the family is frequently blamed as the source of the widespread violence and aggression that is thought to occur today.

Understanding Society, C H Brown

. . . the main functions of the family can be summarised as follows:

1. It provides a way of regulating sexual behaviour.
2. It provides a legitimate basis for the procreation and rearing of children.
3. It provides sustenance and care for its dependent members.
4. It is of primary importance in equipping people to live in a society and thus is passing on culture.
5. It bestows titles, rules and duties on its members which are recognised and approved by society (eg son, husband, wife, mother etc).

Some quotations

Other writers, not attempting definitions, have tried to capture some of the contradictions within family life:

Anna Karenina, Leo Tolstoy

All happy families resemble one another, but each unhappy family is unhappy in its own way.

Physiology of Common Life, G H Lewes

Murder, like talent, occasionally runs in families.

Fruits of the Earth, Andre Gide

Families, I hate you! Shut-in homes, closed doors, jealous possessions of happiness.

Toy Catalogue

Happy families: the ever popular game.

The Happy Life, Charles W Eliot

The security and elevation of the family and family life are the prime objects of civilisation and the ultimate ends of all industry.

The Life of Reason, George Santayana

The family is one of nature's masterpieces.

Into the text

Look closely at the definitions and quotations. Choose one or more that interest you the most, the one(s) that you find the most striking. Write a sentence or two explaining your choice(s). What do you feel about the particular point of view that you have selected?

Share your views with others in your group. From the ideas of your group, agree on one positive statement and one negative statement about families. Write your statements on a large sheet of paper and be prepared to justify your thinking to the rest of the class.

Early childhood: A short story

Approaching the text

The story that follows was written by Frank O'Connor who was born in Ireland in 1903. He wrote a semi-autobiography called *An Only Child* in 1961 and many short stories of which 'My Oedipus Complex' is one. He died in 1966 and his autobiography was published in 1968.

Oedipus was a son born to the King and Queen of Thebes, Laius and Jocasta. When he was born it was predicted that when he grew up, he would murder his father and marry his mother. So, he was abandoned on a hillside to die. He was rescued and raised by shepherds. When he reached adulthood he left his adoptive family and returned, by chance, to Thebes. There he killed a man after a trivial argument. He saved the city of Thebes from destruction by the Sphinx, a monster, and married the widowed Queen who he later discovers is his mother. At the same time he finds out that the man he killed earlier was his father.

The Oedipus complex is a psychological term which refers to a young male child's obsession with his mother.

As you are reading the story, make a note of any words or phrases that date it (for example, *candlelight* in line 4 or *fellow* in line 31).

The hero of the story, Larry, is supposed to be about five years old. Clearly, however, he is not using the language of a five-year-old. Make a note of examples of words or phrases that tell you that he is an adult retelling the events of his father's return from the war.

My Oedipus complex
Frank O'Connor

Father was in the army all through the war – the First War, I mean – so, up to the age of five, I never saw much of him, and what I saw did not worry me. Sometimes I woke and there was a big figure in khaki peering down at me in the candlelight. Sometimes in the early morning I heard the slamming of the front door and the clatter of nailed boots down the cobbles of the lane. These were Father's entrances and exits. Like Santa Claus he came and went mysteriously.

In fact, I rather liked his visits, though it was an uncomfortable squeeze between Mother and him when I got into the big bed in the early morning. He smoked, which gave him a pleasant musty smell, and shaved, an operation of astounding interest. Each time he left a trail of souvenirs – model tanks and Ghurka knives with handles made of bullet cases, and German helmets and cap badges and button-sticks, and all sorts of military equipment – carefully stowed away in a long box on top of the wardrobe, in case they ever came in handy. There was a bit of the magpie about Father; he expected everything to come in handy. When his back was turned, Mother let me get a chair and rummage through his treasures. She didn't seem to think so highly of them as he did.

The war was the most peaceful period of my life. The window of my   20
attic faced south-east. My Mother had curtained it, but that had small
effect. I always woke with the first light and, with all the responsibilities
of the previous day melted, feeling myself rather like the sun, ready to
illumine and rejoice. Life never seemed so simple and clear and full of
possibilities as then. I put my feet out from under the clothes – I called
them Mrs Left and Mrs Right – and invented dramatic situations for
them in which they discussed the problems of the day. At least Mrs Right
did; she was very demonstrative, but I hadn't the same control of Mrs
Left, so she mostly contented herself with nodding agreement.

They discussed what Mother and I should do during the day, what   30
Santa Claus should give a fellow for Christmas, and what steps should
be taken to brighten the home. There was that little matter of the
baby, for instance. Mother and I could never agree about that. Ours was
the only house in the terrace without a new baby, and Mother said we
couldn't afford one till Father came back from the war because they cost
seventeen and six. That showed how simple she was. The Geneys up the
road had a baby, and everyone knew they couldn't afford seventeen and
six. It was probably a cheap baby, and Mother wanted something really
good, but I felt she was too exclusive. The Geneys' baby would have
done us fine.   40

Having settled my plans for the day, I got up, put a chair under the
attic window, and lifted the frame high enough to stick out my head.
The window overlooked the front gardens of the terrace behind ours,
and beyond these it looked over a deep valley to the tall, red-brick houses
terraced up the opposite hillside, which were all still in shadow, while
those at our side of the valley were all lit up, though with long strange
shadows that made them seem unfamiliar, rigid and painted.

After that I went into Mother's room and climbed into the big bed.
She woke and I began to tell her of my schemes. By this time, though
I never seem to have noticed it, I was petrified in my nightshirt, and I   50
thawed as I talked until, the last frost melted, I fell asleep beside her and
woke again only when I heard her below in the kitchen, making the
breakfast.

After breakfast we went into town; heard Mass at St Augustine's and
said a prayer for Father, and did the shopping. If the afternoon was fine
we either went for a walk in the country or a visit to Mother's great
friend in the convent, Mother St Dominic. Mother had them all praying
for Father, and every night, going to bed, I asked God to send him back
safe from the war to us. Little, indeed, did I know what I was praying
for!   60

One morning I got into the big bed, and there, sure enough, was
Father in his usual Santa Claus manner, but later, instead of uniform,
he put on his best blue suit, and Mother was as pleased as anything. I
saw nothing to be pleased about, because, out of uniform, Father was
altogether less interesting, but she only beamed, and explained that our
prayers had been answered, and off we went to Mass to thank God for
having brought Father safely home.

The irony of it! That very day when he came in to dinner he took off
his boots and put on his slippers, donned the dirty old cap he wore

about the house to save him from colds, crossed his legs, and began to   70
talk gravely to Mother, who looked anxious. Naturally, I disliked her
looking anxious, because it destroyed her good looks, so I interrupted
him.

'Just a moment, Larry!' she said gently.

This was only what she said when we had boring visitors, so I attached
no importance to it and went on talking.

'Do be quiet, Larry!' she said impatiently. 'Don't you hear me talking
to Daddy?'

This was the first time I had heard those ominous words, "talking to
Daddy", and I couldn't help feeling that if this was how God answered   80
prayers, He couldn't listen to them very attentively.

'Why are you talking to Daddy?' I asked with as great a show of
indifference as I could muster.

'Because Daddy and I have business to discuss. Now don't interrupt
again!'

In the afternoon, at Mother's request, Father took me for a walk. This
time we went into town instead of out to the country, and I thought at
first, in my usual optimistic way, that it might be an improvement. It was
nothing of the sort. Father and I had quite different notions of a walk
in town. He had no proper interest in trams, ships and horses, and the   90
only thing that seemed to divert him was talking to fellows as old as
himself. When I wanted to stop he simply went on, dragging me behind
him by the hand; when he wanted to stop I had no alternative but to do
the same. I noticed that it seemed to be a sign that he wanted to stop for
a long time whenever he leaned against a wall. The second time I saw
him do it I got wild. He seemed to be settling himself forever. I pulled
him by the coat and trousers, but, unlike Mother who, if you were too
persistent, got into a wax and said: 'Larry, if you don't behave yourself, I'll give you a good slap,' Father had an extraordinary capacity for
amiable inattention. I sized him up and wondered would I cry, but he   100
seemed to be too remote to be annoyed even by that. Really, it was like
going for a walk with a mountain! He either ignored the wrenching and
pummelling entirely, or else glanced down with a grin of amusement
from his peak. I had never met anyone so absorbed in himself as he
seemed.

At teatime, "talking to Daddy" began again, complicated this time by
the fact that he had an evening paper, and every few minutes he put it
down and told Mother something new out of it. I felt this was foul play.
Man for man, I was prepared to compete with him any time for Mother's
attention, but when he had it all made up for him by other people it left   110
me no chance. Several times I tried to change the subject without success.

'You must be quiet while Daddy is reading, Larry,' Mother said
impatiently.

It was clear that she either genuinely liked talking to Father better than
talking to me, or else that he had some terrible hold on her which made
her afraid to admit the truth.

'Mummy,' I said that night when she was tucking me up, 'do you think
if I prayed hard God would send Daddy back to the war?'

She seemed to think about that for a moment.

'No dear,' she said with a smile. 'I don't think he would.'   120
'Why wouldn't he, Mummy?'
'Because there isn't a war any longer, dear.'
'But, Mummy, couldn't God make another war, if He liked?'
'He wouldn't like to, dear. It's not God who makes wars, but bad people.'
'Oh!' I said.

I was disappointed about that. I began to think that God wasn't quite what He was cracked up to be.

Next morning I woke at my usual hour, feeling like a bottle of champagne. I put out my feet and invented a long conversation in which 130
Mrs Right talked of the trouble she had with her own father till she put him in the Home. I didn't quite know what the Home was but it sounded the right place for Father. Then I got my chair and stuck my head out of the attic window. Dawn was just breaking, with a guilty air that made me feel I had caught it in the act. My head bursting with stories and schemes, I stumbled in next door, and in the half-darkness scrambled into the big bed. There was no room at Mother's side so I had to get between her and Father. For the time being I had forgotten about him, and for several minutes I sat bolt upright, racking my brains to know what I could do with him. He was taking up more than his fair share of 140
the bed, and I couldn't get comfortable, so I gave him several kicks that made him grunt and stretch. He made room all right, though. Mother waked and felt for me. I settled back comfortably in the warmth of the bed with my thumb in my mouth.

'Mummy!' I hummed, loudly and contentedly.

'Sssh! dear,' she whispered. 'Don't wake Daddy!'

This was a new development, which threatened to be even more serious than "talking to Daddy". Life without my early-morning conferences was unthinkable.

'Why?' I asked severely.   150

'Because poor Daddy is tired.'

This seemed to me a quite inadequate reason, and I was sickened by the sentimentality of her "poor Daddy". I never liked that sort of gush; it always struck me as insincere.

'Oh!' I said lightly. Then in my most winning tone: 'Do you know where I want to go with you today, Mummy?'

'No, dear,' she sighed.

'I want to go down the Glen and fish for thornybacks with my new net, and then I want to go out to the Fox and Hounds, and –'

'Don't-wake-Daddy!' she hissed angrily, clapping her hand across my 160
mouth.

But it was too late. He was awake, or nearly so. He grunted and reached for the matches. Then he stared incredulously at his watch.

'Like a cup of tea, dear?' asked Mother in a meek, hushed voice I had never heard her use before. It sounded almost as though she were afraid.

'Tea?' he exclaimed indignantly. 'Do you know what the time is?'

'And after that I want to go up the Rathcooney Road,' I said loudly, afraid I'd forget something in all those interruptions.

'Go to sleep at once, Larry!' she said sharply.

I began to snivel. I couldn't concentrate, the way that pair went on, 170
and smothering my early-morning schemes was like burying a family
from the cradle.

Father said nothing, but lit his pipe and sucked it, looking out into the
shadows without minding mother or me. I knew he was mad. Every time
I made a remark Mother hushed me irritably. I was mortified. I felt it
wasn't fair; there was even something sinister in it. Every time I had
pointed out to her the waste of making two beds when we could both
sleep in one, she had told me it was healthier like that, and now here was
this man, this stranger, sleeping with her without the least regard for her
health! 180

He got up early and made tea, but though he brought Mother a cup
he brought none for me.

'Mummy,' I shouted, 'I want a cup of tea, too.'

'Yes, dear,' she said patiently. 'You can drink from Mummy's saucer.'

That settled it. Either Father or I would have to leave the house. I
didn't want to drink from Mother's saucer; I wanted to be treated as an
equal in my own home, so just to spite her, I drank it all and left none
for her. She took that quietly, too.

But that night when she was putting me to bed she said gently:

'Larry, I want you to promise me something.' 190

'What is it?' I asked.

'Not to come in and disturb poor Daddy in the morning. Promise?'

'Poor Daddy' again! I was becoming suspicious of everything involv-
ing that quite impossible man.

'Why?' I asked.

'Because poor Daddy is worried and tired and he doesn't sleep well.'

'Why doesn't he, Mummy?'

'Well, you know, don't you, that while he was at the war Mummy got
the pennies from the Post Office?'

'From Miss MacCarthy?' 200

'That's right. But now, you see, Miss MacCarthy hasn't any more
pennies, so Daddy must go out and find us some. You know what would
happen if he couldn't?'

'No,' I said, 'tell us.'

'Well, I think we might have to go out and beg for them like the poor
old woman on Fridays. We wouldn't like that, would we?'

'No,' I agreed. 'We wouldn't.'

'So you'll promise not to come in and wake him?'

'Promise.'

Mind you, I meant that. I knew pennies were a serious matter, and 210
I was all against having to go out and beg like the old woman on Fridays.
Mother laid out all my toys in a complete ring round the bed so that,
whatever way I got out, I was bound to fall over one of them.

When I woke I remembered my promise all right. I got up and sat on
the floor and played – for hours, it seemed to me. Then I got my chair
and looked out of the attic window for more hours. I wished it was time
for Father to wake; I wished someone would make me a cup of tea. I
didn't feel in the least like the sun: instead, I was bored and so very, very
cold! I simply longed for the warmth and depth of the big featherbed.

At last I could stand it no longer, I went into the next room. As there 220
was still no room at Mother's side I climbed over her and she woke with
a start.

'Larry,' she whispered, gripping my arm very tightly, 'what did you
promise?'

'But I did, Mummy,' I wailed, caught in the very act. 'I was quiet for
ever so long.'

'Oh, dear, and you're perished!' she said sadly, feeling me all over.
'Now, if I let you stay will you promise not to talk?'

'But I want to talk, Mummy,' I wailed.

'That has nothing to do with it,' she said with a firmness that was new 230
to me. 'Daddy wants to sleep. Now, do you understand that?'

I understood it only too well. I wanted to talk, he wanted to
sleep – whose house was it, anyway?

'Mummy,' I said with equal firmness, 'I think it would be healthier for
Daddy to sleep in his own bed.'

That seemed to stagger her, because she said nothing for a while.

'Now, once and for all,' she went on, 'you're to be perfectly quiet or
go back to your own bed. Which is it to be?'

The injustice of it got me down. I had convicted her out of her
own mouth of inconsistency and unreasonableness, and she hadn't even 240
attempted to reply. Full of spite, I gave Father a kick, which she didn't
notice but which made him grunt and open his eyes in alarm.

'What time is it?' he asked in a panic-stricken voice, not looking at Mother but at the door, as if he saw someone there.

'It's early yet,' she replied soothingly. 'It's only the child. Go to sleep again . . . Now Larry,' she added, getting out of bed, 'you've wakened Daddy and you must go back.'

This time, for all her quiet air, I knew she meant it, and knew that my principal rights and privileges were as good as lost unless I asserted them at once. As she lifted me, I gave a screech, enough to wake the dead, not to mind Father. He groaned. 250

'That damn child! Doesn't he ever sleep?'

'It's only a habit, dear,' she said quietly, though I could see she was vexed.

'Well, it's time he got out of it,' shouted Father, beginning to heave in the bed. He suddenly gathered all the bedclothes about him, turned to the wall, and then looked back over his shoulder with nothing showing, only two small, spiteful, dark eyes. The man looked very wicked.

To open the bedroom door, Mother had to let me down, and I broke free and dashed for the farthest corner, screeching. Father sat bolt upright in bed. 260

'Shut up, you little puppy!' he said in a choking voice.

I was so astonished that I stopped screeching. Never, never had anyone spoken to me in that tone before. I looked at him incredulously and saw his face convulsed with rage. It was only then that I fully realised how God had conned me, listening to my prayers for the safe return of this monster.

'Shut up, you!' I bawled, beside myself.

'What's that you said?' shouted Father, making a wild leap out of the bed. 270

'Mick, Mick!' cried Mother. 'Don't you see the child isn't used to you?'

'I see he's better fed than taught,' snarled Father, waving his arms wildly. 'He wants his bottom smacked.'

All his previous shouting was as nothing to these obscene words referring to my person. They really made my blood boil.

'Smack your own!' I screamed hysterically. 'Smack your own! Shut up! Shut up!'

At this he lost his patience and let fly at me. He did it with the lack of conviction you'd expect of a man under Mother's horrified eyes, and it ended up as a mere tap, but the sheer indignity of being struck at all by a stranger, a total stranger who had cajoled his way back from the war into our big bed as a result of my innocent intercession, made me completely dotty. I shrieked and shrieked, and danced in my bare feet, and Father, looking awkward and hairy in nothing but a short grey army shirt, glared down at me like a mountain out for murder. I think it must have been then that I realised he was jealous too. And there stood Mother in her nightdress, looking as if her heart was broken between us. I hoped she felt as she looked. It seemed to me that she deserved it all. 280

From that morning on my life was a hell. Father and I were enemies, open and avowed. We conducted a series of skirmishes against one another, he trying to steal my time with Mother and I his. When she was 290 sitting on my bed, telling me a story, he took to looking for some pair of old boots which he alleged he had left behind him at the beginning of the war. While he talked to Mother I played loudly with my toys to show my total lack of concern. He created a terrible scene one evening when he came in from work and found me at his box, playing with his regimental badges, Ghurka knives, and buttonsticks. Mother got up and took the box from me.

'You mustn't play with Daddy's toys unless he lets you, Larry,' she said   300
severely. 'Daddy doesn't play with yours.'

For some reason Father looked at her as if she had struck him and then turned away with a scowl.

'Those are not toys,' he growled, taking down the box again to see if I had lifted anything. 'Some of those curios are very rare and valuable.'

But as time went on I saw more and more how he managed to alienate Mother and me. What made it worse was that I couldn't grasp his method or see what attraction he had for Mother. In every possible way he was less winning than I. He had a common accent and made noises at his tea. I thought for a while that it might be the newspapers she was   310
interested in, so I made up bits of news of my own to read to her. Then I thought it might be the smoking, which I personally thought attractive, and took his pipes and went round the house dribbling into them till he caught me. I even made noises at my tea, but Mother only told me I was disgusting. It all seemed to hinge round that unhealthy habit of sleeping together, so I made a point of dropping into their bedroom and nosing round, talking to myself, so that they wouldn't know I was watching them, but they were never up to anything that I could see. In the end it beat me. It seemed to depend on being grown-up and giving people rings, and I realised I'd have to wait.   320

But at the same time I wanted him to see that I was only waiting, not giving up the fight. One evening when he was being particularly obnoxious, chattering away well above my head, I let him have it.

'Mummy,' I said, 'do you know what I'm going to do when I grow up?'

'No, dear,' she replied. 'What?'

'I'm going to marry you,' I said quietly.

Father gave a great guffaw out of him, but he didn't take me in. I knew it must be only pretence. And Mother, in spite of everything, was pleased. I felt she was probably relieved to know that one day Father's hold on her would be broken.   330

'Won't that be nice?' she said with a smile.

'It'll be very nice,' I said confidently. 'Because we're going to have lots and lots of babies.'

'That's right, dear,' she said placidly. 'I think we'll have one soon, and then you'll have plenty of company.'

I was no end pleased about that because it showed that in spite of the way she gave in to Father she still considered my wishes. Besides, it would put the Geneys in their place.

It didn't turn out like that, though. To begin with, she was very preoccupied – I supposed about where she would get the seventeen and   340
six – and though Father took to staying out late in the evenings it did me no particular good. She stopped taking me for walks, became as

touchy as blazes, and smacked me for nothing at all. Sometimes I wished I'd never mentioned the confounded baby – I seemed to have a genius for bringing calamity on myself.

And calamity it was! Sonny arrived in the most appalling hullabaloo – even that much he couldn't do without a fuss – and from the first moment I disliked him. He was a difficult child – so far as I was concerned he was always difficult, and demanded far too much attention. Mother was simply silly about him, and couldn't see when he was only 350 showing off. As company he was worse than useless. He slept all day, and I had to go round the house on tiptoe to avoid waking him. It wasn't any longer a question of not waking Father. The slogan now was 'Don't-wake-Sonny'! I couldn't understand why the child wouldn't sleep at the proper time, so whenever Mother's back was turned I woke him. Sometimes to keep him awake I pinched him as well. Mother caught me at it one day and gave me a most unmerciful flaking.

One evening, when Father was coming in from work, I was playing trains in the front garden. I let on not to notice him; instead, I pretended to be talking to myself, and said in a loud voice: 'If another bloody baby 360 comes into this house, I'm going out.'

Father stopped dead and looked at me over his shoulder.

'What was that you said?' he asked sternly.

'I was only talking to myself,' I replied, trying to conceal my panic. 'It's private.'

He turned and went in without a word. Mind you, I intended it as a solemn warning, but its effect was quite different. Father started being quite nice to me. I could understand that, of course. Mother was quite sickening about Sonny. Even at mealtimes she'd get up and gawk at him in the cradle with an idiotic smile, and tell Father to do the same. He was 370 always polite about it, but he looked so puzzled you could see he didn't know what she was talking about. He complained of the way Sonny cried at night, but she only got cross and said that Sonny never cried except when there was something up with him – which was a flaming lie, because Sonny never had anything up with him, and only cried for attention. It was really painful to see how simple-minded she was. Father wasn't attractive, but he had a fine intelligence. He saw through Sonny, and now he knew that I saw through him as well.

One night I woke with a start. There was someone beside me in the bed. For one wild moment I felt sure it must be Mother, having come 380 to her senses and left Father for good, but then I heard Sonny in convulsion in the next room, and Mother saying: 'There! There! There!' and I knew it wasn't she. It was Father. He was lying beside me, wide awake, breathing hard and apparently as mad as hell.

After a while it came to me what he was mad about. It was his turn now. After turning me out of the big bed, he had been turned out himself. Mother had no consideration now for anyone but that poisonous pup, Sonny. I couldn't help feeling sorry for Father. I had been through it all myself, and even at that age I was magnanimous. I began to stroke him down and say: 'There! There!' He wasn't exactly 390 responsive.

'Aren't you asleep either?' he snarled.

'Ah, come on and put your arm around us, can't you?' I said, and he did, in a sort of way. Gingerly, I suppose is how you'd describe it. He was very bony but better than nothing.

At Christmas he went out of his way to buy me a really nice model railway.

Into the text

1 What are Larry's earliest recollections of his father?
2 Why was the war such a good time for Larry? Find examples from the text that explain his attitude towards the war.
3 Larry uses 'prayer' on two occasions, but for different purposes. Find these moments in the text. What do they tell you about Larry's attitude towards prayer?
4 Why do you think the story is called 'My Oedipus Complex'?
5 How does the boy's relationship with his father change during the story? Give examples from the text.
6 The original story of Oedipus was a tragedy. The tone of this story is quite different. At what point did you realise that the story was going to be humorous? What other features of the way in which the story is told make it light-hearted?

Beyond the text

Select one of the following.
1 Choose one of the following episodes and rewrite it from the point of view of the mother or the father:
   a the third morning home after Father's discharge from the army (lines 214 to 289).
   b the arrival of Sonny (lines 346 to 397).
2 Imagine you are a young member of the Geney family. Write about your circumstances and your feeling towards Larry and his family. Remember that Frank O'Connor wrote with adult perceptions but through a child's eyes — you could do the same.
3 Although 'My Oedipus Complex' isn't an autobiographical story, it does rely on memories of childhood. Recall some of your own early childhood memories, paying particular attention to relationships with parents and other members of your family.

Growing up: Non-literary writing

Anthropologists, sociologists and historians also write about family life, often in ways which make us think about what we take for granted.

The next three extracts describe the experiences of growing up in different cultures and in different periods of time. They are unlike 'My Oedipus Complex' in that they communicate facts and information rather than feelings and emotions.

Approaching the text

This extract is from a child care textbook. As you read it, think about the ways in which it conflicts with your experience or confirms it.

_ *Understanding Parenthood and Child Care* _
Margaret Picton

In this country nursery or pre-school education is not compulsory, but when a child reaches the age of five, he is legally compelled to attend an infant school and start the first stage of his primary education.

The compulsory school age is reached at the beginning of the school term following a child's fifth birthday. For example, if a child is five in March, he should start school in April, at the beginning of the summer term. Many education authorities though, do accept a child for primary education at the beginning of the school term in which he has his fifth birthday, but this is dependent upon there being a vacancy in the reception class. A summer-born child may find that there is not a school place   10
available, and he has to wait until September and the beginning of the Autumn term before he can attend school. He may then be over five and a quarter years old, and he will receive only two years infant education before being transferred to the junior school at the age of seven.

During the first years in the primary school, a child continues to learn through his senses. He needs to see, touch, smell, taste and hear things, to be able to understand what they are. He learns through his play to acquire the basic skills needed for reading, writing and number work. A normal young child is full of curiosity, and this can be a motivating force which helps him to learn.   20

There is a gradual growth in abstract reasoning. This develops slowly, as a child realises that he can manipulate objects to solve practical problems. For example, a child will quickly learn how to fit differently shaped pieces into similarly shaped holes. This is the beginning of reasoning.

The young schoolchild shows a greater degree of concentration than the pre-school child, and is less easily distracted. Project work becomes absorbing and attention can be sustained over a period of time.

A child needs to repeat activities and it is by repetition that the learning processes develop, and the memory span increases.   30

A normal six-year-old is an active and energetic individual who can balance on boards, throw and catch a ball with ease, turn somersaults, run, jump, climb, skip with a rope and balance on roller skates. He delights in ball games and can kick a ball well and use a bat. He enjoys all physical activities including music and movement.

Milk teeth start to loosen and fall out around the age of six or seven, and the first permanent teeth begin to appear during this period.

By the age of seven a child can hold and manipulate small objects easily. This is demonstrated in a love for construction kits, such as Meccano, Lego and Sticklebricks and an interest in various handicrafts · 40
such as sewing, knitting and Plasticine modelling.

The young schoolchild shows a marked degree of independence and is usually a self-possessed and confident individual. He has more control over his emotions than during the pre-school period, and is less likely to suffer from temper tantrums, jealousy and sulky displays of obstinacy.

His play is co-operative, and friendships are long-lasting and important. During the first years in primary school, there is little evidence of segregation between the sexes. A boy will play happily with a girl, and will share common interests and activities. Usually around the age of seven, a child will begin to show a preference for friends of the same sex, and groups or gangs may be formed. Jealousy and rivalry frequently arises between groups of children, and this allows the young schoolchild to exhibit aggressive and hostile feelings in a play situation.   50

Into the text

1 From your memories, does the author give an accurate picture of childhood? Do you agree with the author's account of childhood?

2 Is the language used appropriate for a school textbook?

3 One feature of the use of language in this extract is the use of the pronoun 'he' throughout. Choose a couple of paragraphs and rewrite them so that they could refer to either male or female children.

Approaching the text

This extract is an account by an anthropologist (look this word up in a dictionary if you haven't already done so) about the experience of growing up on a South Pacific island. The book from which it was taken was first published in 1928. As you read the text, make a note of any words and phrases that you don't understand.

_____ *Coming of Age in Samoa* _____
Margaret Mead

The reader will remember that the principal activity of the little girls was baby-tending. They could also do reef-fishing, weave a ball and make a pin-wheel, climb a coconut tree, keep themselves afloat in a swimming-hole which changed its level fifteen feet with every wave, grate the skin off a bread fruit or taro, sweep the sanded yard of a house, carry water from the sea, do simple washing, and dance a somewhat individualised *siva*. Their knowledge of the biology of life and death was over-

developed in proportion to their knowledge of the organisation of their
society or any of the niceties of conduct prescribed for their elders. They
were in a position which would be paralleled in our culture if a child had   10
seen birth and death before she was taught not to pass a knife blade first
or how to give change for a shilling. None of these children could speak
the courtesy language, even in its most elementary forms, their knowledge being confined to four or five words of invitation and acceptance.
This ignorance effectively barred them from all the conversations of
their elders upon all ceremonial occasions. Spying on a gathering of
chiefs would have been an unrewarding experience. They knew nothing
of the social organisation of the village beyond knowing which adults
were heads of families and which adult men and women were married.
They used the relationship terms loosely and without any real under-   20
standing, often substituting the term 'sibling of my own sex' where a
sibling of the opposite sex was meant, and when they applied the term
'brother', it was was really a mother's or a father's brother.

All of these children had seen birth and death. They had seen many
dead bodies. They had watched miscarriage and peeped under the arms
of the old women who were washing and commenting on the under-
developed foetus. There was no convention of sending children of the
family away at such times, although the hordes of neighbouring children
were scattered with a shower of stones if any of the older women could
take time from the more absorbing events to hurl them. But the feeling   30
here was that children were noisy and troublesome; there was no desire
to protect them from shock or keep them in ignorance. About half the
children had seen a partly developed foetus, which the Samoans fear will
otherwise be born as an avenging ghost, cut from a woman's body in the
open grave. If shock is the result of early experiences with birth, death,
or sex activities, it should surely be manifest here in this post-mortem
Caesarian where grief for the dead, fear of death, a sense of horror
and a dread of contamination from contact with the dead, the open,
unconcealed operation and the sight of a distorted, repulsive foetus all
combine to render the experience indelible. An only slightly less emo-   40
tionally charged experience was the often witnessed operation of cutting
open any dead body to search out the cause of death. These operations
performed in the shallow open grave, beneath a glaring noon day sun,
with a frightened, excited crowd watching in horrid fascination, are
hardly orderly or unemotional initiations into the details of biology
and death, and yet they seem to leave no bad effects on the children's
emotional make-up. Possibly the adult attitude that these are horrible
but perfectly natural, non-unique occurrences, forming a legitimate part
of a child's experiences, may sufficiently account for the lack of bad
results. Children take an intense interest in life and death, and they are   50
more proportionately obsessed by it than are the adults who divide their
horror between the death of a young neighbour in child-bed and the fact
that the high chief has been insulted by some breach of etiquette in the
neighbouring village. The intricacies of the social life are a closed book
to the child and a correspondingly fascinating field of exploration in
later life, while the facts of life and death are shorn of all mystery at an
early age.

Into the text

1 In groups, pool the words you do not understand. Discuss possible meanings and then check in a dictionary any that you still feel unsure about.

2 What does the writer find surprising about what these young Samoan girls know and don't know?

3 From the evidence in the passage, what do you understand by the phrase 'courtesy language'?

4 What is the attitude of the adult Samoans towards the children in the community? Find examples from the text.

5 What are the differences between the Samoans' attitude towards death and the one that you are familiar with? How do you account for the differences?

6 What sort of audience do you think 'Coming of Age in Samoa' was written for?

7 The writing could be described as being 'detached': the actual content is quite gory, but the language used is distant and impersonal. Why do you think Margaret Mead wrote in this way?

8 Identify the key differences between children growing up in a British culture, as described in the extract from *Understanding Parenthood and Child Care*, and the experience of Samoan girls.

Approaching the text

The following extract is based on a documentary television series about changes that have taken place in women's lives over the last 70 years. Although it is still written in a non-literary style, it is aimed at a wider audience and the language is generally less complicated and detached. Angela Holdsworth writes in a journalistic style and includes a personal narrative spoken by a working class woman. Note the differences in style between this spoken account and the linking written account of the author.

Out of the Doll's House
Angela Holdsworth

In working class families, children were left entirely to mother. In the early years of this century, there was no talk of stimulating play or entertaining or amusing children. On the contrary, one or two elderly ladies remember that when they were toddlers they used to be strapped into a chair for hours on end to keep them 'out of harm's way while mother got on'. Children were left to their own devices and by the age of six or seven they were expected to look after themselves and, when not at school, run errands for the family. Ideally, they kept out of the way, bothering the grown-ups as little as possible.

Some writers suggest that mothers in the past loved their children less   10
than today, that either they were afraid of becoming too attached to a

child who might be 'taken from them' or that, in a large family, there
was less room for individual affection. Our own interviews suggest that
this is far from the truth. Women still speak with tears in their eyes of
a child lost sixty years ago. At the beginning of this century, it was quite
common for children to die from infectious diseases and babies were
particularly vulnerable. One in six, registered alive at birth, never
reached its first birthday and the number who died at birth without ever
being registered is unknown.

Rose Ashton's baby sister was one of many whose birth went   20
unrecorded and whose death was unmarked by any headstone. In 1904
Rose was called to her mother's bedroom where she saw her newborn
sister lying dead on the pillow, 'looking like a little doll, a beautiful
thing'. Rose was told by her mother to collect a soap box from the
grocer, put the baby inside and take it to the gravedigger for burial.
Wanting to do more for her tiny sister, Rose tore the lining out of her
father's coat to upholster the soap box and only when she had it looking
pretty did she set off for the graveyard with her baby sister tucked into
her makeshift coffin. The gravedigger was not at all surprised to see
Rose, clutching the small box, and pointed her towards a heap of similar   30
boxes and packets near the church. Upset and puzzled, Rose asked
where he was going to bury all the tiny babies. '*Well, lass,*' Rose
remembers the gravedigger explaining. '*Y'see, people can't afford to buy
graves these days so when a public grave is full and ready for filling we
put one on each end till we get rid of them. They can't afford a private
grave so we put them in at the foot or the head,*' he said and *I came back
broken-hearted for this little doll.* Officials at that time were not too
worried about babies who were stillborn or which died in their first
month like Rose's little sister. Most assumed when babies died in their
first few weeks that they had a congenital weakness and their dying was   40
simply part of the process of natural selection. They were more
concerned about those who died in the following months.

Concern about the wastage of infant life intensified in the years
preceding the First World War. Medical Officers of Health were
convinced that if mothers were better educated in the arts of mothering,
fewer babies would die. They were convinced there were too many
incompetent mothers who, through ignorance and carelessness,
jeopardized the lives of their children. Diarrhoea, thought to be caught
from germs on dirty feeding-bottles or dummies, was the main killer of
small babies. The cheapest and simplest solution seemed to be to educate   50
women in hygiene, encourage them to breast-feed their young and keep
their houses cleaner, particularly by getting rid of flies (a huge menace
in the days when the horse was the main means of transport). In fact,
sub-standard sanitation caused many of the problems – towns like Hull,
which had a large percentage of insanitary privies, also had high infant
mortality – but improved sanitation was a long-term and far more
costly project than teaching women how to be better mothers. Mother-
hood was to be looked on not just as a personal duty but as a national
one. Women were expected to take pride in being mothers of the race
and they had to learn how to do the job properly.   60

Into the text

1 What features of the language of Rose Ashton's story make it different from Angela Holdsworth's account?

2 Even though Angela Holdsworth says that '. . . officials were not too worried about babies who were stillborn or which died in the first month like Rose's little sister' (lines 37–9), the incident of the soap-box burial would still have caused great scandal in some sections of society.

   a In groups, prepare a report of between 200 and 300 words that would appear in a tabloid newspaper (eg *Sun, Star, Mirror*) telling the story of baby Ashton's burial as if it had occurred in the present time. You will have to make sure that you record the views of all of the people referred to and that you use language that tabloid newspapers would use. Where necessary, invent other details which you think would make the story more sensational.

   b When you have written your reports, present them to the rest of the class and consider in what ways they differ from the original account (think about layout, audience, tone, choice of vocabulary, sentence structure).

Falling in and out of love: Poetic writing

Approaching the text

So far in this unit, you have looked at literary and non-literary writing. In this next section, you will be looking at poetic writing. Before you actually read any poems, list four or five words or phrases that describe what poetry is, and how it differs from prose, whether literary or non-literary.

Read the poems, aloud if you want, and share your ideas about them, recording what you consider to be important. You may find it useful to refer to *On reading a poem* on page 220 in the Reference Section before you start.

You will almost certainly have seen columns of classified advertisements in newspapers from people seeking partners, for example

Warm, shy, single, 22-year-old male seeks bright attractive female for friendship, possible lasting relationship.

The writer of the following poem has read some of these advertisements and has written a poem about them.

Lonely Hearts

Wendy Cope

Can someone make my simple wish come true?
Male biker seeks female for touring fun.
Do you live in North London? Is it you?

Gay vegetarian whose friends are few,
I'm into music, Shakespeare and the sun.
Can someone make my simple wish come true?

Executive in search of something new –
Perhaps bisexual woman, arty, young.
Do you live in North London? Is it you?

Successful, straight and solvent? I am too –
Attractive Jewish lady with a son.
Can someone make my simple wish come true?

I'm Libran, inexperienced and blue –
Need slim non-smoker, under twenty-one.
Do you live in North London? Is it you?

Please write (with photo) to Box 152.
Who knows where it may lead once we've begun?
Can you make my simple wish come true?
Do you live in North London? Is it you?

Into the text

1 How many characters can you identify in this poem? How do they differ from each other? In what way(s) are they similar?
2 What would you say is Wendy Cope's attitude towards the people in the poem?
3 Poems contain patterns — of words, of lines and of sounds. What patterns can you identify in this poem? How is the poem different from the 'Lonely hearts' advertisement on page 31?
4 Using a similar structure to the poem, write another stanza (perhaps advertising yourself).

The Picnic
John Logan

It is the picnic with Ruth in the spring.
Ruth was third on my list of seven girls
But the first two were gone (Betty) or else
Had someone (Ellen had accepted Doug).
Indian Gully the last day of school;   5
Girls make the lunches for the boys too.
I wrote a note to Ruth in algebra class
Day before the test. She smiled, and nodded.
We left the cars and walked through the young corn
The shoots green as paint and the leaves like tongues   10
Trembling. Beyond the fence where we stood
Some wild strawberry flowered by an elm tree
And Jack-in-the-pulpit was olive ripe.
A blackbird fled as I crossed, and showed
A spot of gold or red under its quick wing.   15
I held the wire for Ruth and watched the whip
Of her long, striped skirt as she followed.
Three freckles blossomed on her thin, white back
Underneath the loop where the blouse buttoned.
We went for our lunch away from the rest,   20
Stretched in the new grass, our heads close
Over unknown things wrapped up in wax papers.
Ruth tried for the same, I forget what it was,
And our hands were together. She laughed,
And a breeze caught the edge of her little   25
Collar and the edge of her brown, loose hair
That touched my cheek. I turned my face into
The gentle fall. I saw how sweet it smelled.
She didn't move her head or take her hand.
I felt a soft caving in my stomach   30
As at the top of the highest slide
When I had been a child, but was not afraid,
And did not know why my eyes moved with wet
As I brushed her cheek with my lips and brushed
Her lips with my own lips. She said to me   35
Jack, Jack, different than I had ever heard,
Because she wasn't calling me, I think,
Or telling me. She used my name to
Talk in another way I wanted to know.
She laughed again and then she took her hand;   40
I gave her what we both had touched – can't
Remember what it was, and we ate the lunch.
Afterward we walked in the small, cool creek
Our shoes off, her skirt hitched, and she smiling,
My pants rolled, and then we climbed up the high   45
Side of Indian Gully and looked

Where we had been, our hands together again.
It was then some bright thing came in my eyes,
Starting at the back of them and flowing
Suddenly through my head and down my arms   50
And stomach and my bare legs that seemed not
To stop in feet, not to feel the red earth
Of the Gully, as though we hung in a
Touch of birds. There was a word in my throat
With the feeling and I knew the first time   55
What it meant and I said, it's beautiful.
Yes, she said, and I felt the sound and word
In my hand join the sound and word in hers
As in one name said, or in one cupped hand.
We put back on our shoes and socks and we   60
Sat in the grass awhile, crosslegged, under
Á blowing tree, not saying anything.
And Ruth played with shells she found in the creek,
As I watched. Her small wrist which was so sweet
To me turned by her breast and the shells dropped   65
Green, white, blue, easily into her lap,
Passing light through themselves. She gave the pale
Shells to me, and got up and touched her hips
With her light hands, and we walked down slowly
To play the school games with the others.   70

Into the text

1 Identify some of the details that Jack sees in Indian Gully.

2 What might they tell us about the feelings Jack has on this day?

3 What suggests that 'The Picnic' is set in America?

4 Look again at the lines beginning 'Jack, Jack, . . .' (lines 36–9). What do you think is meant by these lines?

5 What makes this a poem as opposed to a passage of prose?

6 Write 300 to 500 words describing the outing from Ruth's point of view. You can write poetry or prose.

In the Midnight Hour
Adrian Henri

When we meet
in the midnight hour
country girl
I will bring you nightflowers
coloured like your eyes   5
in the moonlight
in the midnight
hour

I remember

Your cold hand   10
held for a moment among strangers
held for a moment among dripping trees
in the midnight hour

I remember

Your eyes coloured like the autumn landscape   15
walking down muddy lanes
watching sheep eating yellow roses
walking in city squares in winter rain
kissing in darkened hallways
walking in empty suburban streets   20
saying goodnight in deserted alleyways

in the midnight hour

Andy Williams singing 'We'll keep a Welcome in the Hillsides'
    for us
When I meet you at the station   25
The Beatles singing 'We Can Work It Out' with James Ensor
    at the harmonium
Rita Hayworth in a nightclub singing 'Amada Mia'

I will send you armadas
of love vast argosies of flowers   30
in the midnight hour
country girl

when we meet
in the
moonlight   35
midnight
hour
country girl

I will bring you

yellow   40
white
eyes
bright
moon
light   45
mid
night
flowers
in the midnight hour.

Into the text

1 This is a poem about lovers' meetings. List some of the features of language and settings in the poem which might create the romantic atmosphere.

2 Apart from the fact that Adrian Henri tells us that the girl is a country girl, what other evidence is there in the poem that tells us this?

3 Writers use images — metaphor and simile — to add to the meaning of their writing. Similes use the words 'as' and 'like'. Can you find examples in this poem? There are two examples of metaphor in the poem. Can you find them?

4 In the stanza beginning 'Andy Williams . . .' Adrian Henri refers to characters you may not have heard of. What, if anything, does this stanza contribute to the poem as a whole?

5 Why do you think Adrian Henri laid the poem out in this way?

Waiting

Peter Haworth

Waiting
Seven o'clock she said
But she's not here
The sun is bright
In the distance   5
Clouds are gathering
It's ten past
There is no sign
The trees and grass sway
Whispering their secrets   10
To each other
From the playground
The sounds of children's laughter

Echoes in my ears
Cars pass   15
People pass
I am unnoticed
Perhaps I
Have become part of the lamp post
Where we have met   20
So many times
I'll give her till twenty-past
The clouds take the sun from my view
The skies darken
I shiver in a deep coldness   25
Which suddenly surrounds me
I turn
but wait
I see a lonely figure
Approaching   30
I recognise
Her best friend
I realise
What will be said
I can't bear to hear it   35
So I turn
And run

Into the text

1 In this poem, as in 'The Picnic' on page 33, there are many references to things in the 'landscape'. Here they serve a different purpose. What do you think that might be?

2 At what point in the poem do you realise that the girl is not going to come?

3 Why does he say 'I have become part of the lamp post . . .' (lines 18–19)?

4 This poem tells a simple story. It also evokes a mood but the writer does not tell us directly how he feels. What means does he use to communicate his feelings to us?

Approaching the text

Andrew Marvell was born in Hull in 1621, five years after Shakespeare's death. Although he lived and wrote 350 years ago, Marvell deals with experiences which are relevant to our own times. In this poem the narrator is trying to seduce a young 'Lady' who is resisting his advances. In the first part of the poem he wittily says that her shyness would not be a problem if he could court her for ever when time would not have an effect on either of them. In the second part of the poem, he points out the reality of the situation: that their lives are short and unless she agrees to his overtures, it could be too late; she will grow old and die, missing her chance of fulfilment. As you read the poem, be alert to all the references to time in it.

To his Coy Mistress
Andrew Marvell

Had we but world enough, and time,
This coyness, Lady, were no crime.
We would sit down and think which way
To walk and pass our love's long day.
Thou by the Indian Ganges' side   5
Shouldst rubies find; I by the tide
Of Humber would complain. I would
Love you ten years before the Flood
And you should, if you please, refuse
Till the conversion of the Jews.   10
My vegetable love would grow
Vaster than empires, and more slow;
An hundred years would go to praise
Thine eyes and on thy forehead gaze;
Two hundred to adore each breast,   15
But thirty thousand to the rest;
An age at least to every part,
And the last age should show your heart.
For, Lady, you deserve this state,
Nor would I love at lower rate.   20

But at my back I always hear
Time's wingéd chariot hurrying near;
And yonder all before us lie
Deserts of vast eternity.
Thy beauty shall no more be found,   25
Nor, in thy marbled vault, shall sound
My echoing song; then worms shall try
That longed preserved virginity,
And your quaint honour turn to dust,
And into ashes all my lust: 30
The grave's a fine and private place,
But none, I think, do there embrace.

Now therefore, while the youthful hue
Sits on thy skin like morning dew,
And while thy willing soul transpires   35
At every pore with instant fires,
Now let us sport us while we may,
And now, like amorous birds of prey,
Rather at once our time devour
Than languish in his slow-chapped power.   40
Let us roll all our strength and all
Our sweetness up into one ball,
And tear our pleasures with rough strife
Through the iron gates of life:
Thus, though we cannot make our sun   45
Stand still, yet we will make him run.

Into the text

1 What do you think the following words and phrases
mean within the context of the poem:
 • coyness (line 2)
 • My vegetable love (line 11)
 • Time's wingéd chariot (line 22)
 • Deserts of vast eternity (line 24)
 • Now let us sport us while we may (line 37)
 • the iron gates of life (line 44).

2 Look closely at the section between line 25 (Thy
beauty . . .) and line 32 (. . . do there embrace.). An
understanding of these lines provides the key to the
meaning of the whole poem. What case do you think
Marvell is arguing in these lines?

3 What attitude towards women do you think this poem
reveals?

Mohammed Ibrahim Speaks
Martha Beidler

*told by a Man of the
Arab Motier Tribe
of Upper Egypt*

'I have two wives,
I have had three.
The first one, Zeynab, I divorced:
   There was a wedding in the town,
   And I forbade her going, lest   5
The men might look at her.
She disobeyed me. Veiled,
She walked among the women,
Thinking I would not know her.
But what other woman walks like Zeynab?   10
Three times I told her 'I divorce you,'
And I sent her back to her father's house.

My present wives obey me as they ought.
If I should say to them, 'These stones are bread,'
They'd eat the stones.   15
But in the night, my thoughts return to Zeynab.
Truly she was light-hearted,
And her eyes were like black pearls
Within their shells.'

Into the text

1 What kind of person is Zeynab? In what way is she different from Mohammed's other two wives?
2 Compare the first three and last seven lines. By close reference, how do they differ in describing Mohammed's attitude towards Zeynab? What does this tell us about Mohammed?
3 Publicly, Mohammed Ibrahim has to announce his divorce. What kind of influences force him into this situation? In what way do his private thoughts differ from his public action?

Approaching the text

The following two poems are about relationships ending – about one person leaving the other.

Read them both carefully and then identify the similarities and the differences between them.

A Happening
Nina Cassian

Yesterday I watched an amazing fight
between a woman in love and a man
who wasn't, her hair agitated,
and her mouth interrupted by white teeth.
She talked and talked – he didn't. She talked furiously,   5
striking expired time with words.
There was no sound of shields.
Time totally disarmed!
She had her arguments, he did not.
He was leaving her for another woman;   10
He was guilty – so was the other woman,
But the woman who loved was the innocent party.
Her words had a natural nobleness,
The mud of passion left only cast gold.
To avoid her eyes, he looked at his hands –   15
noticing a certain contrast between them.

It was a ridiculously unfair battle,
the air whistled as if clutching a line
of the thousand arrows never reaching their target.
Everything about seemed to sink – to decline.   20

Separation
Julie Harrison

She sat quietly
As he strode into the room
Slamming the door
His eyes cold black granite
As he stared at her.   5
She wouldn't look at him.
He threw down his briefcase
Crossed to the armchair
Picked up his paper
Scanned the headlines   10
Not really seeing.
She stood up
Glanced through the window
Walked to the door and quietly said
'It's all for the best.'   15
His head snapped round as she walked
through the door
And proceeded slowly up the stairs
To the bedroom

Where suitcases waited   20
Already packed
Beneath their marriage photograph.
She put on her new coat
Recently bought by him
As a bribe   25
Wincing as it touched fresh bruises
and swellings,
Picked up the suitcases and walked to
the hall.
He stood waiting   30
'You can't leave me, I love you.'
She smiled bitterly.
A hand went up to her blackened cheek
And she touched it gently.
She stepped towards the front door   35
Moving slowly
He took a quick step forward, and
faltered
Staring at his outstretched hands.
He watched as she twisted the door knob   40
Stepped through the door
Then turned back for the suitcases.
Their eyes met
Hers were the first to fall away
She picked up the suitcases   45
And walked out of his life.

Into the text

1 In 'A Happening', Nina Cassian uses a recurring image to emphasise the emotional conflict being described. Find examples of this image. What is it an image of? Why is it appropriate?

2 In 'Separation', Julie Harrison, a schoolgirl, concentrates on the behaviour of her characters. How would you describe this? Give some examples. What does it tell us about their mood?

3 In what ways are the poems similar? In what ways are they different?

4 Which poem do you prefer? For what reasons?

Beyond the text

1 By close reference to the first poem ('The Happening'), but inventing detail where necessary, either:
   a describe what the man would say to the 'other woman';
   or
   b what the 'woman in love' would say to a close friend about the 'happening'.

2 Write the story of 'Separation' from the man's point of view.

3 Using either poetry or prose, write about your own experience of the end of a relationship.

Simple Lyric
Brian Patten

When I think of her sparkling face
And of her body that rocked this way and that,
When I think of her laughter,
Her jubilance that filled me,
It's a wonder I'm not gone mad. 5

She is away and I cannot do what I want.
Other faces pale when I get close.
She is away and I cannot breathe her in.

The space her leaving has created
I have attempted to fill 10
With bodies that numbed upon touching,
Among them I expected her opposite,
And found only forgeries.

Her wholeness I know to be a fiction of my making,
Still I cannot dismiss the longing for her; 15
It is a craving for sensation new flesh
Cannot wholly calm or cancel,
It is perhaps for more of her.

At night above the parks the stars are swarming.
The streets are thick with nostalgia; 20
I move through senseless routine and insensitive chatter
As if her going did not matter.
She is away and I cannot breathe her in.
I am ill simply through wanting her.

Into the text

1 What impression of the girl do you get from the first stanza?

2 How do other women compare with the poet's recollection of 'her'?

3 What do you think Patten means by the line 'Her wholeness I know to be a fiction of my making' (line 14)?

4 In what ways does the poet describe his acute sense of loss?

Parenthood

Approaching the text

DH Lawrence was born in Eastwood, Nottinghamshire, in 1885, the son of a coal miner. He was a novelist, poet and artist. Many of his works offended middle-class English society. Even as recently as 1963 when Penguin Books wanted to publish *Lady Chatterley's Lover* in paperback, attempts were made to suppress his writing. He died in 1930 after spending the last years of his life in self-imposed exile.

The Rainbow, first published in 1915, describes three generations of the Brangwen family in Nottinghamshire, living through a period of social upheaval due to the impact of industrialisation. The young man, Will, and his wife, Anna, are coming to terms, in different ways, with the arrival of their first child, Ursula. As you read the extract, notice the ways in which the father's attitude towards the child changes.

The Rainbow
D H Lawrence

From the first, the baby stirred in the young father a deep, strong emotion he dared scarcely acknowledge, it was so strong and came out of the dark of him. When he heard the child cry, a terror possessed him, because of the answering echo from the unfathomed distances in himself. Must he know in himself such distances, perilous and imminent?

He had the infant in his arms, he walked backwards and forwards troubled by the crying of his own flesh and blood. This was his own flesh and blood crying! His soul rose against the voice suddenly breaking out from him, from the distances in him.   10

Sometimes in the night, the child cried and cried, when the night was heavy and sleep oppressed him. And half asleep, he stretched out his hand to put it over the baby's face to stop the crying. But something arrested his hand: the very inhumanness of the intolerable, continuous crying arrested him. It was so impersonal, without cause or object. Yet he echoed to it directly, his soul answered its madness. It filled him with terror, almost with frenzy.

He learned to acquiesce to this, to submit to the awful, obliterated sources which were the origin of his living tissue. He was not what he conceived himself to be! Then he was what he was, unknown, potent,   20 dark.

He became accustomed to the child, he knew how to lift and balance the little body. The baby had a beautiful, rounded head that moved him passionately. He would have fought to the last drop to defend that exquisite, perfect round head.

He learned to know the little hands and feet, the strange, unseeing, golden-brown eyes, the mouth that opened only to cry, or to suck, or to show a queer, toothless laugh. He could almost understand even the dangling legs, which at first had created in him a feeling of aversion. They could kick in their queer little way, they had their own softness.   30

One evening, suddenly, he saw the tiny, living thing rolling naked in the mother's lap, and he was sick, it was so utterly helpless and vulnerable and extraneous; in a world of hard surfaces and varying altitudes, it lay vulnerable and naked at every point. Yet it was quite blithe. And yet, in its blind, awful crying, was there not the blind, far-off terror of its own vulnerable nakedness, the terror of being so utterly delivered over, helpless at every point. He could not bear to hear it crying. His heart strained and stood on guard against the whole universe.

But he waited for the dread of these days to pass; he saw the joy   40 coming. He saw the lovely, creamy, cool little ear of the baby, a bit of dark hair rubbed to a bronze floss, like bronze-dust. And he waited, for the child to become his, to look at him and answer him.

It had a separate being, but it was his own child. His flesh and blood vibrated to it. He caught the baby to his breast with his passionate, clapping laugh. And the infant knew him.

As the newly-opened, newly-dawned eyes looked at him, he wanted them to perceive him, to recognise him. Then he was verified. The child knew him, a queer contortion of laughter came on its face for him. He caught it to his breast, clapping with a triumphant laugh. 50

The golden-brown eyes of the child gradually lit up and dilated at the sight of the dark-glowing face of the youth. It knew its mother better, it wanted its mother more. But the brightest, sharpest little ecstasy was for the father.

It began to be strong, to move vigorously and freely, to make sounds like words. It was a baby girl now. Already it knew his strong hands, it exulted in his strong clasp, it laughed and crowed when he played with it.

And his heart grew red-hot with passionate feeling for the child. She was not much more than a year old when the second baby was born. 60 Then he took Ursula for his own. She his first little girl. He had set his heart on her.

Into the text

1 Identify, from the first and last paragraphs, the phrases which confirm the changes in Will's attitude towards his daughter.
2 List the words and phrases used to describe the child. What do they have in common? Is there a change in emphasis within the extract?
3 The child is referred to as 'it' until line 61. Why do you think this is so?
4 The mother is hardly mentioned in this extract. Write a paragraph describing her feelings about Will's relationship with the child.

Approaching the text

The English Language has many varieties: these are called *dialects*. Your origins (place of birth, class) will determine the dialect you use. A widely used dialect, and one which the National Curriculum expects all pupils to have access to, is Standard English: the language of the media, business and professions. This is not to say that other dialects are inferior.

The poem that follows is written in a dialect described as 'patois' and spoken by some members of the West Indian British community. It deals with the issue of parenthood in ways which are very different from the previous extract.

Sonny's Lettah

Linton Kwesi Johnson

Anti-Sus poem

Brixton Prison
Jebb Avenue
London SW2
England

Dear Mama,
Good Day.
I hope dat wen
deze few lines reach y'u,
they may find y'u in di bes' af helt.   5

Mama,
I really doan know how ti tell y'u dis,
cause I did mek a salim pramis
fi tek care a lickle Jim
an' try mi bes' fi luk out fi him.   10

Mama,
Ah really did try mi bes',
but none-di-les',
mi sarry fi tell y'u seh
poor lickle Jim get arres'.   15

It woz di miggle a di rush howah
wen everybady jus' a hus'le a bus'le
fi goh home fi dem evenin' showah;
mi an' Jim stan-up
waitin' pan a bus,   20
nat causin' no fus',
wen all am a sudden
a police van pull-up.

Out jump t'ree policeman,
di 'hole a dem carryin' batan.   25
Dem waak straight up to mi an' Jim.
One a dem hol' an to Jim
seh him tekin him in;

Jim tell him fi let goh a him
far him noh dhu not'n',   30
an him naw t'ief,
nat even a but'n.
Jim start to wriggle.
Di police start to giggle.
Mama,   35
mek Ah tell y'u whey dem dhu to Jim;

Mama,
mek Ah tell y'u whey dem dhu to Jim;
dem t'ump him in him belly
an' it turn to jelly   40
dem lick him pan hi back
an' him rib get pap
dem lik him pan him he'd
but it tuff like le'd
dem kick him in him seed   45
an' it started to bleed

Mama
Ah jus' could'n' stan-up deh
an' noh dhu not'n:

soh mi jook one in him eye   50
an' him started to cry;
mi t'ump one in him mout'
an' him started to shout
mi kick one pan him shin
an' him started to spin   55
mi t'ump him pan him chin
an' him drap pan a bin
an' crash
an' de'd.

Mama,   60
more policeman come dung
an' beat mi to di grung:
dem charge Jim fi sus
dem charge mi fi murdah.

Mama,   65
doan fret,
doan get depres'
an' doun-hearted
Be af good courage
till I hear fram you.   70

I remain,
your son,
Sonny.

Into the text

1 Read the poem out aloud. The phonetic spelling and the punctuation may help you to understand it.
2 Rewrite the poem in Standard English as a letter.
3 Construct a Non-Standard/Standard Dictionary which lists and explains all of the unfamiliar words and phrases in the poem.

The exorcism: A drama script

Approaching the text

Plays are meant to be performed by actors on the stage. A good performance of a play will help to interpret the text for the audience by use of movement, speed of delivery, emphasis, the design of the set, costumes, etc. When you read a play, therefore, you have to try to recreate a sense of the play in performance which means that you should be alert to all of the clues the writer gives you, eg pauses, indications of mood, actions, interpretation, instructions to actors as to how lines should be delivered.

In this extract from *Who's Afraid of Virginia Woolf*, George is a middle-aged university lecturer married to Martha, the daughter of the university Principal. They have a very stormy relationship and on this particular evening, they have been to a party and invited Nick, a new lecturer, and his wife, Honey, for more drinks at their home. Alcohol has affected everyone and George and Martha, as is customary, are sniping at each other.

As you read the play, try to recreate the atmosphere of a group of spiteful young children playing games that can, so easily, get out of hand.

Who's Afraid of Virginia Woolf

Edward Albee

NICK	Is the game over?
HONEY	Yes! Yes, it is.
GEORGE	Ho-ho! Not by a long shot. [*to Martha*] We got a little surprise for you, baby. It's about Sunny-Jim.
MARTHA	No more, George.
GEORGE	YES!
NICK	Leave her be!
GEORGE	I'M RUNNING THIS SHOW! [*to Martha*] Sweetheart, I'm afraid I've got some bad news for you . . . for us, of course. Some rather sad news. 10 [*Honey begins weeping, head in hands.*]
MARTHA	[*afraid, suspicious*] What is this?
GEORGE	[*oh, so patiently*] Well, Martha, while you were out of the room, while the . . . two of you were out of the room . . . I mean, I don't know where, hell, you both must have been somewhere [*little laugh*]. . . . While you were out of the room, for a while . . . well, Missy and I were sittin' here havin' a little talk, you know: a chaw and a talk . . . and the doorbell rang. . . .
HONEY	[*head still in hands*] Chimed.
GEORGE	Chimed . . . and . . . well, it's hard to tell you, Martha. . . . 20
MARTHA	[*a strange throaty voice*] Tell me.
HONEY	Please . . . don't.
MARTHA	Tell me.
GEORGE	. . . and . . . what it was . . . it was good old Western Union, some little boy about seventy.
MARTHA	[*involved*] Crazy Billy?
GEORGE	Yes, Martha, that's right . . . Crazy Billy . . . and he had a telegram, and it was for us, and I have to tell you about it.
MARTHA	[*as if from a distance*] Why didn't they phone it? Why did they bring it; why didn't they telephone it? 30
GEORGE	Some telegrams you have to deliver, Martha; some telegrams you can't phone.
MARTHA	[*rising*] What do you mean?
GEORGE	Martha . . . I can hardly bring myself to say it . . .
HONEY	Don't.
GEORGE	[*to Honey*] Do you want to do it?
HONEY	[*defending herself against an attack of bees*] No no no no no.
GEORGE	[*sighing heavily*] All right. Well, Martha . . . I'm afraid our boy isn't coming home for his birthday.
MARTHA	Of course he is. 40
GEORGE	No, Martha.
MARTHA	Of course he is. I say he is!
GEORGE	He . . . can't.
MARTHA	He is! I say so!

GEORGE	Martha . . . [*long pause*] . . . our son is . . . dead. [*Silence*] He was . . . killed . . . late in the afternoon . . . [*Silence*] [*a tiny chuckle*] on a country road, with his learner's permit in his pocket, he swerved, to avoid a porcupine, and drove straight into a . . .
MARTHA	[*rigid fury*] YOU . . . CAN'T . . . DO . . . THAT! 50
GEORGE	. . . large tree.
MARTHA	YOU CANNOT DO THAT!
NICK	[*softly*] Oh my God. [*Honey is weeping louder*]
GEORGE	[*quietly, dispassionately*] I thought you should know.
NICK	Oh my God, no.
MARTHA	[*quivering with rage and loss*] NO! NO! YOU CANNOT DO THAT! YOU CAN'T DECIDE THAT FOR YOUR- SELF! I WILL NOT LET YOU DO THAT!
GEORGE	We'll have to leave around noon, I suppose. . . .
MARTHA	I WILL NOT LET YOU DECIDE THESE THINGS! 60
GEORGE	. . . because there are matters of identification, naturally, and arrangements to be made. . . .
MARTHA	[*leaping at George, but ineffectual*] YOU CAN'T DO THIS! [*Nick rises, grabs hold of Martha, pins her arms behind her back*] I WON'T LET YOU DO THIS, GET YOUR HANDS OFF ME!
GEORGE	[*as Nick holds on; right in Martha's face*] You don't seem to understand, Martha; I haven't done anything. Now, pull yourself together. Our son is DEAD! Can you get that into your head?
MARTHA	YOU CAN'T DECIDE THESE THINGS. 70
NICK	Lady, please.
MARTHA	LET ME GO!
GEORGE	Now listen, Martha; listen carefully. We got a telegram; there was a car accident, and he's dead. POUF! Just like that! Now, how do you like it?
MARTHA	[*a howl which weakens into a moan*] NOOOOOOooooooo.
GEORGE	[*to Nick*] Let her go. [*Martha slumps to the floor in a sitting position*] She'll be right now.
MARTHA	[*pathetic*] No; no, he is *not* dead; he is not *dead*.
GEORGE	He is dead. Kyrie, eleison. Christie, eleison. Kyrie, eleison. 80
MARTHA	You can*not*. You may not decide these things.
NICK	[*leaning over her; tenderly*] He hasn't decided anything, lady. It's not his doing. He doesn't have the power. . . .
GEORGE	That's right, Martha; I'm not a God. I don't have the power over life and death, do I?
MARTHA	YOU CAN'T KILL HIM! YOU CAN'T HAVE HIM DIE!
HONEY	Lady . . . please. . . .
MARTHA	You CAN'T!
GEORGE	There was a telegram, Martha.
MARTHA	[*up; facing him*] Show it to me! Show me the telegram! 90
GEORGE	[*long pause; then with a straight face*] I ate it.
MARTHA	[*a pause; then with the greatest disbelief possible, tinged with hysteria*] What did you just say to me?

GEORGE [*barely able to stop exploding with laughter*] I . . . ate . . . it. [*Martha stares at him for a long moment, then spits in his face.*]

GEORGE [*with a smile*] Good for you, Martha.

NICK [*to George*] Do you think that's the way to treat her at a time like this? Making an ugly goddam joke like that? Hunh?

GEORGE [*snapping his fingers at Honey*] Did I eat the telegram or did I not?

HONEY [*terrified*] Yes; yes, you ate it. I watched . . . I watched 100
you . . . you . . . you ate it all down.

GEORGE [*prompting*] . . . like a good boy.

HONEY . . . like a . . . g-g-g-good . . . boy. Yes.

MARTHA [*to George, coldly*] You're not going to get away with this.

GEORGE [*with disgust*] YOU KNOW THE RULES, MARTHA! FOR CHRIST'S SAKE, YOU KNOW THE RULES!

MARTHA NO!

NICK [*with the beginnings of knowledge he cannot face*] What are you two talking about?

GEORGE I can kill him, Martha, if I want to. 110

MARTHA HE IS OUR CHILD!

GEORGE Oh yes, and you bore him, and it was a good delivery. . . .

MARTHA HE IS OUR CHILD!

GEORGE	AND I HAVE KILLED HIM!
MARTHA	NO!
GEORGE	YES!
	[*long silence*]
NICK	[*very quietly*] I think I understand this.
GEORGE	[*ibid*] Do you?
NICK	[*ibid*] Jesus Christ, I think I understand this.
GEORGE	[*ibid*] Good for you, buster.
NICK	[*violently*] JESUS CHRIST I THINK I UNDERSTAND THIS!
MARTHA	[*great sadness and loss*] You have no right . . . you have no right at all . . . .
GEORGE	[*tenderly*] I have the right, Martha. We never spoke of it; that's all. I could kill him any time I wanted to.
MARTHA	But why? Why?
GEORGE	You broke our rule, baby. You mentioned him . . . you mentioned him to someone else.
MARTHA	[*tearfully*] I did *not*. I never did.
GEORGE	Yes, you did.
MARTHA	Who? WHO?!
HONEY	[*crying*] To me. You mentioned him to me.
MARTHA	[*crying*] I FORGET! Sometimes . . . sometimes when it's night, when it's late, and . . . and everybody else is . . . talking . . . I forget and I . . . want to mention him . . . but I . . . HOLD ON . . . I hold on . . . but I've wanted to . . . so often . . . oh, George, you've *pushed* it . . . there was no need . . . there was no need for *this*. I *mentioned* him . . . all right . . . but you didn't have to push it over the EDGE. You didn't have to . . . kill him.
GEORGE	Requiescat in pace.
HONEY	Amen.
MARTHA	You didn't have to have him die, George.
GEORGE	Requiem aeternam dona eis, Domine.
HONEY	Et lux perpetua luceat eis.
MARTHA	That wasn't . . . needed.
	[*a long silence*]
GEORGE	[*softly*] It will be dawn soon. I think the party's over.
NICK	[*to George: quietly*] You couldn't have . . . any?
GEORGE	*We* couldn't.
MARTHA	[*a hint of communion in this*] *We* couldn't.
GEORGE	[*to Nick and Honey*] Home to bed, children; it's way past your bedtime.
NICK	[*his hand out to Honey*] Honey?
HONEY	[*rising, moving to him*] Yes.
GEORGE	[*Martha is sitting on the floor by a chair now*] You two go now.
NICK	Yes.
HONEY	Yes.
NICK	I'd like to . . . .
GEORGE	Good night.

120

130

140

150

160

NICK	[*pause*] Good night.	
	[*Nick and Honey exit; George closes the door after them; looks round the room; sighs, picks up a glass or two, takes them to the bar. This whole last section very softly, very slowly*]	
GEORGE	Do you want anything, Martha?	
MARTHA	[*still looking away*] No . . . nothing.	
GEORGE	All right. [*Pause*] Time for bed.	
MARTHA	Yes.	
GEORGE	Are you tired?	
MARTHA	Yes.	
GEORGE	I am.	
MARTHA	Yes.	170
GEORGE	Sunday tomorrow; all day.	
MARTHA	Yes.	
	[*A long silence between them*]	
MARTHA	Did you . . . did you . . . have to?	
GEORGE	[*pause*] Yes.	
MARTHA	It was . . . ? You had to?	
GEORGE	[*pause*] Yes.	
MARTHA	I don't know.	
GEORGE	It was . . . time.	
MARTHA	Was it?	
GEORGE	Yes.	180
MARTHA	[*Pause*] I'm cold.	
GEORGE	It's late.	
MARTHA	Yes.	
GEORGE	[*long silence*] It will be better.	
MARTHA	[*long silence*] I don't . . . know.	
GEORGE	It will be . . . maybe.	
MARTHA	I'm . . . not . . . sure.	
GEORGE	No.	
MARTHA	Just . . . us?	
GEORGE	Yes.	190
MARTHA	I don't suppose, maybe, we could	
GEORGE	No, Martha.	
MARTHA	Yes. No.	
GEORGE	Are you all right?	
MARTHA	Yes. No.	
GEORGE	[*puts his hand gently on her shoulder; she puts her head back and he sings to her, very softly*] Who's afraid of Virginia Woolf Virginia Woolf Virginia Woolf?	
MARTHA	I . . . am . . . George	
GEORGE	Who's afraid of Virginia Woolf . . . ?	200
MARTHA	I . . . am . . . George . . . I . . . am	
	[*George nods, slowly*]	
	[*Silence; tableau*]	

Into the text

1 In what ways, if at all, did the stage directions help you to interpret the extract?

2 Why do you think George 'chuckles' when he describes the circumstances of his son's death? (line 46)

3 What do you think Martha meant when she shouted:
   - 'YOU . . . CAN'T . . . DO . . . THAT!' (line 50)
   - 'YOU CANNOT DO THAT!' (line 52)
   - 'NO! NO! YOU CANNOT DO THAT! YOU CAN'T DECIDE THAT FOR YOURSELF! I WILL NOT LET YOU DO THAT!' (lines 56–8)?

4 At lines 82–3, Nick does not realise the truth of the situation.
   a At what point do we know he realises?
   b At what point in the extract did you realise that 'Sunny-Jim' does not really exist?
   c Does Honey realise this at any point?

5 What effect do the words 'I ate it' (lines 93–4) have on
   a you,
   b Martha?
   Why does George say 'Good for you, Martha' when she spits in his face?

6 George tells Martha that 'YOU KNOW THE RULES' (lines 105–6) What do you know to be the one rule that Martha broke?

7 How do you think Nick was going to end the sentence 'I'd like to . . .' (line 160) Would what he was going to say be appropriate?

8 How would you describe the relationship between George and Martha at the end of the play?

9 George and Honey use Greek and Latin phrases on three occasions in the text (lines 142, 145 and 146). Find out what they mean and where they come from. What do they contribute to your understanding of the characters and situation? In what way does this help you to understand why this section of the play is called 'The Exorcism'?

10 This play was written by an American. American English is a variety of English with its own grammar, vocabulary, use of idiom, etc. What evidence can you find of this in this extract?

Assignments

Throughout this unit, you have had the opportunity to explore, in writing, some of your ideas about family life. Now that you have read all of the extracts and some of the suggested wider reading, you may wish to consider 'the family' in general terms.

1 We said in the Introduction that everybody is exposed to a view of family life through TV advertisements and other media images.

As preparation for this assignment, collect examples of some of these – particularly TV advertisements.

    a Write brief descriptions including, if you can, transcripts of the words used.

    b Consider who the advertisements are aimed at. What difference (if any) does the target audience make to the content and style of the advertisements?

    c What assumptions do the advertisers make about the structure of a typical family?

    d Is there any conflict in the advertisement? If so, how is it resolved?

    e Is there any affection shown? If so, how?

    f What social class do the families belong to? How do you know?

By making close reference to the texts you have read, the advertisements you have investigated and to your own ideas, write an essay entitled 'Love and hate: the myth and reality of family life'.

2 Poets and lyricists have always written about love: not telling love stories but exploring the strong emotions that close relationships generate. Why do you think that poets have chosen love as a major theme of their writing? With this question in mind choose at least three poems (from those you have read in this unit, wider reading or even pop lyrics if you wish) and:

    a describe in detail what the poet is saying

    b comment on the use of language: can you find any patterns?

    c consider how successful each poem is in expressing some aspect of love.

3 The following extract is set in Rhodesia (now Zimbabwe) in 1950. Mary, a city girl, has recently married a poor white farmer and is finding it difficult to adjust to life in the country. Here, she and her husband Dick are arguing about their black houseboy who doesn't like Mary and wants to return to his village. Read the passage carefully and answer the questions that follow.

The Grass is Singing
Doris Lessing

'It's my house,' said Mary. 'He's my boy, not yours. Don't interfere.'

    'Listen to me,' said Dick curtly. 'I work hard enough, don't I? All day I am down on the lands with these lazy black savages, fighting them to get some work out of them. You know that. I won't come back home to this damned fight, fight, fight in the house. Do you understand? I will not have it. And you should learn sense. If you want to get work out of them you have to know how to manage them. You shouldn't expect too much. They are nothing but savages after all.' Thus Dick, who had never stopped to reflect that these same savages had cooked for him better than

his wife did, had run his house, had given him a comfortable existence, 10
as far as his pinched life could be comfortable, for years.

Mary was beside herself. She said, wanting to hurt him, really wanting
to hurt him for the first time, because of this new arrogance of his, 'You
expect a lot from me, don't you?' On the brink of disaster, she pulled
herself up, but could not stop completely, and after a hesitation went on,
'You expect such a lot! You expect me to live like a poor white in this
pokey little place of yours. You expect me to cook myself every day
because you won't put in ceilings . . .'. She was speaking in a new voice
for her, a voice she had never used before in her life. It was taken direct
from her mother, when she had had those scenes over money with her 20
father. It was not the voice of Mary, the individual (who after all did not
care . . . whether the native stayed or went), but the voice of the suffering
female, who wanted to show her husband she just would not be treated
like that. In a moment she would begin to cry, as her mother had cried
on these occasions, in a kind of dignified, martyred rage.

Dick said curtly, white with fury, 'I told you when I married you what
you could expect. You can't accuse me of telling you lies. I explained
everything to you. And there are farmers' wives all over the country
living no better, and not making such a fuss. And as for ceilings, you can
whistle for them. I have lived in this house for six years and it hasn't hurt 30
me. You can make the best of it.'

She gasped in astonishment. Never had he spoken like that to her. And
inside she went hard and cold against him, and nothing would melt her
until he said he was sorry and craved her forgiveness.

'That boy will stay now, I've seen to that. Now treat him properly and
don't make a fool of yourself again,' said Dick.

She went straight into the kitchen, gave the boy the money he was
owed, counting out the shillings as if she grudged them, and dismissed
him. She returned cold and victorious. But Dick did not acknowledge
her victory. 40

'It is not me you are hurting, it is yourself,' he said. 'If you go on like
this, you'll never get any servants. They soon learn the women who don't
know how to treat their boys.'

She got the supper herself, struggling with the stove, and afterwards
when Dick had gone to bed early, as he always did, she remained alone
in the little front room. After a while, feeling caged, she went out into
the dark outside the house, and walked up and down the path between
the borders of white stones which gleamed faintly through the dark,
trying to catch a breath of cool air to soothe her hot cheeks. Lightning
was flickering gently over the kopjes; there was a dull red glow where 50
the fire burned; and overhead it was dark and stuffy. She was tense with
hatred. Then she began to picture herself walking there up and down in
the darkness, with the hated bush all around her, outside that pigsty he
called a house, having to do all her own work – while only a few months
ago she had been living her own life in town, surrounded by friends who
loved her and needed her. She began to cry, weakening into self-pity. She
cried for hours, till she could walk no more. She staggered back into bed,
feeling bruised and beaten. The tension between them lasted for an
intolerable week, until at last the rains fell, and the air grew cool and

relaxed. And he had not apologized. The incident was simply not men-   60
tioned. Unresolved and unacknowledged, the conflict was put behind
them, and they went on as if it had not happened. But it had changed
them both.

a '... it had changed them both.' What evidence can you find in the
passage that this is a turning-point in Mary and Dick's relationship?
b In the last paragraph, how does the writer communicate Mary's mood?
c What insight does the extract give you into the attitudes of whites to
blacks in southern Africa at this time?
d Can you find any parallels between Mary's situation and that of the
servant? What conclusions do you draw from this?
e Unlike the servant, Mary can protest – but how effective is this? What
do you think the future holds for Mary and Dick?
f Relationships can go wrong for a number of reasons. In this extract the
characters try to carry on as if nothing has happened which in the long
run often makes things far worse. It is often better to face up to problems
even if it means splitting-up. Choose one of the following situations and
describe how you would bring the relationship to an end as sensitively as
you can:
i   you have fallen in love with your partner's best friend
ii your partner is becoming too possessive, not willing to give you any
    freedom or independence
iii you want to leave your home town (perhaps to go to University, to
    work abroad)
iv invent a situation of your own.
4 a Look back at the definition that you wrote down at the beginning of
the unit. Having worked through the unit, is there anything that you
would like to add or change?
b Look at the definitions on page 58. Consider each one of them in turn
and in the light of your reading, say what you think to be missing from
them, and how they could be improved.
c Which extract most accurately represents your view of family life?
Explain your choice.

Belief and conflict: Ideology and the individual

Contents

Introduction

This unit is concerned with what people believe and how beliefs determine the way in which people act towards one another. People have a variety of beliefs shaped by many things: race, family, age, peer groups, religion, creed, politics. Sometimes, these beliefs or ideologies can bring people into conflict with others, either because they are out of step with the majority or they deliberately choose to challenge them.

Belief and conflict can operate on several levels. When people act individually, the conflict is restricted to the people directly involved. For instance, two people who violently disagree about an issue are likely only to affect themselves, unless they deliberately choose to involve others. Social minorities, rooted in particular beliefs (racial, religious or political), are often themselves victims of oppression and exploitation. They can find themselves in conflict with the majority views. Governments, especially those with strongly held ideological views, can come into conflict with others having different opinions. In such cases, Governments gain support for their actions because of the reservoirs of patriotism which nations possess.

Patriotism can sometimes lead people to commit actions which in other circumstances they might not commit: for example, in the Mai Lai massacre in Vietnam in 1969, a whole village of men, women and children were killed by American troops. Other beliefs can be equally as powerful: many awful acts have been committed for racial and religious reasons. Some people may regard these atrocities as the consequence of propaganda and indoctrination.

Some definitions

You will come across some words with which you may be unfamiliar during the course of this unit. Here are some definitions which you may find useful:

Anarchy   want of government in society; lawless disorder in a country; a political theory, which would dispense with all laws, founding authority on the individual conscience.

Armageddon   scene of the final struggle between the powers of good and evil; a great war or battle of nations.

Belief   persuasion of the truth of anything; faith; the opinion or doctrine believed.

Conflict   violent collision, a struggle or contest; a state of being at odds with.

Creed   a system of belief.

Exploitation   the act of using for selfish purposes.

Government   act of governing; exercise of authority; the system of governing in a state or community; the ruling power in a state; the executive power.

Holocaust a huge slaughter or destruction of life with particular reference to the Nazi 'Final Solution' which caused the deaths of six million Jews before and during World War II.

Ideology a body of ideas, usually political and/or economic, forming the basis of a national or sectarian policy; a way of thinking.

Indoctrination the act of persuading others of a point of view.

Oppression harshness, severity, tyranny.

Patriotism the belief that a country deserves uncritical service and support.

Propaganda a persuasive way of expressing an ideology which may be only partially true or not true.

War a state of conflict; a contest between states or between parties within a state (civil war) carried on by arms; any long continued struggle.

Human rights

As a striking example of what can happen when an individual comes into conflict with a government, the following passage, written in prison for the author, pleads for justice.

'It is impossible to see respect for human rights and the rule of law when a human being is detained for a solid year without ever being accused of any crime let alone being tried and convicted.

I am of the considered opinion which prevails after exhaustive thinking, that if Independence means the substitution of indigenous tyranny for alien rule then Doctor Banda has not only desecrated the cause of human rights but betrayed humanism and his own people.

I wish I was taken to court, given a fair trial, given an opportunity to defend myself and then discharged or punished depending on whether or not my innocence had been established or my guilt passed beyond any reasonable shadow of doubt.' (Allie Dessu, Zomba Central Detention, 5 February 1974–22 January 1975)

An attitude survey

Read each of the statements in the *Attitude Survey* on your own and in silence. On a photocopy, tick the box which best shows your attitude towards each statement.

In groups, compare your responses with your classmates'. Take each statement in turn. For each one, add up the number of ticks in each of the five columns. Which statements had the greatest degree of unanimity? Which had the least? Were you able to resolve any disagreements? How do you account for the differences in opinion between the members of your group?

Any differences that you have within your group could be regarded as a conflict of ideology. The following extracts are about a variety of conflicts

An attitude survey

	Strongly agree	Agree	Don't know	Disagree	Strongly disagree
1 I am prepared to argue for what I believe in.					
2 I dislike being made to do what I would not choose to do.					
3 I know what I believe – nobody can convince me that I am wrong.					
4 I am interested in other people's ideas and opinions.					
5 'If you can't beat 'em, join 'em.'					
6 Society needs laws to guarantee order.					
7 My opinions are important – they deserve a hearing.					
8 I sometimes pretend to agree with others just to keep the peace.					
9 I would be prepared to fight for what I believe in.					
10 In war, any action is justifiable in pursuit of victory.					

	Strongly agree	Agree	Don't know	Disagree	Strongly disagree
11 *Dulce et decorum est, pro patria mori* (it is sweet and fitting to die for one's country).					
12 'Your country needs YOU!' (Recruiting Poster First World War).					
13 The prospect of nuclear war frightens me.					
14 'Anything for a quiet life.'					
15 There is no such thing as 'a just war'.					
16 I am tolerant even of things I disagree with.					
17 I am prepared to kill somebody if ordered to do so.					
18 I love my country.					
19 'Love thine enemies as thyself' (*The New Testament*).					
20 'An eye for an eye, a tooth for a tooth' (*The Old Testament*).					

of ideology – all rooted in disagreements similar to the ones you may have had.

Keep your attitude survey and the analysis of your group's response as you will return to them later in the unit.

The abuse of power: A short story

Approaching the text

Graham Greene was born in 1904 and died in 1991. He was a novelist and short story writer. 'The Destructors' was first published in 1954. While on the one hand it stands on its own as a description of a piece of wanton vandalism, it can also be seen as a reflection on the events of the previous two decades; ie the rise of Adolf Hitler, the growth of Nazi Germany and the victimisation of the Jews.

As you read the story, pay particular attention to the way in which T, the central character, gains and sustains his influence over the other members of the gang, with startling results.

The Destructors
Graham Greene

1

It was on the eve of August Bank Holiday that the latest recruit became the leader of the Wormsley Common Gang. No one was surprised except Mike, but Mike at the age of nine was surprised by everything. 'If you don't shut your mouth,' somebody once said to him, 'you'll get a frog down it.' After that Mike kept his teeth tightly clamped except when the surprise was too great.

The new recruit had been with the gang since the beginning of the summer holidays, and there were possibilities about his brooding silence that all recognized. He never wasted a word even to tell his name until that was required of him by the rules. When he said 'Trevor' it was a   10
statement of fact, not as it would have been with the others a statement of shame or defiance. Nor did anyone laugh except Mike, who finding himself without support and meeting the dark gaze of the newcomer opened his mouth and was quiet again. There was every reason why T, as he was afterwards referred to, should have been the object of mockery – there was his name (and they substituted the initial because otherwise they had no excuse not to laugh at it), the fact that his father, a former architect and present clerk, had 'come down in the world' and that his mother considered herself better than the neighbours. What but an odd quality of danger, of the unpredictable, established him in the   20
gang without any ignoble ceremony of initiation?

The gang met every morning in an impromptu car-park, the site of the last bomb of the first blitz. The leader, who was known as Blackie, claimed to have heard it fall, and no one was precise enough in his dates to point out that he would have been one year old and fast asleep on the down platform of Wormsley Common Underground Station. On one side of the car-park leant the first occupied house, No. 3, of the shattered Northwood Terrace – literally leant, for it had suffered from the blast of the bomb and the side walls were supported on wooden struts. A smaller bomb and incendiaries had fallen beyond, so that the house stuck up like a jagged tooth and carried on the further wall relics of its neighbour, a dado, the remains of a fireplace. T, whose words were almost confined to voting 'Yes' or 'No' to the plan of operations proposed each day by Blackie, once startled the whole gang by saying broodingly, 'Wren built that house, father says.'

'Who's Wren?'

'The man who built St Paul's.'

'Who cares?' Blackie said. 'It's only Old Misery's.'

Old Misery – whose real name was Thomas – had once been a builder and decorator. He lived alone in the crippled house, doing for himself: once a week you could see him coming back across the common with bread and vegetables, and once as the boys played in the car-park he put his head over the smashed wall of his garden and looked at them.

'Been to the lav,' one of the boys said, for it was common knowledge that since the bombs fell something had gone wrong with the pipes of the house and Old Misery was too mean to spend money on the property. He could do the redecorating himself at cost price, but had never learnt plumbing. The lav was a wooden shed at the bottom of the narrow garden with a star-shaped hole in the door: it had escaped the blast which had smashed the house next door and sucked out the window-frames of No. 3.

The next time the gang became aware of Mr Thomas was more surprising. Blackie, Mike and a thin yellow boy, who for some reason was called by his surname Summers, met him on the common coming back from the market. Mr Thomas stopped them. He said glumly, 'You belong to the lot that play on the car-park?'

Mike was about to answer when Blackie stopped him. As the leader he had responsibilities. 'Suppose we are?' he said ambiguously.

'I got some chocolates,' Mr Thomas said. 'Don't like 'em myself. Here you are. Not enough to go round, I don't suppose. There never is,' he   60
added with sombre conviction. He handed over three packets of Smarties.

The gang was puzzled and perturbed by this action and tried to explain it away. 'Bet someone dropped them and he picked 'em up,' somebody suggested.

.'Pinched 'em and then got in a bleeding funk,' another thought aloud.

'It's a bribe,' Summers said. 'He wants us to stop bouncing balls on his wall.'

'We'll show him we don't take bribes,' Blackie said, and they sacrificed the whole morning to the game of bouncing that only Mike was young   70
enough to enjoy. There was no sign of Mr Thomas.

Next day T astonished them all. He was late at the rendezvous, and the voting for the day's exploit took place without him. At Blackie's suggestion the gang was to disperse in pairs, take buses at random and see how many free rides could be snatched from unwary conductors (the operation was to be carried out in pairs to avoid cheating). They were drawing lots for their companions when T arrived.

'Where have you been, T?' Blackie asked. 'You can't vote now. You know the rules.'

'I've been *there*,' T said. He looked at the ground, as though he had   80
thoughts to hide.

'Where?'

'At Old Misery's.' Mike's mouth opened and then hurriedly closed again with a click. He had remembered the frog.

'At Old Misery's?' Blackie said. There was nothing in the rules against it, but he had a sensation that T was treading on dangerous ground. He asked hopefully, 'Did you break in?'

'No. I rang the bell.'

'And what did you say?'

'I said I wanted to see his house.'   90

'What did he do?'

'He showed it me.'

'Pinch anything?'

'No.'

'What did you do it for then?'

The gang had gathered round: it was as though an impromptu court were about to form and try some case of deviation. T said, 'It's a beautiful house,' and still watching the ground, meeting no one's eyes, he licked his lips first one way, then the other.

'What do you mean, a beautiful house?' Blackie asked with scorn.   100

'It's got a staircase two hundred years old like a corkscrew. Nothing holds it up.'

'What do you mean, nothing holds it up. Does it float?'

'It's to do with opposite forces, Old Misery said.'

'What else?'

'There's panelling.'

'Like in the Blue Boar?'

'Two hundred years old.'

'Is Old Misery two hundred years old?'

Mike laughed suddenly and then was quiet again. The meeting was in a serious mood. For the first time since T had strolled into the car-park on the first day of the holidays his position was in danger. It only needed a single use of his real name and the gang would be at his heels.

'What did you do it for?' Blackie asked. He was just, he had no jealousy, he was anxious to retain T in the gang if he could. It was the word 'beautiful' that worried him – that belonged to a class world that you could still see parodied at the Wormsley Common Empire by a man wearing a top hat and a monocle, with a haw-haw accent. He was tempted to say, "My dear Trevor, old chap," and unleash his hell hounds. 'If you'd broken in,' he said sadly – that indeed would have been an exploit worthy of the gang.

'This was better,' T said. 'I found out things.' He continued to stare at his feet, not meeting anybody's eye, as though he were absorbed in some dream he was unwilling – or ashamed – to share.

'What things?'

'Old Misery's going to be away all tomorrow and Bank Holiday.'

Blackie said with relief, 'You mean we could break in?'

'And pinch things?' somebody asked.

Blackie said, 'Nobody's going to pinch things. Breaking in – that's good enough, isn't it? We don't want any court stuff.'

'I don't want to pinch anything,' T said. 'I've got a better idea.'

'What is it?'

T raised eyes, as grey and disturbed as the drab August day. 'We'll pull it down,' he said. 'We'll destroy it.'

Blackie gave a single hoot of laughter and then, like Mike, fell quiet, daunted by the serious implacable gaze. 'What'd the police be doing all the time?' he said.

'They'd never know. We'd do it from inside. I've found a way in.' He said with a sort of intensity, 'We'd be like worms, don't you see, in an apple. When we came out again there'd be nothing there, no staircase, no panels, nothing but just walls, and then we'd make the walls fall down – somehow.'

'We'd go to jug,' Blackie said.

'Who's to prove? And anyway we wouldn't have pinched anything.' He added without the smallest flicker of glee, 'There wouldn't be anything to pinch after we'd finished.'

'I've never heard of going to prison for breaking things,' Summers said.

'There wouldn't be time,' Blackie said. 'I've seen housebreakers at work.'

110

120

130

140

150

'There are twelve of us,' T said. 'We'd organise.'

'None of us know how . . .'

'I know,' T said. He looked across at Blackie. 'Have you got a better plan?'

'Today,' Mike said tactlessly, 'we're pinching free rides . . .'

'Free rides,' T said. 'Kid stuff. You can stand down, Blackie, if you'd rather . . .'

'The gang's got to vote.'

'Put it up then.'

Blackie said uneasily, 'It's proposed that tomorrow and Monday we   160
destroy Old Misery's house.'

'Here, here,' said a fat boy called Joe.

'Who's in favour?'

T said, 'It's carried.'

'How do we start?' Summers asked.

'He'll tell you,' Blackie said. It was the end of his leadership. He went away to the back of the car-park and began to kick a stone, dribbling it this way and that. There was only one old Morris in the park, for few cars were left there except lorries: without an attendant there was no safety. He took a flying kick at the car and scraped a little paint off the   170
rear mudguard. Beyond, paying no more attention to him than to a stranger, the gang had gathered round T; Blackie was dimly aware of the fickleness of favour. He thought of going home, of never returning, of letting them all discover the hollowness of T's leadership, but suppose after all what T proposed was possible – nothing like it had ever been done before. The fame of the Wormsley Common car-park gang would surely reach around London. There would be headlines in the papers. Even the grown-up gangs who ran the betting at the all-in wrestling and the barrow-boys would hear with respect of how Old Misery's house had been destroyed. Driven by the pure, simple and altruistic ambition of   180
fame for the gang, Blackie came back to where T stood in the shadow of Old-Misery's wall.

T was giving his orders with decision: it was as though this plan had been with him all his life, pondered through the seasons, now in his fifteenth year crystallized with the pain of puberty. 'You,' he said to Mike, 'bring some big nails, the biggest you can find, and a hammer. Anybody who can, better bring a hammer and a screwdriver. We'll need plenty of them. Chisels too. We can't have too many chisels. Can anybody bring a saw?'

'I can,' Mike said.   190

'Not a child's saw,' T said. 'A real saw.'

Blackie realised he had raised his hand like any ordinary member of the gang.

'Right, you bring one, Blackie. But now there's a difficulty. We want a hacksaw.'

'What's a hacksaw?' someone asked.

'You can get 'em at Woolworth's,' Summers said.

The fat boy called Joe said gloomily, 'I knew it would end in a collection.'

'I'll get one myself,' T said. 'I don't want your money. But I can't buy 200
a sledge-hammer.'

Blackie said, 'They're working on No. 15. I know where they'll leave
their stuff for Bank Holiday.'

'Then that's all,' T said. 'We meet here at nine sharp.'

'I've got to go to church,' Mike said.

'Come over the wall and whistle. We'll let you in.'

2

On Sunday morning all were punctual except Blackie, even Mike.
Mike had a stroke of luck. His mother felt ill, his father was tired after
Saturday night, and he was told to go to church alone with many
warnings of what would happen if he strayed. Blackie had difficulty in 210
smuggling out the saw, and then in finding the sledge-hammer at the
back of No. 15. He approached the house from a lane at the rear of the
garden, for fear of the policeman's beat along the main road. The tired
evergreens kept off a stormy sun; another wet Bank Holiday was being
prepared over the Atlantic, beginning in swirls of dust under the trees.
Blackie climbed the wall into Misery's garden.

There was no sign of anybody anywhere. The lav stood like a tomb
in a neglected graveyard. The curtains were drawn. The house slept.
Blackie lumbered nearer with the saw and the sledge-hammer. Perhaps
after all nobody had turned up: the plan had been a wild invention: they 220
had woken wiser. But when he came close to the back door he could hear
a confusion of sound hardly louder than a hive in swarm: a clickety-
clack, a bang bang, a scraping, a creaking, a sudden painful crack. He
thought: it's true, and whistled.

They opened the back door to him and he came in. He had at once
the impression of organization, very different from the old happy-go-
lucky ways under his leadership. For a while he wandered up and down
stairs looking for T. Nobody addressed him: he had a sense of great
urgency, and already he could begin to see the plan. The interior of
the house was being carefully demolished without touching the walls. 230
Summers with hammer and chisel was ripping out the skirting-boards in
the ground-floor dining-room: he had already smashed the panels of the
door. In the same room Joe was heaving up the parquet blocks, exposing
the soft wood floorboards over the cellar. Coils of wire came out of the
damaged skirting and Mike sat happily on the floor clipping the wires.

On the curved stairs two of the gang were working hard with an
inadequate child's saw on the bannisters – when they saw Blackie's big
saw they signalled for it wordlessly. When he next saw them a quarter
of the bannisters had been dropped into the hall. He found T at last in
the bathroom – he sat moodily in the least cared-for room in the house, 240
listening to the sounds coming up from below.

'You've really done it,' Blackie said with awe. 'What's going to
happen?'

'We've only just begun,' T said. He looked at the sledge-hammer and
gave his instructions. 'You stay here and break the bath and the wash-
basin. Don't bother about the pipes. They come later.'

Mike appeared at the door. 'I've finished the wires, T,' he said.

'Good. You've just got to go wandering round now. The kitchen's in the basement. Smash all the china and glass and bottles you can lay hold of. Don't turn on the taps – we don't want a flood – yet. Then go into all the rooms and turn out the drawers. If they are locked get one of the others to break them open. Tear up any papers you find and smash all the ornaments. Better take a carving knife with you from the kitchen. The bedroom's opposite here. Open the pillows and tear up the sheets. That's enough for the moment. And you, Blackie, when you've finished in here crack the plaster in the passage up with your sledge-hammer.' 250

'What are you going to do?' Blackie asked.

'I'm looking for something special,' T said.

It was nearly lunch-time before Blackie had finished and went in search of T. Chaos had advanced. The kitchen was a shambles of broken glass and china. The dining-room was stripped of parquet, the skirting was up, the door had been taken off its hinges, and the destroyers had moved up a floor. Streaks of light came in through the closed shutters where they worked with the seriousness of creators – and destruction after all is a form of creation. A kind of imagination had seen this house as it had now become. 260

Mike said, 'I've got to go home for dinner.'

'Who else?' T asked, but all the others on one excuse or another had brought provisions with them.

They squatted in the ruins of the room and swapped unwanted 270
sandwiches. Half an hour for lunch and they were at work again. By the
time Mike returned they were on the top floor, and by six the superficial
damage was completed. The doors were all off, all the skirtings raised,
the furniture pillaged and ripped and smashed – no one could have slept
in the house except on a bed of broken plaster. T gave his orders – eight
o'clock next morning, and to escape notice they climbed singly over
the garden wall, into the car-park. Only Blackie and T were left: the
light had nearly gone, and when they touched a switch, nothing worked
– Mike had done his job thoroughly.

'Did you find anything special?' Blackie asked.   280

T nodded. 'Come over here,' he said, 'and look.' Out of both pockets
he drew bundles of pound notes. 'Old Misery's savings,' he said. 'Mike
ripped out the mattress, but he missed them.'

'What are you going to do? Share them?'

'We aren't thieves,' T said. 'Nobody's going to steal anything from this
house. I kept these for you and me – a celebration.' He knelt down on
the floor and counted them out – there were seventy in all. 'We'll burn
them,' he said, 'one by one,' and taking it in turns they held a note
upwards and lit the top corner, so that the flame burnt slowly towards
their fingers. The grey ash floated above them and fell on their heads like 290
age. 'I'd like to see Old Misery's face when we are through,' T said.

'You hate him a lot?' Blackie asked.

'Of course I don't hate him,' T said. 'There'd be no fun if I hated him.'
The last burning note illuminated his brooding face. 'All this hate and
love,' he said, 'it's soft, it's hooey. There's only things, Blackie,' and he
looked round the room crowded with the unfamiliar shadows of half
things, broken things, former things. 'I'll race you home, Blackie,' he
said.

3

Next morning the serious destruction started. Two were missing –
Mike and another boy whose parents were off to Southend and Brighton 300
in spite of the slow warm drops that had begun to fall and the rumble
of thunder in the estuary like the first guns of the old blitz. 'We've got
to hurry,' T said.

Summers was restive. 'Haven't we done enough?' he asked. 'I've been
given a bob for slot machines. This is like work.'

'We've hardly started,' T said. 'Why, there's all the floors left, and the
stairs. We haven't taken out a single window. You voted like the others.
We are going to *destroy* this house. There won't be anything left when
we've finished.'

They began again on the first floor picking up the top floorboards next 310
to the outer wall, leaving the joists exposed. Then they sawed through
the joists and retreated into the hall, as what was left of the floor heeled
and sank. They had learnt with practice, and the second floor collapsed
more easily. By the evening an odd exhilaration seized them as they
looked down the great hollow of the house. They ran risks and made

mistakes: when they thought of the windows it was too late to reach them. 'Cor,' Joe said, and dropped a penny down into the dry rubble-filled well. It cracked and span amongst the broken glass.

'Why did we start this?' Summers asked with astonishment; T was already on the ground, digging at the rubble, clearing a space along the 320 outer wall. 'Turn on the taps,' he said. 'It's too dark for anyone to see now, and in the morning it won't matter.' The water overtook them on the stairs and fell through the floorless rooms.

It was then they heard Mike's whistle at the back. 'Something's wrong,' Blackie said. They could hear his urgent breathing as they unlocked the door.

'The bogies?' Summers asked.

'Old Misery,' Mike said. 'He's on his way,' he said with pride.

'But why?' T said. 'He told me . . .' He protested with the fury of the child he had never been, 'It isn't fair.'   330

'He was down at Southend,' Mike said, 'and he was on the train coming back. Said it was too cold and wet.' He paused and gazed at the water. 'My, you've had a storm here. Is the roof leaking?'

'How long will he be?'

'Five minutes. I gave Ma the slip and ran.'

'We better clear,' Summers said. 'We've done enough, anyway.'

'Oh no, we haven't. Anybody could do this' – 'this' was the shattered hollowed house with nothing left but the walls. Yet walls could be preserved. Facades were valuable. They could build inside again more beautifully than before. This could again be a home. He said angrily, 340 'We've got to finish. Don't move. Let me think.'

'There's no time,' a boy said.

'There's got to be a way,' T said. 'We couldn't have got this far . . .'

'We've done a lot,' Blackie said.

'No. No, we haven't. Somebody watch the front.'

'We can't do any more.'

'He may come in at the back.'

'Watch the back too.' T began to plead. 'Just give me a minute and I'll fix it. I swear I'll fix it.' But his authority had gone with his ambiguity. He was only one of the gang. 'Please,' he said.   350

'Please,' Summers mimicked him, and then suddenly struck home with the fatal name. 'Run along home, Trevor.'

T stood with his back to the rubble like a boxer knocked groggy against the ropes. He had no words as his dreams shook and slid. Then Blackie acted before the gang had time to laugh, pushing Summers backwards. 'I'll watch the front, T,' he said, and cautiously he opened the shutters of the hall. The grey wet common stretched ahead, and the lamps gleamed in the puddles. 'Someone's coming, T. No, it's not him. What's your plan, T?'

'Tell Mike to go out to the lav and hide close beside it. When he hears 360 me whistle he's got to count to ten and start to shout.'

'Shout what?'

'Oh, "Help", anything.'

'You hear, Mike,' Blackie said. He was the leader again. He took a quick look between the shutters. 'He's coming, T.'

'Quick, Mike. The lav. Stay here, Blackie, all of you, till I yell.'

'Where are you going, T?'

'Don't worry. I'll see to this. I said I would, didn't I?'

Old Misery came limping off the common. He had mud on his shoes and he stopped to scrape them on the pavement's edge. He didn't want to soil his house, which stood jagged and dark between the bomb-sites, saved so narrowly, as he believed, from destruction. Even the fan-light had been left unbroken by the bomb's blast. Somewhere somebody whistled. Old Misery looked sharply round. He didn't trust whistles. A child was shouting: it seemed to come from his own garden. Then a boy ran into the road from the car-park. 'Mr Thomas,' he called, 'Mr Thomas.'

'What is it?'

'I'm terribly sorry, Mr Thomas. One of us got taken short, and we thought you wouldn't mind, and now he can't get out.'

'What do you mean, boy?'

'He's got stuck in your lav.'

'He'd no business . . . Haven't I seen you before?'

'You showed me your house.'

'So I did. So I did. That doesn't give you the right to . . .'

'Do hurry, Mr Thomas. He'll suffocate.'

'Nonsense. He can't suffocate. Wait till I put my bag in.'

'I'll carry your bag.'

'Oh no, you don't. I carry my own.'

'This way, Mr Thomas.'

'I can't get in the garden that way. I've got to go through the house.'

'But you *can* get in the garden this way, Mr Thomas. We often do.'

'You often do?' He followed the boy with a scandalized fascination. 'When? What right . . . ?'

'Do you see . . . ? the wall's low.'

'I'm not going to climb walls into my own garden. It's absurd.'

'This is how we do it. One foot here, one foot there, and over.'

The boy's face peered down, an arm shot out, and Mr Thomas found his bag taken and deposited on the other side of the wall.

'Give me back my bag,' Mr Thomas said. From the loo a boy yelled and yelled. 'I'll call the police.'

'Your bag's alright, Mr Thomas. Look. One foot there. On your right. Now just above. To your left.' Mr Thomas climbed over his own garden wall. 'Here's your bag, Mr Thomas.'

'I'll have the wall built up,' Mr Thomas said. 'I'll not have you boys coming over here, using my loo.' He stumbled on the path, but the boy caught his elbow and supported him. 'Thank you, thank you, my boy,' he murmured automatically. Somebody shouted again through the dark. 'I'm coming, I'm coming,' Mr Thomas called. He said to the boy beside him, 'I'm not unreasonable. Been a boy myself. As long as things are done regular. I don't mind you playing round the place Saturday mornings. Sometimes I like company. Only it's got to be regular. One of you asks leave and I say Yes. Sometimes I'll say No. Won't feel like it. And you come in at the front door and out at the back. No garden walls.'

'Do get him out, Mr Thomas.'

'He won't come to any harm in my loo,' Mr Thomas said, stumbling
slowly down the garden. 'Oh, my rheumatics,' he said. 'Always get 'em
on Bank Holiday. I've got to be careful. There's loose stones here. Give
me your hand. Do you know what my horoscope said yesterday?   420
"Abstain from any dealings in first half of week. Danger of serious
crash." That might be on this path,' Mr Thomas said. 'They speak in
parables and double meanings.' He paused at the door of the loo.
'What's the matter in there?' he called. There was no reply.

'Perhaps he's fainted,' the boy said.

'Not in my loo. Here, you, come out,' Mr Thomas said, and giving
a great jerk at the door he nearly fell on his back when it swung easily
open. A hand first supported him and then pushed him hard. His head
hit the opposite wall and he sat heavily down. His bag hit his feet. A
hand whipped the key out of the lock and the door slammed. 'Let me   430
out,' he called, and heard the key turn in the lock. 'A serious crash,' he
thought, and felt dithery and confused and old.

A voice spoke to him softly through the star-shaped hole in the door.
'Don't worry, Mr Thomas,' it said, 'we won't hurt you, not if you stay
quiet.'

Mr Thomas put his head between his hands and pondered. He had
noticed that there was only one lorry in the car-park, and he felt certain
that the driver would not come for it before the morning. Nobody could
hear him from the road in front, and the lane at the back was seldom
used. Anyone who passed there would be hurrying home and would not   440
pause for what they would certainly take to be drunken cries. And if he
did call "Help", who, on a lonely Bank Holiday evening, would have the
courage to investigate? Mr Thomas sat on the loo and pondered with the
wisdom of age.

After a while it seemed to him that there were sounds in the silence
– they were faint and came from the direction of his house. He stood
up and peered through the ventilation-hole – between the cracks in one
of the shutters he saw a light, not the light of a lamp, but the waver-
ing light that a candle might give. Then he thought he heard the sound
of hammering and scraping and chipping. He thought of burglars –   450
perhaps they had employed the boy as a scout, but why should burglars
engage in what sounded more and more like a stealthy form of car-
pentry? Mr Thomas let out an experimental yell, but nobody answered.
The noise could not even have reached his enemies.

4

Mike had gone home to bed, but the rest stayed. The question of
leadership no longer concerned the gang. With nails, chisels, screw-
drivers, anything that was sharp and penetrating, they moved around
the inner walls worrying at the mortar between the bricks. They started
too high, and it was Blackie who hit on the damp course and realised
the work could be halved if they weakened the joints immediately above.   460
It was a long, tiring, unamusing job, but at last it was finished. The
gutted house stood there balanced on a few inches of mortar between the

damp course and the bricks.

There remained the most dangerous task of all, out in the open at the edge of the bomb-site. Summers was sent to watch the road for passers-by, and Mr Thomas, sitting on the loo, heard clearly now the sound of sawing. It no longer came from the house, and that a little reassured him. He felt less concerned. Perhaps the other noises too had no significance.

A voice spoke to him through the hole. 'Mr Thomas.'

'Let me out,' Mr Thomas said sternly.   470

'Here's a blanket,' the voice said, and a long grey sausage was worked through the hole and fell in swathes over Mr Thomas's head.

'There's nothing personal,' the voice said. 'We want you to be comfortable tonight.'

'Tonight,' Mr Thomas repeated incredulously.

'Catch,' the voice said. 'Penny buns – we've buttered them, and sausage-rolls. We don't want you to starve, Mr Thomas.'

Mr Thomas pleaded desperately. 'A joke's a joke, boy. Let me out and I won't say a thing. I've got rheumatics. I got to sleep comfortable.'

'You wouldn't be comfortable, not in your house, you wouldn't. Not 480 now.'

'What do you mean, boy?' But the footsteps receded. There was only the silence of the night: no sound of sawing. Mr Thomas tried one more yell, but he was daunted and rebuked by the silence – a long way off an owl hooted and made away again on its muffled flight through the soundless world.

At seven next morning the driver came to fetch his lorry. He climbed into the seat and tried to start the engine. He was vaguely aware of a voice shouting, but it didn't concern him. At last the engine responded and he backed the lorry until it touched the great wooden shore that 490 supported Mr Thomas's house. That way he could drive right out and down the street without reversing. The lorry moved forward, was momentarily checked as though something were pulling it from behind, and then went on to the sound of a long rumbling crash. The driver was astonished to see bricks bouncing ahead of him, while stones hit the roof of his cab. He put on his brakes. When he climbed out the whole landscape had suddenly altered. There was no house beside the car-park, only a hill of rubble. He went round and examined the back of his lorry for damage, and found a rope tied there that was still twisted at the other end round part of a wooden strut.   500

The driver again became aware of somebody shouting. It came from the wooden erection which was the nearest thing to a house in that desolation of broken-brick. The driver climbed the smashed wall and unlocked the door. Mr Thomas came out of the loo. He was wearing a grey blanket to which flakes of pastry adhered. He gave a sobbing cry. 'My house,' he said. 'Where's my house?'

'Search me,' the driver said. His eyes lit on the remains of a bath and what had once been a dresser and he began to laugh. There wasn't anything left anywhere.

'How dare you laugh,' Mr Thomas said. 'It was my house. My house.' 510

'I'm sorry,' the driver said, making heroic efforts, but when he remembered the sudden check of his lorry, the crash of bricks falling, he became convulsed again. One moment the house had stood there with such dignity between the bomb-sites like a man in a top hat, and then, bang, crash, there wasn't anything left – not anything. He said, 'I'm sorry. I can't help it, Mr Thomas. There's nothing personal, but you got to admit it's funny.'

Into the text

1   We are told on page 64 that the new member of the gang, T, very quickly becomes its leader.
Re-read lines 78 to 166. How does T manage this so quickly?

2   'It's a bribe,' says Summers on line 67 when Mr Thomas gives them some chocolates.
  a   Do you think it was a bribe?
  b   Where did Mr Thomas get the Smarties from?
  c   Why did the boys choose to play the bouncing game against Mr Thomas' wall?

3   'It's a beautiful house,' (lines 97–8). 'We'll pull it down. We'll destroy it.' (lines 133–4) Why does T want to destroy something beautiful? Why do the gang go along with him so readily?

4   Why do you think that Blackie and T are so determined that nothing should be stolen? (Ignore that fact that they fear going to prison.) Look again at lines 129 ff. and 285 ff.

5   When Blackie first arrives at the house on the morning of the Bank Holiday he has '. . . at once the impression of organisation.' (lines 225–6). We are told that '. . . destruction after all is a form of creation.' (lines 264–5). What does this tell you about T?

6   On two occasions, T seems to be in danger of losing his authority. Find each example and try to explain what happened and how T dealt with the challenge.

7   Why is Old Misery so easily taken in by T when he returns home?

8   Why, at the end of the story, did the lorry driver laugh at Mr Thomas?

9   On the next page are four lists of words that may be used to describe the four individuals/groups that appear in the story. Look at each list closely and decide which character each list refers to: Old Misery, the Driver, the Gang, T. Then look back at the passage and find evidence to support the inclusion of each word.

planner	easily led	respecter of	indifferent
efficient	intimidated	order	blind
organised	anonymous	kind	complacent
almost	looking for	reasonable	cruel
laughable	adventure	disorganized	
serious	childish	vulnerable	
minded	irresponsible	passive	
unemotional		polite	
unfeeling		trusting	
amoral		boring	
active		uninteresting	
charismatic			

10 The words in the list above can combine to represent an ideology – a way of thinking. The main conflict in the story appears to be between the beliefs of T and Old Misery. Consider each of the characters and their attitude of mind. Describe them in detail. What do you like and dislike about each of them? Which one would you trust the most? Which one would you be prepared to follow?

Out of the text

1 Imagine you are one of the anonymous members of the gang and you are having to explain to an angry adult (parent, policeman) what happened to the house and how you became involved in its destruction. Make sure that you describe in detail the events as they unfolded and your feelings about what was going on.

2 The lorry driver doesn't seem to be very sympathetic towards the plight of Mr Thomas. Write the conversation that you might have with the lorry driver, explaining to him why you think that his attitude was so wrong.

The individual and the state

We take for granted what we mean by the 'state', but it is, in fact, a highly complex idea. Sometimes, it is used as another word for 'nation' or 'country'. At other times, however, it describes the relationship between the government and the governed; this can be either good or bad. For instance, in South Africa, the state represents different things to the minority white population and to the majority black population. To the former, it provides security, protection and privilege; to the latter, oppression and exploitation.

Below is a list of words and phrases that use the word 'state'. These words can have positive, neutral or negative associations. In pairs, make three columns headed by the three words **Positive**, **Neutral** and **Negative**. Assign the words from the list to the appropriate column. You may want to put some words in more than one column.

state secret; statesman; stateless person; United States of America; State Opening of Parliament; state terrorism; the ship of state; state bureaucracy; Head of State; state tyranny; statehood; Secretary of State; Nation State; a state coach; State Department; state police; state repression; the Welfare State; nanny state; state interference.

Our ideal state

Writers over the centuries have expressed various views about the nature and function of the state:

> 'Our object in the construction of the state is the greatest happiness of the whole, and not that of any one class.' (Plato)

> 'The very idea of the power and the right of the people to establish government, presupposes the duty of every individual to obey the established government.' (George Washington)

> 'Government and co-operation are in all things the laws of life; anarchy and competition, the laws of death.' (John Ruskin)

> 'The worst enemy of life, freedom and the common decencies is total anarchy; their second worst enemy is total efficiency.' (Aldous Huxley)

> 'Liberty is the right to do whatever the law permits.' (Montesquieu)

Reach agreement about how to complete the following sentence:
'Our ideal state will give us, its citizens ....
in return for .... '

Approaching the text
The following poem by W H Auden was published in 1940 when state power was becoming more pervasive in some European countries. He envisages a time in the future when the state controls every aspect of people's lives. As you read the poem, make note of all of the agencies of the state that Auden refers to, which shape the unknown citizen's existence.

The Unknown Citizen

WH Auden

To JS/07/M/378
This Marble Monument
is erected by the State

He was found by the Bureau of Statistics to be
One against whom there was no official complaint,
And all the reports on his conduct agree
That, in the modern sense of an old-fashioned word, he was a saint,
For in everything he did he served the Greater Community.   5
Except for the War till the day he retired
He worked in a factory and never got fired,
But satisfied his employers, Fudge Motors Inc.
Yet he wasn't a scab or odd in his views,
For his Union reports that he paid his dues,   10
(Our report on his Union shows it was sound)
And our Social Psychology workers found
That he was popular with his mates and liked a drink.
The Press are convinced that he bought a paper every day
And that his reactions to advertisements were normal in every way. 15
Policies taken out in his name prove that he was fully insured,
And his Health-card shows he was once in hospital but left it cured.
Both Producers Research and High-Grade Living declare
He was fully sensible to the advantages of the Instalment Plan
And had everything necessary to the Modern Man,   20
A phonograph, a radio, a car and a frigidaire.
Our researchers into Public Opinion are content
That he held the proper opinions for the time of year;
When there was peace, he was for peace; when there was war, he went.
He was married and added five children to his population,   25
Which our Eugenist says was the right number for a parent of his
    generation,
And our teachers report that he never interfered with their education.
Was he free? Was he happy? The question is absurd:
Had anything been wrong, we should certainly have heard.   30

Into the text

1 What do you think are the functions of all of the agencies listed? You may need to refer to a dictionary.

2 Who is 'speaking' in this poem? What tone is employed?

3 This poem is the official view of JS/07/M/378. What epitaph would the unknown citizen write for himself?

4 In the light of your responses to the previous two questions, what do you think was Auden's purpose in writing this poem? What is Auden's attitude towards the state?

A rebuke and a warning: Poetic writing

Approaching the text

Poets, like other writers, are interested in conflicts of belief and their consequences. What they can do is speak out very passionately about the human suffering caused in this way. The poems that follow express their concern about the waste of human life which wars bring about. World War I poet, Wilfred Owen, said that poetry had a special role: '. . . not to glorify war, but to provide a memorial to all those who have died by putting forward a plea for those still fighting. War poetry is not consolation, it is a rebuke and a warning.'

The way in which a poet uses language appeals not only to the intellect but also to the emotions and therefore a poet is able to arouse the readers' pity, anger and disgust.

_____ *The Charge of the Light Brigade* _____
Alfred, Lord Tennyson

Half a league, half a league,
Half a league onward,
All in the valley of Death
    Rode the six hundred.
'Forward, the Light Brigade!   5
Charge for the guns!' he said.
Into the valley of Death
    Rode the six hundred.

'Forward, the Light Brigade!'
Was there a man dismayed?   10
Not though the soldier knew
    Someone had blundered.
Theirs not to make reply,
Theirs not to reason why,
Theirs but to do and die.   15
Into the valley of Death
    Rode the six hundred.

Cannon to right of them,
Cannon to left of them,
Cannon in front of them   20
    Volleyed and thundered;
Stormed at with shot and shell,
Boldly they rode and well,
Into the jaws of Death,
Into the mouth of hell   25
    Rode the six hundred.

Flashed all their sabres bare,
Flashed as they turned in air,
Sabring the gunners there
Charging an army, while   30
  All the world wondered.
Plunged in the battery-smoke
Right through the line they broke;
Cossack and Russian
Reeled from the sabre-stroke   35
  Shattered and sundered.
Then they rode back, but not,
  Not the six hundred.

Cannon to right of them,
Cannon to left of them,   40
Cannon behind them
  Volleyed and thundered;
Stormed at with shot and shell,
While horse and hero fell,
They that had fought so well   45
Came through the jaws of Death,
Back from the mouth of hell,
All that was left of them,
  Left of six hundred.

When can their glory fade?   50
O the wild charge they made!
  All the world wondered.
Honour the charge they made!
Honour the Light Brigade,
  Noble six hundred!   55

Into the text

1 This poem describes a disastrous charge made by British cavalry against Russian guns during the Crimean War in 1854. What evidence can you find to show that the poem is:
   a a celebration of heroism?
   b a critical comment on the charge?
2 Identify the repetitions that occur. Why does Tennyson use this technique? What does the poem gain from the use of repetition?

High Wood
Philip Johnstone

Ladies and gentlemen, this is High Wood,
Called by the French, Bois de Fourneaux,
The famous spot which in Nineteen-Sixteen,
July, August and September was the scene
Of long and bitterly contested strife,   5
By reason of its high commanding site.
Observe the effect of shell-fire in the trees
Standing and fallen; here is wire; this trench
For months inhabited, twelve times changed hands;
(They soon fall in), used later as a grave.   10
It has been said on good authority
That in the fighting for this patch of wood
Were killed somewhere above eight thousand men,
Of whom the greater part were buried here,
This mound on which you stand being . . .   15
                              Madame, please,
You are requested kindly not to touch
Or take away the Company's property
As souvenirs; you'll find we have on sale
A large variety, all guaranteed.   20
As I was saying, all this as it was,
This is an unknown British officer,
The tunic having lately rotted off.
Please follow me – this way . . .
                    the *path, sir, please*,   25
The ground which was secured at great expense
The Company keeps absolutely untouched,
And in that dug-out (genuine) we provide
Refreshments at a reasonable rate.
You are requested not to leave about   30
Paper, or ginger-beer bottles, or orange-peel,
There are waste-paper baskets at the gate.

Into the text

1   Who is the narrator of this poem? Whose voice do we
    hear?
2   There are three points of view in this poem: the tour
    guide, the tourists and the poet. What are the three
    different attitudes towards this World War I site? Use
    evidence from the text to support your answer.

Night Patrol

Alan Ross

We sail at dusk. The red moon,
Rising in a paper lantern, sets fire
To the water, the black headland disappears,
Sullen in shadow, clenched like a paw.

The docks grow flat, rubbered with mist.   5
Cranes, like tall drunks, hang
Over the railway. The unloading of coal
Continues under blue arc-lights.

Turning south, the moon like a rouged face
Between masts, the knotted aerials swing   10
Taut against the horizon, the bag
Of sea crumpled in the spray-flecked blackness.

Towards midnight the cold stars, high
Over Europe, freeze on the sky,
Stigmata above the flickering lights   15
Of Holland. Flashes of gunfire

Lick out over meditative coastlines, betraying
The stillness. Taking up position, night falls
Exhausted about us. The wakes
Of gunboats sew the green dark with speed.   20

From Dunkirk red flames open fanwise
In spokes of light: like the rising moon
Setting fire to the sky, the remote
Image of death burns on the water.

The slow muffle of hours. Clouds grow visible.   25
Altering course the moon congeals on a new
Bearing. Northwards again, and Europe recedes
With the first sharp splinters of Dawn.

The orange sky lies over the harbour
Derricks and pylons like scarecrows   30
Black in the early light. And minesweepers
Pass us, moving out slowly to the North Sea.

Into the text   1 What do you understand by the following lines:
    a '. . . the moon like a rouged face' (line 9)
    b 'The wakes
       Of gunboats sew the green dark with speed.' (lines
       19–20)

c '. . . red flames open fanwise
    In spokes of light . . .' (lines 21–2)
d '. . . the remote
    Image of death burns on the water.' (lines 23–4)
e '. . . the moon congeals on a new
    Bearing.' (lines 26–7)

2 The poet contrasts the activity of humans with the stillness of the natural sea and landscape. Find examples
  of this.
3 What do you think the poet's attitude towards war is?

Approaching the text

This poem deals with the threat of nuclear war which, as Tom Lehrer
argues, would spell the end of human life on Earth. The prospect is so
appalling that the poet could only respond with black humour.

_____ *We will all go together when we go* _____
Tom Lehrer

When you attend a funeral
It is sad to think that sooner or
Later those who love you will do the same for you
And you may have thought it tragic
Not to mention other adjec-   5
Tives to think of all the weeping they will do
But don't you worry
No more ashes, no more sackcloth
And an armband made of black cloth
Will some day never more adorn a sleeve   10
For if the bomb that drops on you
Gets your friends and neighbours, too
There'll be nobody left behind to grieve

And we will all go together when we go
What a comforting fact that is to know   15
Universal bereavement
An aspiring achievement
Yes, we will all go together when we go

We will all go together when we go
All suffused with an incandescent glow   20
No one will have the endurance
To collect on his insurance
Lloyds of London will be loaded when they go

We will all fry together when we fry
We'll be French fried potatoes by and by   25
There will be no more misery
When the world is our rotisserie
We will all fry together when we fry

Down by the old maelstrom
There'll be a storm before the calm   30

And we will all bake together when we bake
There'll be nobody present at the wake
With complete participation
In that grand incineration
Nearly three billion hunks of well-done steak   35

And we will all char together when we char
And let there be no moaning at the bar
Just sing out a Te Deum
When you see that ICBM
And the party will be 'Come as you are!'   40

We will all burn together when we burn
There'll be no need to stand and wait your turn
When it's time for the fall-out
And St Peter called us all out
We'll just drop our agendas and adjourn   45

You will all go directly to your respective Valhallas
Go directly, do not pass 'GO', do not collect two hundred dollars

And we will all go together when we go
Every Hottentot and every Eskimo
When the air becomes uraneous   50
We will all go simultaneous
Yes, we all will go together when we all go together
Yes, we all will go together when we go

Into the text

1 Find some examples of Lehrer's use of black humour. Do you think that the humorous approach detracts from the message in any way?

2 This is a song. How can you tell?

The Responsibility

Peter Appleton

I am the man who gives the word,
If it should come, to use the bomb.

I am the man who spreads the word
From him to them if it should come.

I am the man who gets the word   5
From him who spreads the word from him.

I am the man who drops the Bomb
If ordered by the one who's heard
From him who merely spreads the word
The first one gives if it should come.   10

I am the man who loads the Bomb
That he must drop should orders come
From him who gets the word passed on
By one who waits to hear from him.

I am the man who makes the Bomb   15
That he must load for him to drop
If told by one who gets the word
From one who passes it from him.

I am the man who fills the till,
Who pays the tax, who foots the bill   20
That guarantees the Bomb he makes
For him to load for him to drop
If orders come from one who gets
The word passed on to him by one
Who waits to hear it from the man   25
Who gives the word to use the Bomb

I am the man behind it all
I am the one responsible.

Into the text

1 The structure of the poem is based on a children's
nursery rhyme. Do you know what it is? Why does the
poet use this rhythm?

2 Who does Peter Appleton say is '. . . the one responsible' (line 28)? Do you agree with him?

3 In a group, prepare a reading which brings out the
nature of the poem and the points it is making.

_ *Appendix IV: Requirements in the Shelter* _
Adrian Mitchell

'Clothing
Cooking equipment
Food
Furniture
Hygiene   5
Lighting
Medical
Shrouds'

What?

'Shrouds.   10
Several large, strong, black plastic bags and a reel of 2-inch, or wider,
adhesive tape can make adequate air-tight containers for deceased
persons until the situation permits burial.'

No I will not put my lovely wife into a large strong black plastic bag
No I will not put my lovely children into large strong black plastic bags   15
No I will not put my lovely dog or my lovely cats into large strong black
plastic bags

I will embrace them until I am filled with their radiation

Then I will carry them, one by one,
Through the black landscape   20
And lay them gently at the concrete door
Of the concrete block
Where the colonels
And the chief detectives
And the MPs   25
And the Regional Commissioners
Are biding their time
And then I will lie down with my wife and children and my dog and my
                                                                    cats

and we will wait for the door to open   30

Into the text   1 What is the overall tone of the poem?
                      2 In what way does the official voice in the poem con-
                         trast with the poet's own voice?

Approaching the text

The Vietnam War, the setting for this poem, was the first war to be fought in the television age: pictures appeared on news programmes night after night – this contributed to the loss of the will to win among the American people.

As you read the poem, try to imagine the pictures that Tom Earley's words suggest.

Pictures in the Paper
Tom Earley

Bewildered girl, her vulnerable face
reflecting nightmare war, her little hand
in bloodstained bandage inexpertly dressed,
she limps along half leaning on a stick,
her wounds ill bound in military haste,   5
parents already dead in battle wreck
of jungle town now named Dong Xoai.

And sadder pictures that could make you cry:
grim soldiers shoot deserters in a ditch,
cold blooded, singly, while the others watch;   10
emaciated mother, staring wild
and streaming tears, enfolds her murdered child.

The poetry, he said, is in the pity.
We need another Wilfred Owen now.

Into the text
1 Identify some of the details in the poem that move Tom Earley to 'pity' (line 13).
2 What do you think the last two lines mean?
3 How does the poet seek to arouse pity in the reader?

Geography Lesson
Zulfikar Ghose

When the jet sprang into the sky,
it was clear why the city
had developed the way it had,
seeing it scaled six inches to the mile.
There seemed an inevitability   5
About what on the ground had looked haphazard,
unplanned and without style
when the jet sprang into the sky.

When the jet reached ten thousand feet,
it was clear why the country   10
had cities where rivers ran
and why the valleys were populated.
the logic of Geography –
that land and water attracted man –
was clearly delineated   15
when the jet reached ten thousand feet.

When the jet rose to six miles high,
it was clear that the earth was round
and that it had more sea than land.
But it was difficult to understand   20
why the men on earth found
causes to hate each other, to build
walls across cities and kill.
From the height, it was not clear why.

Out of the text
1 Why is the poem called 'Geography Lesson'?
2 What, from the aircraft, did Zulfikar Ghose find clear? What was difficult to understand?
3 What evidence is there of optimism in the poem?

Approaching the text

The context for the following poem is a struggle for independence in which, it is often claimed, there are no innocent victims: everybody is a legitimate target. The poem uses a form of language often adopted by those organisations claiming responsibility for murderous actions.

_____ *Communiqué to a child* _____
Jim Burns

First of all you must not complain.
The bomb that blew off your left leg,
and tore away one of your eyes,
was placed by some of our volunteers
to obtain maximum psychological effect   5
in the struggle to achieve our demands.
It was not our intention to maim
or kill anyone, and we regret the death
of your mother. However, you must
accept that there are no innocents   10
in a situation such as this.
So, adjust to your present condition,
and do not condemn us. As you
limp into the future your one eye
will enable you to see things clearly,   15
and you will evaluate the event
with the wisdom of age. You will
begin to understand why it happened.
Only an adult can possibly know this,
and apply reasoning to the suffering.   20

Out of the text

1 Does the language of the poem convince you that '. . . there are no innocents/in a situation such as this.' (lines 10–11)?
2 At what point in the poem do you detect the narrator's feeling of guilt about what has happened?
3 What do you think the last two lines of the poem mean?
4 What evidence is there to suggest that Jim Burns isn't convinced by the arguments that the terrorists use?

The time comes in the life of any nation: Political rhetoric

Approaching the text

You will probably have heard of Nelson Mandela, one of the leaders of the African National Congress, who until his release in 1990 had been in prison in South Africa for 27 years.

The following extract is taken from a transcript of what he said at his trial in 1964. As you read the passage, consider how he justifies the actions of the African National Congress.

_____ *No Easy Walk to Freedom* _____
Nelson Mandela

The African National Congress was formed in 1912 to defend the rights
of the African people which had been seriously curtailed by the South
Africa Act, and which were then being threatened by the Native Land
Act. For thirty-seven years – that is until 1949 – it adhered strictly
to a constitutional struggle. It put forward demands and resolutions;
it sent delegations to the Government in the belief that African grie-
vances could be settled through peaceful discussion and that Africans
could advance gradually to full political rights. But White Governments
remained unmoved, and the rights of the Africans became less instead
of becoming greater. In the words of my leader, Chief Lutuli, who   10
became President of the ANC in 1952, and who was later awarded the
Nobel Peace Prize:

'Who will deny that thirty years of my life have been spent knocking
in vain, patiently, moderately, and modestly at a closed and barred
door? What have been the fruits of moderation? The past thirty years
have seen the greatest number of laws restricting our rights and progress,
until today we have reached a stage where we have almost no rights at
all.'

. . . At the beginning of June 1961, after a long and anxious
assessment of the South Africa situation, I, and some colleagues, came 20
to the conclusion that as violence in this country was inevitable, it would
be unrealistic and wrong for African leaders to continue preaching
peace and non-violence at a time when the Government met our peaceful
demands with force.

This conclusion was not easily arrived at. It was only when all else had
failed, when all channels of peaceful protest had been barred to us, that
the decision was made to embark on violent forms of political struggle,
and to form *Umkhonto we Sizwe*. (*The spear of the Nation*). We did so
not because we desired such a course, but solely because the Government had left us with no other choice. In the Manifesto of *Umkhonto*   30
published on 16th December, 1961, which is Exhibit AD, we said:
   'The time comes in the life of any nation when there remain only two
choices – submit or fight. That time has now come to South Africa. We
shall not submit and we have no choice but to hit back by all means in
our power in defence of our people, our future and our freedom.'
   . . . Four forms of violence were possible. There is sabotage, there is
guerilla warfare, there is terrorism, and there is open revolution. We
chose to adopt the first method and to exhaust it before taking any other
decision.

Into the text

1 Among other things, this is a political speech, aimed
   at a wider audience than just the courtroom. What
   evidence can you find, however, that tells you that
   Mandela is conducting his defence in court?
2 In what ways in the speech does Mandela justify
   resorting to violence?
3 Write a brief description of what you consider the four
   forms of violence to be.

Approaching the text

Nelson Mandela was sentenced to life imprisonment after having been
accused of attempting to overthrow the South African Government. In 1985
Prime Minister Botha offered to free Mandela if he renounced all further
violence. Mandela's response was given by his daughter, Zindzi, at a mass
rally in Soweto.

My Father Speaks
Zindzi Mandela

On Friday my mother and our attorney saw my father at Pollsmoor Prison to obtain his answer to Botha's offer of conditional release. The prison authorities attempted to stop this statement being made but he would have none of this and made it clear that he would make the statement to you, the people.

Strangers like Bethell from England . . . have in recent weeks been authorized by Pretoria to see my father without restriction, yet Pretoria cannot allow you, the people, to hear what he has to say directly. He should be here himself to tell you what he thinks of this statement by Botha. He is not allowed to do so. My mother who also heard his words   10
is also not allowed to speak to you today.

My father and his comrades at Pollsmoor Prison send their greetings to you, the freedom-loving people of this our tragic land, in the full confidence that you will carry on the struggle for freedom. . . .

My father and his comrades wish to make this statement to you, the people, first. They are clear that they are accountable to you and to you alone, and that you should hear their views directly and not through others.

My father speaks not only for himself and for his comrades at Pollsmoor Prison but he hopes he speaks for all those in jail for their   20
opposition to apartheid, for all those who are banished, for all those who are in exile, for all those who suffer under apartheid, for all those who are opponents of apartheid and for all those who are oppressed and exploited.

Throughout our struggle there have been puppets who have claimed to speak for you. They have made this claim, both here and abroad. They are of no consequence. My father and his colleagues will not be like them.

My father says 'I am a member of the African National Congress. I have always been a member of the African National Congress and I will   30
remain a member of the African National Congress until the day I die. Oliver Tambo is much more than a brother to me. He is my greatest friend and comrade for nearly fifty years. If there is anyone amongst you who cherishes my freedom, Oliver Tambo cherishes it more and I know that he would give his life to see me free.

'There is no difference between his views and mine.'

My father says, 'I am surprised at the conditions the government wants to impose on me. I am not a violent man. My colleagues and I wrote in 1952 to Malan asking for a round-table conference to find a solution to the problems of our country but that was ignored. When   40
Strijdom was in power, we made the same offer. Again it was ignored. When Verwoerd was in power we asked for a national convention for all the people in South Africa to decide on their future. This, too, was in vain.

'It was only when all other forms of resistance were no longer open to us that we turned to armed struggle.

'I cherish my own freedom dearly but I care even more for your freedom. Too many have died since I went to prison. Too many have suffered for their love of freedom. I owe it to their widows, to their orphans, to their mothers and to their fathers who have grieved and wept for them. Not only have I suffered during these long, lonely, wasted   60 years. I am not less life-loving than you are. But I cannot sell my birthright, nor am I prepared to sell the birthright of the people, to be free. I am in prison as the representative of the people and of your organisation, the African National Congress, which was banned. What freedom am I being offered whilst the organisation of the people remains banned? What freedom am I being offered when I may be arrested on a pass offence? What freedom am I being offered to live my life as a family with my dear wife who remains in banishment in Brandfort? What freedom am I being offered when I must ask for permission to live in an urban area? What freedom am I being offered when I need a stamp   70 in my pass to seek work? What freedom am I being offered when my very South African citizenship is not respected?

'Only free men can negotiate. Prisoners cannot enter into contracts. . . .'

My father says, 'I cannot and will not give any undertaking at a time when I and you, the people, are not free. Your freedom and mine cannot be separated, I will return.'

(from *South Africa* by Graham Leach)

Into the text

1 Because of South African laws, it would have been illegal for Zindzi to read Mandela's own words. From the evidence of the transcript, would you consider that Zindzi was breaking the law? How would she defend herself against the charge?

2 From this speech, do you get any feeling of the sort of person that Zindzi Mandela is?

3 Why exactly does Mandela refuse Botha's offer of conditional release?

Approaching the text

The following passage is a published transcript of the speech made by Nelson Mandela in Cape Town on 11th February, 1990 following his unconditional release.

We have waited too long for our freedom ...
Nelson Mandela

Friends, Comrades and Fellow South Africans,

I greet you in the name of peace, democracy and freedom for all. I stand here before you, not as a prophet, but as a humble servant of you, the people.

Your tireless and heroic sacrifices have made it possible for me to be here today. I therefore place the remaining years of my life in your hands.

On this day of my release I extend my sincere and warmest gratitude to the millions of my compatriots and those in every corner of the globe who have campaigned tirelessly for my release.   10

I extend special greetings to the people of Cape Town, the city which has been my home for three decades. Your mass marches and other forms of struggle have served as a constant source of strength to all political prisoners.

I salute the African National Congress. It has fulfilled our every expectation in its role as leader of the great march to freedom.

I salute our President, Comrade Oliver Tambo, for leading the ANC even under the most difficult circumstances. I salute the rank and file members of the ANC. You have sacrificed life and limb in the pursuit of the noble cause of our struggle.   20

I salute combatants of Umkhonto we Sizwe, like Solomon Mahlangu and Ashley Kriel, who have paid the ultimate price for the freedom of all South Africans.

I salute the South African Communist Party for its sterling contribution to the struggle for democracy. You have survived 40 years of unrelenting persecution. The memory of great communists like Moses Kotane, Yusuf Dadoo, Bram Fischer and Moses Mabhida will be cherished for generations to come. I salute General Secretary Joe Slovo – one of our finest patriots. We are heartened by the fact that the alliance between ourselves and the Party remains as strong as it always 30 was.

I salute the United Democratic Front, Cosatu, the National Education Crisis Committee, the South African Youth Congress, the Transvaal and Natal Indian Congresses and the many other formations of the Mass Democratic Movement.

Conscience of whites

I also salute the Black Sash and the National Union of South African Students. We note with pride that you have acted as the conscience of white South Africans. Even during the darkest days in the history of your struggle you held the flag of liberty high. The large-scale mass mobilisa- 40 tion of the past few years is one of the key factors which led to the opening of the final chapter of our struggle.

I extend my greetings to the working class of our country. Your organised strength is the pride of our movement. You remain the most dependable force in the struggle to end exploitation and oppression.

I pay tribute to the many religious communities who carry the campaign for justice forward when the organisations of our people were silenced.

I greet the traditional leaders of our country. Many among you continue to walk in the footsteps of great heroes like Hintsa and 50 Sekhukhuni.

I pay tribute to the endless heroism of the youth. You, the young lions, have energised our entire struggle.

I pay tribute to the mothers and wives and sisters of our nation. You are the rock-hard foundation of our struggle. Apartheid has inflicted more pain on you than on anyone else.

Frontline sacrifices

On this occasion we thank the world community for their great contribution to the anti-apartheid struggle. Without your support our struggle would not have reached this advanced stage. The sacrifices of 60 the Front Line States will be remembered by South Africans forever.

My salutations will be incomplete without expressing my deep appreciation for the strength given to me during my long and lonely years in prison by my beloved wife and family. I am convinced that your pain and suffering was far greater than my own.

Before I go any further, I wish to make the point that I intend making only a few preliminary comments at this stage. I will make a more public statement only after I have had the opportunity to consult with my comrades.

Today the majority of South Africans, black and white, recognise that 70 apartheid has no future. It has to be ended by our own decisive mass action in order to build peace and security. The mass campaign of defiance and other actions of our organisation and people can only culminate with the establishment of democracy.

The apartheid destruction to our sub-continent is incalculable. The fabric of family life of millions of our people has been shattered. Millions are homeless and unemployed, our economy lies in ruins and our people are embroiled in political strife.

Armed struggle – No option but to continue
Our resort to the armed struggle in 1960, with the formation of the   80
military wing of the ANC, Umkhonto we Sizwe, was a purely defensive action against the violence of apartheid.

The factors which necessitated the armed struggle still exist today. We have no option but to continue. We express the hope that a climate conducive to a negotiated settlement will be created soon so that there may no longer be the need for the armed struggle.

I am a loyal and disciplined member of the African National Congress. I am therefore in full agreement with all of its objectives, strategies and tactics.

The need to unite the people of our country is as important a task now   90
as it has always been. No individual leader is able to take on this enormous task on his own.

It is our task as leaders to place our views before our organisation and to allow the democratic structures to decide on the way forward. On the question of democratic practice, I feel duty-bound to make the point that the leader of the movement is a person who has been democratically elected at a national conference. This is a principle which must be upheld without any exceptions.

Insistence on a meeting
Today I wish to report to you that my talks with the government have   100
been aimed at normalising the political situation in the country. We have not as yet begun discussing the basic demands of the struggle. I wish to stress that I, myself, have at no time entered into negotiation about the future of our country, except to insist on a meeting between the ANC and the government.

Mr De Klerk has gone further than any other Nationalist President in taking real steps to normalise the situation.

However, there are further steps as outlined in the Harare Declaration that have to be met before negotiations on the basic demand of our people can begin.   110

I reiterate our call for, *inter alia*, the immediate ending of the State of Emergency and the freeing of all, and not only some, political prisoners.

Only such a normalised situation which allows for free political activity, can allow us to consult our people in order to obtain a mandate.

Not behind the backs of the people
The people need to be consulted on who will negotiate and on the content of such negotiations. Negotiations cannot take place above the

heads or behind the backs of our people.

It is our belief that the future of our country can only be determined by a body which is democratically elected on a non-racial basis.   120

Negotiations on the dismantling of apartheid will have to address the overwhelming demands of our people for a democratic, non-racial and unitary South Africa.

There must be an end to white monopoly on political power and a fundamental restructuring of our political and economic system to ensure that the inequalities of apartheid are addressed and our society thoroughly democratised.

It must be added that Mr De Klerk himself is a man of integrity who is acutely aware of the danger of a public figure not honouring his undertakings.   130

But as an organisation we base our policy and strategies on the harsh reality we are faced with and this reality is that we are still suffering under the policy of the Nationalist government. Our struggle has reached a decisive moment. We call on our people to seize this moment so that the process towards democracy is rapid and uninterrupted.

We have waited too long for our freedom. We can no longer wait. Now is the time to intensify the struggle on all fronts.

To relax our effort now would be a mistake which generations to come will not be able to forgive.

The sight of freedom   140

The sight of freedom looming on the horizon should encourage us to redouble our efforts. It is only through disciplined mass action that our victory can be assured.

We call on our white compatriots to join us in the shaping of a new South Africa. The freedom movement is a political home for you too. We call on the international community to continue the campaign to isolate the apartheid regime.

To lift sanctions now would be to run the risk of aborting the process towards the complete eradication of apartheid. Our march to freedom is irreversible. We must not allow fear to stand in our way.   150

Universal suffrage on a common voters' roll in a united, democratic and non-racial South Africa is the only way to peace and racial harmony.

In conclusion, I wish to quote my own words during my trial in 1964. They are as true today as they were then, I quote:
'I have fought against white domination and I have fought against black domination. I have carried the ideal of a democratic and free society in which all persons live together in harmony and with equal opportunity. It is an ideal which I hope to live for and to achieve. But, if needs be, it is an ideal for which I am prepared to die.'

I hope you will disperse with dignity and not a single one of you should   160 do anything which will make other people say that we can't control our own people.

Into the text

1 Imagine you are a news reporter at the scene in Cape Town when this speech was delivered. Write a 400-word report covering the main issues addressed by Mandela.

2 What evidence can you find in all three passages that they are transcripts of spoken language? Look at their style of delivery and use of language, for example.

3 What conclusions would you draw about the character of Nelson Mandela?

Freedom fighter or terrorist: Contradictions in language

Friend or foe?

The words in the following list have all been used to describe people in conflict with others. Look carefully at the words and then:

a decide who the target is (it could be other individuals; groups; authority; government; a foreign government).

b decide whether you feel favourable or unfavourable towards each one.

c attempt a short definition.

d give an example (if possible) of a group or organisation the descriptions may apply to.

agitator; anarchist; demonstrator; dissident; freedom fighter; guerilla; hooligan; martyr; pacifist; protester; patriot; radical; red; resistance fighter; revolutionary; rioter; soldier; terrorist; traitor.

What does this exercise tell you about the way in which language can be used to manipulate the ideas of others?

Now read the following passage:

_ *When is a Freedom Fighter just another Terrorist?* _
Nigel Fountain

We all know where we stand on terrorism. It is awful, and it kills people. Our Prime Minister, in common with leaders East and West, says she won't talk to anyone involved in such acts.

I know a man who used to have an interesting job. He went round factories and threatened their owners. He told them that if they didn't wreck their production lines, he knew some people who would blow their premises up. The proprietors tended to go along with his suggestion.

So was he a terrorist? To his enemies he was, but they were the bad guys. He was working with the French Resistance and what he was doing was helping to defeat Hitler.   10

On Monday the House of Commons discussed the role of the British Army special forces unit, the SAS, in training guerillas in Thailand who work with the Khmer Rouge. They are the people who, when they ruled Cambodia in the 1970s, killed more than one million fellow citizens.

They like to call themselves freedom fighters. Most people would call them terrorists, with leaders who could give Hitler a run for his money.

But one person's freedom fighter is indeed someone else's terrorist. In Zimbabwe the British Army is helping train soldiers to fight the Renamo group in Mozambique. Renamo burn, kill and destroy in Mozambique and Zimbabwe, and they have to be defeated. Renamo has been backed by the white South African government.

Hold on, it gets more complicated. In South Africa the government still says it won't talk to the African National Congress. It calls that organisation – which seeks an end to the apartheid regime – a terrorist group.

And back in Zimbabwe, the soldiers the British are training were themselves called terrorists, by many British papers and politicians up to 10 years ago. In those days the Zimbabweans were fighting to end white minority rule in their country.

Let's look at another continent. In Nicaragua the government is fighting the Contras. According to former United States President Reagan, the Contras are the moral equivalents of the revolutionaries who threw out the British and set up the US. To most people in Nicaragua the Contras are terrorists, who have murdered civilians and destroyed homes, hospitals and farms. But some of their leaders have visited Britain, even made appearances at Conservative Party conference fringe meetings.

But it is the Middle East that most papers, and many people, see as the centre of world terrorism. Remember *Back to the Future*? When Michael J Fox escaped to the past he was fleeing from a gun-waving Arab. And in the Middle East there have been many terrible and horrific events. The destruction of the Pan American jumbo jet at Lockerbie was probably planned there; planes have been highjacked; hostages taken, and the Lebanon is the centre of a civil war between two groups often described as terrorists.

One permanent part of the Middle East crisis has been the struggle between the state of Israel and the Palestine Liberation Organisation. The PLO has, in the past, been responsible for terrorist acts, but it says it has abandoned such tactics.

The Palestinians want their own state. Israel refuses to talk to the PLO and the Prime Minister, Yitzhak Shamir, says he won't talk to terrorists.

More than 40 years ago the United Nations sent a Swedish diplomat, Folke Bernadotte, to mediate between the Israelis and the Palestinians. He was murdered by a terrorist group. One of the three men who gave the order for his death was Yitzhak Shamir.

The Israeli leader would probably argue that such actions weren't terrorism, but part of the struggle to make Israel secure. But then people who commit such acts always believe they have good reasons. The road to hell is paved with them.

So, despite horror of terrorist acts, despite the violence and misery they cause, politicians do talk to terrorists. Sometimes, as with the Contras, they call them freedom fighters, sometimes they say they changed their ways.

The leader of Kenya's struggle for independence was Jomo Kenyatta. In the 1950s the British called him a terrorist. By the 1970s he was shaking hands with the Queen, and a revered national leader.

So does it mean there's no good, no bad, just shades in between? No, but it does mean that when someone is described as a terrorist, it's worth wondering who is providing the description, and why.   70
(reproduced from *The Guardian*, 15 November, 1989)

Into the text

1 The title 'When is a Freedom Fighter just another Terrorist?' highlights the contradiction involved in applying labels to people who choose violence to gain their political ends. Find a number of examples of this contradiction.

2 From evidence in the passage, what does a terrorist have to do to gain respectability and recognition by other governments?

3 Who do you think that this passage is aimed at? Justify your conclusion with specific reference to the style of the passage.

4 Look closely again at the first three paragraphs. How does the writer gain your attention? Is it effective?

5 Does reading this passage make you want to change your mind about where you put some of the words in the previous exercise, 'Friend or Foe?'?

Assignments

1 Re-read the statement written by Allie Dessu from the Introduction (page 61). Write an extended piece reflecting on the thoughts and feelings of a person like Allie Dessu, imprisoned without trial, not knowing what you are accused of, not knowing how long your ordeal is going to last, or not knowing whether anybody is aware of your fate.

2 The following extract is taken from *The Monocled Mutineer* by William Allison and John Fairley.

The extract is a quotation from bandleader Victor Silvester, and describes his experiences during World War I.

The first man I had to help to kill was a private in my own regiment, the Argyll and Sutherland Highlanders, a fact which filled me with even greater shame. He was said to have fled in the face of the enemy.

We marched to a quarry outside Etaples at first dawn. The victim was brought out from a shed and led struggling to a chair to which he was then bound and a white handkerchief placed over his heart as our target area.

Mortified by the sight of the poor wretch tugging at his bonds, twelve of us, on the order, raised our rifles unsteadily. Some of the men, unable to face their ordeal, had got themselves drunk overnight. They could not have aimed straight if they had tried, and, contrary to popular belief, all twelve rifles were loaded. The condemned man had also been plied with whisky during the night, but he had remained sober through fear.

The tears were rolling down my cheeks as he went on attempting to free himself from the ropes attaching him to the chair. I aimed blindly and when the gunsmoke had cleared away we were further horrified to see that, although wounded, the intended victim was still alive. Still blindfolded, he was attempting to make a run for it still strapped to the chair. The blood was running freely from a chest wound. An officer in charge stepped forward to put the finishing touch with a revolver held to the poor man's temple.

He had only once cried out and that was when he shouted the one word 'Mother'. He could not have been very much older than me. We were told later that in fact he had been suffering from shell-shock, a condition not recognised by the army in 1917.

By the time I had taken part in four more such dawn executions, I did not have to feign illness. Like the other executioners, I was screaming in my sleep and physically ill every day. I was put into a hospital and strapped down to the bed to prevent me running away. I was then sent away from Etaples and all its horrors to the Italian Front. The simple business of being twice wounded there was less injurious by far than all the mental scars that Etaples left with me for the rest of my life.

a Write a letter of protest to a newspaper or a Member of Parliament expressing your outrage at the events described.

b Imagine you were one of the guards in charge of the prisoner during the night before the execution. Describe your experience.

3 Look back at the *Attitude Survey* that you did at the beginning of the unit. Think again about each of the 20 statements. Identify five of them about which you now feel differently. For each statement, write a paragraph explaining your new position and saying why you have changed your mind.

Truths and persuasion: Language and the hidden agenda

Contents

Introduction

The National Curriculum for English says, 'In both fiction and non-fiction texts, [pupils] should be taught to use information or contextual clues to deduce authorial points of view. Non-literary texts used should include persuasive writing eg advertisements, leader columns from newspapers, campaign literature from pressure groups . . .' (Programmes of Study for Reading, para 25). In other words, the National Curriculum recognises that much writing, both fiction and non-fiction, seeks to convince us of something. Sometimes it is clear that this is going on, but sometimes it is less so. In either case, as readers, we need to be alert to the kind of language that writers use.

This unit explores how a range of writers use various techniques to persuade us of their points of view. Behind the title *Truths and persuasion* is an awareness that a number of different truths can co-exist: truths are not absolute. Successful writers can convince us that this variety exists.

We come across the language of persuasion every day of our lives: at home, in the street, in the playground, watching TV, reading the newspapers and reading novels, for example. Before we begin to look at some examples of written persuasion, make a list of people who might try to persuade you to do something. From your lists, try to answer the following questions:

- Who benefits, if you are persuaded?
- What purpose did the persuaders have?
- What was the outcome?
- Which persuaders are the most successful, and why?
- What techniques (kinds of language, tone, images, etc) did they use?

Sometimes, the benefits, the purposes and the outcomes are not clear. While an advertisement for soap powder has an obvious purpose, some written literature seeks to persuade you indirectly, ie by the writer using fiction to argue a case.

Some definitions and descriptions

There are a number of ways in which we can be persuaded through the medium of print. The following list of definitions will be helpful to you as you consider the different ways by which appeals for your support can be made.

Advertisement   a public announcement (especially used in newspapers, on posters, by television, etc)

Communication and Persuasion, G H Jamieson
The deployment of persuasion for commercial gain is not an entirely new phenomenon; in a primitive way it can be seen to have its origins in the selling of wares in the market place. However, our interest here lies in the more specialised and professional uses of advertising, particularly as it is practised by big business through its formal agencies. Criticism of advertis-

ing generally begins from a negative bias, but it is worth recalling that a large proportion of advertising is informative in its content, for example advertising in the technical press. This point is mentioned not for the purpose of justifying advertising, but to create some form of balance in its assessment. It is often difficult to separate the informative from the persuasive in messages or advertisements; the informative can be persuasive, and conversely, that which is persuasive by intent may also be informative.

Indoctrination   to teach, instruct; to imbue with a doctrine, idea or opinion.

The Dictionary of Education, Derek Rowntree
Teaching of a particular doctrine or belief in such a way that the learner has no opportunity to consider it critically or compare it to other doctrines of beliefs.

Manifesto   public declaration of policy by sovereign, state, political party, candidate, etc.

Parable   narrative of imagined events used to represent moral or spiritual truths.

Persuasion   the act of causing to have belief (of fact, that thing is so); to induce (person to do, into action); to convince (of thing, that).

Polemic   controversial discussion.

A Handbook to Literature, C Hugh Holman
A vigorously argumentative work, setting forth its author's attitudes on a highly controversial subject, usually on religion, social issues, economics, or politics.

Propaganda   association or organised scheme for propagation of a doctrine or practice; (usually derogatory) doctrines, information thus propagated etc.

Communication and Persuasion, G H Jamieson
The term propaganda has gathered to itself sinister overtones, owing to its connections with totalitarian systems of government, and yet its origins lie in religious affairs. The term propaganda was derived from the proceedings of the Roman Catholic Church, which promulgated a 'Congregatio de Propaganda Fide' in the seventeenth century for the purpose of coordinating its missionary activities. The Soviet-Marxist concept of propaganda still possesses this sense of missionary zeal, and it was confirmed in a report in the Times newspaper on 22 February, 1978 which quoted the editor-in-chief of Pravda as saying, 'Our aim is propaganda, the propaganda of the Party and State. We do not hide this.' This interpretation carries with it an educational motive, which is quite contrary to the interpretation placed upon propaganda in western, democratic societies. But it is an interpretation which is quite openly proclaimed. It could be hypothesised that the covert censorship, practised by editors of the press in 'open' societies, creates distortion which is only different in kind from that in the press of authoritarian states.

Find examples of each of these forms of persuasion. You may need to go to your library, or other subject departments in your school.
Your task now is to persuade a group of people to do one of the following:
- send their children to your school
- close a local nuclear-waste dump
- buy an ozone-friendly fridge
- build a sports centre.

You could use one or more of the techniques of persuasion described above. You can include drawings, posters, storyboards and text but your final display must not exceed one side of A1 paper. You will come back to this display towards the end of the work on this unit.

Decision time

Approaching the text

During the course of our lives, people will try to persuade us to do many things. We have to make decisions. These decisions can have major implications for our future. In this story, James Joyce explores the predicament of a girl making one of these decisions. Throughout the story she compares her life so far with the attractions of the future that has been offered to her.

As you read the story, make a note of her reasons for staying and her reasons for leaving Dublin.

Eveline
James Joyce

She sat at the window watching the evening invade the avenue. Her head was leaned against the window curtains, and in her nostrils was the odour of dusty cretonne. She was tired.

Few people passed. The man out of the last house passed on his way home; she heard his footsteps clacking along the concrete pavement and afterwards crunching on the cinder path before the new red houses. One time there used to be a field there in which they used to play every evening with other people's children. Then a man from Belfast bought the field and built houses in it – not like their little brown houses, but bright brick houses with shining roofs. The children of the avenue used   10

to play together in that field – the Devines, the Waters, the Dunns, little Keogh the cripple, she and her brothers and sisters. Ernest, however, never played: he was too grown up. Her father used often to hunt them in out of the field with his blackthorn stick; but usually little Keogh used to keep *nix* and call out when he saw her father coming. Still they seemed to have been rather happy then. Her father was not so bad then; and besides, her mother was alive. That was a long time ago; she and her brothers and sisters were all grown up; her mother was dead. Tizzie Dunn was dead, too, and the Waters had gone back to England. Everything changes. Now she was going to go away like the others, to   20
leave her home.

Home! She looked round the room, reviewing all its familiar objects which she had dusted once a week for so many years, wondering where on earth all the dust came from. Perhaps she would never see again those familiar objects from which she had never dreamed of being divided. And yet during all those years she had never found out the name of the priest whose yellowing photograph hung on the wall above the broken harmonium beside the coloured print of the promises made to Blessed Margaret Mary Alacoque. He had been a school friend of her father. Whenever he showed the photograph to a visitor her father used to pass   30
it with a casual word:

‘He is in Melbourne now.’

She had consented to go away, to leave her home. Was that wise? She tried to weigh each side of the question. In her home anyway she had shelter and food; she had those whom she had known all her life about her. Of course she had to work hard, both in the house and at business. What would they say of her in the Stores when they found out that she had run away with a fellow? Say she was a fool, perhaps; and her place would be filled up by advertisement. Miss Gavan would be glad. She had always had an edge on her, especially whenever there were people   40
listening.

‘Miss Hill, don’t you see these ladies are waiting?’

‘Look lively, Miss Hill, please.’

She would not cry many tears at leaving the Stores.

But in her new home, in a distant unknown country, it would not be like that. Then she would be married – she, Eveline. People would treat her with respect then. She would not be treated as her mother had been. Even now, though she was over nineteen, she sometimes felt herself in danger of her father’s violence. She knew it was that that had given her the palpitations. When they were growing up he had never gone for her,   50
but he used to go for Harry and Ernest, because she was a girl; but latterly he had begun to threaten her and say what he would do to her only for her dead mother’s sake. And now she had nobody to protect her, Ernest was dead and Harry, who was in the church decorating business, was nearly always down somewhere in the country. Besides, the invariable squabble for money on Saturday nights had begun to weary her unspeakably. She always gave her entire wages – seven shillings – and Harry always sent up what he could, but the trouble was to get any money from her father. He said she used to squander the money, that she had no head, that he wasn’t going to give   60

her his hard-earned money to throw about the streets, and much more, for he was usually fairly bad on Saturday night. In the end he would give her the money and ask her had she any intention of buying Sunday's dinner. Then she had to rush out as quickly as she could and do her marketing, holding her black leather purse tightly in her hand as she elbowed her way through the crowds and returning home late under her load of provisions. She had hard work to keep the house together and to see that the two young children who had been left to her charge went to school regularly and got their meals regularly. It was hard work – a hard life – but now that she was about to leave it she did not find it a   70
wholly undesirable life.

She was about to explore another life with Frank. Frank was very kind, manly, open-hearted. She was to go away with him by the night-boat to be his wife and to live with him in Buenos Ayres, where he had a home waiting for her. How well she remembered the first time she had seen him; he was lodging in a house on the main road where she used to visit. It seemed a few weeks ago. He was standing at the gate, his peaked cap pushed back on his head and his hair tumbled forward over a face of bronze. Then they had come to know each other. He used to meet her outside the Stores every evening and see her home. He took her   80
to see *The Bohemian Girl* and she felt elated as she sat in an unaccustomed part of the theatre with him. He was awfully fond of music and sang a little. People knew that they were courting, and, when he sang about the lass that loves a sailor, she always felt pleasantly confused. He used to call her Poppens out of fun. First of all it had been an excitement for her to have a fellow and then she had begun to like him. He had tales of distant countries. He had started as a deck boy at a pound a month on a ship of the Allan Line going out to Canada. He told her the names of the ships he had been on and the names of the different services. He had sailed through the Straits of Magellan and he told her stories of the   90
terrible Patagonians. He had fallen on his feet in Buenos Ayres, he said, and had come over to the old country just for a holiday. Of course, her father had found out the affair and had forbidden her to have anything to say to him.

'I know these sailor chaps,' he said.

One day he had quarrelled with Frank, and after that she had to meet her lover secretly.

The evening deepened in the avenue. The white of two letters in her lap grew indistinct. One was to Harry; the other was to her father. Ernest had been her favourite, but she liked Harry too. Her father was becoming old lately, she noticed; he would miss her. Sometimes he could be very nice. Not long before, when she had been laid up for a day, he had read her out a ghost story and made toast for her at the fire. Another day, when their mother was alive, they had all gone for a picnic to the Hill of Howth. She remembered her father putting on her mother's bonnet to make the children laugh.

Her time was running out, but she continued to sit by the window, leaning her head against the window curtain, inhaling the odour of dusty cretonne. Down far in the avenue she could hear a street organ playing. She knew the air. Strange that it should come that very night to remind her of the promise to her mother, her promise to keep the home together as long as she could. She remembered the last night of her mother's illness; she was again in the close, dark room at the other side of the hall and outside she heard a melancholy air of Italy. The organ-player had been ordered to go away and given sixpence. She remembered her father strutting back into the sick-room saying:

'Damned Italians! coming over here!'

As she mused, the pitiful vision of her mother's life laid its spell on the very quick of her being – that life of commonplace sacrifices closing in final craziness. She trembled as she heard again her mother's voice saying constantly with foolish insistence:

'Derevaun Seraun! Derevaun Seraun!'

She stood up in a sudden impulse of terror. Escape! She must escape! Frank would save her. He would give her life, perhaps love, too. But she wanted to live. Why should she be unhappy? She had a right to happiness. Frank would take her in his arms, fold her in his arms. He would save her.

She stood among the swaying crowd in the station at the North Wall. He held her hand and she knew that he was speaking to her, saying something about the passage over and over again. The station was full of soldiers with brown baggages. Through the wide doors of the sheds she caught a glimpse of the black mass of the boat, lying in beside the quay wall, with illumined portholes. She answered nothing. She felt her cheek pale and cold and, out of a maze of distress, she prayed to God to direct her, to show her what was her duty. The boat blew a long mournful whistle into the mist. If she went, tomorrow she would be on the sea with Frank, steaming towards Buenos Ayres. Their passage had been booked. Could she still draw back after all he had done for her? Her distress awoke a nausea in her body and she kept moving her lips in silent fervent prayer.

A bell clanged upon her heart. She felt him seize her hand:

'Come!'

All the seas of the world tumbled about her heart. He was drawing her into them: he would drown her. She gripped with both hands at the iron railing.

'Come!'

No! No! No! It was impossible. Her hands clutched the iron in frenzy.
Amid the seas she sent a cry of anguish.

'Eveline! Evvy!'

He rushed beyond the barrier and called to her to follow. He was 150
shouted at to go on, but he still called to her. She set her white face to
him, passive, like a helpless animal. Her eyes gave him no sign of love
or farewell or recognition.

Into the text

1 What evidence is there in the text that tells you that this story was written in the early twentieth century?

2 Almost certainly, you will have found more reasons for Eveline to go to Buenos Ayres than to stay in Dublin. Why then, do you think that she refuses to get on the boat? There is one phrase in the story that explains why. Which line is it?

3 What do you think about her decision? How would she justify it to Frank?

4 What do you understand by the lines 'She set her white face to him, passive, like a helpless animal. Her eyes gave him no sign of love or farewell or recognition' (lines 151–3)?

5 Pick out some of the details that Joyce mentions about the room that Eveline is sitting in. What do they tell us about the kind of life that Eveline has?

6 Imagine you are Eveline. Write a letter to Frank explaining the reasons for your decision not to board the boat.

7 Think about the arguments that Frank might have used to persuade Eveline to go to Buenos Ayres, if he had got the chance, before the boat was due to sail. Write the conversation either as dialogue or as narrative.

Severely workful: Polemical language

The following extracts, written over a period of 130 years, are descriptions of industrial landscapes. In each case, the writer feels very strongly about the scene being described and a clear point of view emerges. This point of view is not stated directly but is implied by the ways in which the writer chooses to describe the scene by the use of imagery, selection of detail, emphasis and repetition, and tone. These are from works of literature. Non-literary polemic, like a political pamphlet, would be more direct in its approach.

Approaching the text

In the first extract, Charles Dickens describes a northern industrial town (possibly Manchester or Preston). Many Victorians were both fascinated and appalled by the growth of the new industrial towns. Dickens, and other writers, wanted to shake their readers out of their complacency about the living and working conditions of the newly urbanised populations.

One image of this town that Dickens uses in the first paragraph to shock his readers is that of the jungle: a stark contrast to the widely held view that these towns represented the great achievements of Victorian civilisation. As you read the passage, make a note of the words used to develop this image.

Hard Times
Charles Dickens (1854)

It was a town of red brick, or of brick that would have been red if the smoke and ashes had allowed it; but, as matters stood it was a town of unnatural red and black like the painted face of a savage. It was a town of machinery and tall chimneys, out of which interminable serpents of smoke trailed themselves for ever and ever, and never got uncoiled. It had a black canal in it, and a river that ran purple with ill-smelling dye, and vast piles of building full of windows where there was a rattling and a trembling all day long, and where the piston of the steam-engine worked monotonously up and down, like the head of an elephant in a state of melancholy madness. It contained several large streets all very   10 like one another, and many small streets still more like one another, inhabited by people equally like one another, who all went in and out at the same hours, with the same sound upon the same pavements, to do the same work, and to whom every day was the same as yesterday and tomorrow, and every year the counterpart of the last and the next . . .

. . . You saw nothing in Coketown but what was severely workful. If the members of a religious persuasion built a chapel there – as the members of eighteen religious persuasions had done – they made it a pious warehouse of red brick, with sometimes (but this is only in highly   20 ornamental examples) a bell in a bird-cage on the top of it. The solitary exception was the New Church; a stuccoed edifice with a square steeple over the door, terminating in four short pinnacles like florid wooden legs. All the public inscriptions in the town were painted alike, in severe characters of black and white. The jail might have been the infirmary, the infirmary might have been the jail, the town-hall might have been either, or both, or anything else, for anything that appeared to the contrary in the graces of their construction. Fact, fact, fact, everywhere in the material aspect of the town; fact, fact, fact, everywhere in the immaterial.   30

Into the text

1 You have noted words and phrases that describe Coketown in terms of a jungle. The unexpected thing about this image is that the jungle has been 'tamed' and mechanised: '. . . interminable serpents of smoke trailed themselves for ever and ever, and never got uncoiled.' (lines 4–5); '. . . the piston of the steam-engine worked monotonously up and down, like the head of an elephant in a state of melancholy madness.' (lines 8–10). In what other ways does Dickens reinforce the image of Coketown being uniform and inhuman? Find examples from the text.

2 Find examples of words and phrases in the text that suggest to you that this was not written in the twentieth century.

3 What do you understand by the following:
   a interminable serpents (line 4)?
   b severely workful (line 17)?
   c pious warehouse (line 20)?
   d fact, fact, fact (lines 28, 29)?

Approaching the text

During the nineteenth century, a tradition was established by writers like Dickens who condemned the consequences of industrialisation. Later writers drew on and developed the ideas and images used by earlier writers. What evidence can you find in the following passage, written seventy years after *Hard Times*, that Lawrence is continuing this tradition? In what way does Lawrence develop the tradition?

_____ *Lady Chatterley's Lover* _____
DH Lawrence (1928)

The car ploughed uphill through the long squalid straggle of Tevershall, the blackened brick dwellings, the black slate roofs glistening their sharp edges, the mud black with coal-dust, the pavements wet and black. It was as if dismalness had soaked through and through everything. The utter negation of natural beauty, the utter negation of the gladness of life, the utter absence of the instinct for shapely beauty which every bird and beast has, the utter death of the human intuitive faculty was appalling. The stacks of soap in the grocers' shops! the rhubarb and lemons in the greengrocers! the awful hats in the milliners! all went by ugly, ugly, ugly, followed by the plaster-and-gilt horror of the cinema with its wet picture announcements, 'A Woman's Love!', and the new big Primitive chapel, primitive enough in its stark brick and big panes

10

of greenish and raspberry glass in the windows. The Wesleyan chapel, higher up, was of blackened brick and stood behind iron railings and blackened shrubs. The Congregational chapel, which thought itself superior, was built of rusticated sandstone and had a steeple, but not a very high one. Just beyond were the new school buildings, expensive pink brick, and gravelled playground inside iron railings, all very imposing, and mixing the suggestion of a chapel and a prison. Standard Five girls were having a singing lesson, just finishing the la-me-doh-   20
la exercises and beginning a 'sweet children's song'. Anything more unlike song, spontaneous song, would be impossible to imagine: a strange bawling yell that followed the outlines of a tune. It was not like savages: savages have subtle rhythms. It was not like animals: animals *mean* something when they yell. It was like nothing on earth, and it was called singing. Connie sat and listened with her heart in her boots, as Field was filling petrol. What could possibly become of such a people, a people in whom the living intuitive faculty was dead as nails, and only queer mechanical yells and uncanny will-power remained?

Into the text

1 What use does Lawrence make of colour? What effect does it have on you?
2 Find examples from this passage that are similar to those used by Dickens in *Hard Times* when describing Coketown. What references tell you that Lawrence was writing about the twentieth century?
3 What other features of the language tell you that the vision of Tevershall makes the narrator angry?

Approaching the text

In the two previous passages, Dickens and Lawrence present nature as having been defeated by industry and mechanisation. What evidence can you find in this poem, written by Ted Hughes, of the same thinking?

Hill-Stone Was Content
Ted Hughes (1979)

Hill-stone was content
To be cut, to be carted
And fixed in its new place.

It let itself be conscripted
Into mills. And it stayed in position   5
Defending this slavery against all.

It forgot its wild roots
Its earth-song
In cement and the drum-song of looms.

And inside the mills mankind 10
With bodies that came and went
Stayed in position, fixed like the stones
Trembling in the song of the looms.

And they too became four-cornered, stony

In their long, darkening stand 15
Against the guerilla patience
Of the soft hill-water.

Into the text

1 What is the author saying in this poem? Put the poem into your own words.

2 How are Hughes' conclusions about the conflict between the natural and the man-made different from those of Dickens and Lawrence? Find evidence in the poem.

3 Why does the poet start the poem with an 'invented' word and end with another?

4 Look back at the definition of polemic writing given on page 105. To what extent do you think each of these are examples of polemic writing? Which do you consider to have the most impact? Why?

5 Bearing in mind what you have read and discussed about the nature of polemic, write a description of a scene with which you are familiar (eg breaktime at school, a football match, a disco) which gives the reader a clear point of view without actually *stating directly* what the view is.

Bound up his wounds: A parable

Approaching the text

Before you go on to this next section, look back at the dictionary's definition of parable on page 105. Religious leaders often tell stories in order to persuade their listeners that some conduct is more preferable than others. A famous parable narrated by Jesus is that of the Good Samaritan. He told this story to a Jewish priest who was trying to catch him out.

_____ *The Parable of the Good Samaritan* _____
The Revised English Bible (1989)

Lŭke 10.30 '. . . A man was on his way from Jerusalem down to Jericho when he was set upon by robbers, who stripped and beat him, and went off leaving him half dead.

.31 It so happened that a priest was going down by the same road, and when he saw him, he went past on the other side.

.32 So too a Levite came to the place, and when he saw him went past on the other side.

.33 But a Samaritan who was going that way came upon him, and when he saw him he was moved to pity.

.34 He went up and bandaged his wounds, bathing them with oil and wine. Then he lifted him on to his own beast, brought him to an inn, and looked after him.

.35 Next day he produced two silver pieces and gave them to the innkeeper, and said, "Look after him; and if you spend more, I will repay you on my way back.'

.36 Which of these three do you think was neighbour to the man who fell into the hands of the robbers?'

.37 He answered, 'The one who showed him kindness.' Jesus said to him, 'Go and do as he did.'

Into the text

1 What do you think is the point of this story?

2 In what ways is this story more powerful than simply saying 'Love thy neighbour'?

This version of the story appears in the most recent official English Bible first published in 1989. Over the years people have felt the need to revise the Bible in order to make its message more accessible to its readers. When these changes take place, however, they are rarely greeted with enthusiasm.

New Bible aims at "man in the pew"

John Ezard

AN EMINENT Hebrew scholar pushed a button yesterday and started a mass print run for a new official English Bible, the latest in a process which will have stripped church worship of much of its most familiar language within a generation.

The Revised English Bible, which publishes its first 300,000 copies on September 27, drops "thee" and "thou" as antiquated, cuts familiar words from the 23rd Psalm, and omits the phrase "still waters".

The new version will be publicised as carrying Christianity into the 21st century with a single ecumenical form of words.

It is the first text since the Reformation 400 years ago to be planned by all leading British church groups, including Roman Catholics.

The new text, disclosed to the Guardian yesterday when production was started by the Bath Press, is the result of 15 years of work by teams headed by the former Archbishop of Canterbury, Lord Coggan. The Bible follows its predecessor, the still controversial New English Bible, published 30 years ago, in translating Christ's last cry from the Cross as "It is accomplished", instead of "It is finished" – the version in the Authorised King James' Bible. "Finished" is said to sound "too workaday".

The revised Bible makes St Paul address his epistles to "brothers and sisters" or "friends", although the original text's word is admitted to mean "brothers", the King James' Bible translation.

The project director, Professor William Duff McHardy, former Regius Professor of Hebrew at Oxford, said it was clear in context that St Paul meant to address women as well as men. The change was to cater for "the sexist language lobby".

Translators had also been careful about using the word "gay", but no substitute for "kingdom" of heaven had proved feasible.

The words in the Authorised Version of the 23rd psalm, "though I walk through the valley of the shadow of death", were rendered in the New English Bible as "though I walk through a valley dark as death". In the revised Bible, this passage becomes: "Were I to walk through a valley of deepest darkness". Professor McHardy said the reference to death misread the Hebrew.

"He leadeth me beside the still waters" becomes "he leads me to waters where I may rest".

"It's a version for the man in the pew, not for the highly educated person," Professor McHardy added. "It's very much a question of compromise."

The joint publishers, the Oxford and Cambridge University Presses, expect the new version rapidly to supersede the New English Bible and to reach a world market of millions.

Metamorphosis of the 23rd Psalm:

Authorised Version: The Lord is my shepherd; I shall not want. He maketh me to lie down in green pastures; he leadeth me beside the still waters. He restoreth my soul; he leadeth me in the paths of righteousness for his name's sake.

Yea, though I walk through the valley of the shadow of death, I will fear no evil; for thou art with me; thy rod and thy staff, they comfort me.

New English Bible: The Lord is my shepherd; I shall want nothing. He makes me lie down in green pastures, and leads me beside the waters of peace; he renews life within me and for his name's sake guides me in the right path. Even though I walk through a valley as dark as death I fear no evil, thy staff and thy crook are my comfort.

Revised English Bible: 'The Lord is my shepherd; I lack for nothing. He makes me lie down in green pastures, he leads me to water where I may rest; he revives my spirit; for his name's sake he leads me in the right paths. Even were I to walk through a valley of deepest darkness I should fear no harm for you are with me; your shepherd's staff and crook comfort me.

Here are some letters that appeared in *The Guardian* after the original article. Which do you find to be the most persuasive, and why?

Behold there came a word from the person in the pew

IF the Revised English Bible (Guardian, July 29) has catered for the "sexist language lobby", why is it aimed at the "man in the pew"?
Rebecca Bunting

WHAT has "the man in the pew" done to deserve the Revised English Bible? It seems that meaning and poetry have been thrown out together with "thee" and "thou." I suppose that "anti-quated" hymns will be next in line for this kind of editorial butchery. Shall we suffer from "revised" George Herbert?

Teach me, my God and King.

In all things you to see.
And what I do in anything
To do it as for me.
Anne Serraillier,

I SEE no new revolution in Bible Translation. Thees and Thous are decidedly thin on the ground even in the ageing Revised Standard Version, and as for supersed-ing the New English Bible, this may be the official attempt, but "independent" translations effectively drove NEB off the shelves years ago.

Here in theological college the standard text is RSV, as it most literally follows the original Hebrew and Greek, but for lay reading of the Bible, the two translations which dominate the market are the New International Version as a scholarly text and the highly readable Good News Bible.

The best of the rest for my money are The Jerusalem Bible for its down-to-earth approach (a light is hidden not under a bushel but a tub), and the Living Bible, a para-phrase which a reader of the Daily Mirror really would be able to follow with ease, however much over-educated scholars might criticise its style. That translation in par-ticular really is a Bible for "the man [sic] in the pew." A translation using construc-tions like "Even were I" is still stuck in the lecture room.
Mike Hampson

Language changes

Approaching the text

You are now going to read three more versions of this same story. They were published in 1380, 1611 and 1901. During this period, the English Language changed in a variety of ways: words (their meanings and spellings); punctuation; and word order (syntax). Read these versions carefully, making notes as you go along.

The Wiclif Version (1380)

Luke 10.30 . . . A man cam doun from ierusalem in to ierico, and filde among theues/ and thei robbeden hym, and woundiden hym, and wenten aweie: and leften the man half alyue

.31 and it bifelle that a preest cam doun the same weie and passid forth whanne he hadde seen hym

.32 also a dekene whanne he was bisidis the place, and saie hym: passid forth/

.33 but a samaritan goynge the weie: cam bisidis hym/ and he saie hym and hadde rewthe on hym,

.34 _ cam to hym and bounde his woundis togidre/ and heeld ynne oile and wyne: and leid hym on his beest, and ledde in to an ostrie, and dide the cure of hym

.35 and another dai he brou _ te forth tweie pens and _ af to the ostler and seide/ haue the cure of hym/ and what euer thou shalt seue ouer: I schal _ ilde to thee whanne I come a _ en

.36 who of these thre semeth to thee: was nei _ bore to hym that fille among theues? and he seide/ he that dide merci in to hym

.37 and ihesus seide to hym/ go thou and do thou on like maner.

The Authorised Version (1611)

Luke 10.30 . . . A certaine man went downe from Hierusalem to Iericho, and fel among theeues, which stripped him of his raiment, and wounded him, and departed, leauing him half dead.

.31 And by chance there came downe a certain Priest that way; and when he saw him, he passed by on the other side.

.32 And likewise a Leuite, when hee was at the place, came and looked on him, and passed by on the other side.

.33 But a certaine Samaritane, as he iourneyed, came where he was; and when he saw him, hee had compassion on him,

.34 And went to him, and bound vp his wounds, powring in oyle and wine, and set him on his owne beast, and brought him to an Inne, and tooke care of him.

.35 And on the morrow when he departed, hee tooke out two pence,

and gaue them to the hoste, and sayd vnto him, Take care of him: and whatsoeuer thou spendest more, when I come againe, I will repay thee.
.36 Which now of these three, thinkest thou, was neighbour vnto him that fell among the thieues?
.37 And he said, He that showed mercie on him. Then said Jesus vnto him, Go, and doe thou likewise.

The Revised Version (1901)

Luke 10.30 . . . A certain man was going down from Jerusalem to Jericho; and he fell among robbers, which both stripped him and beat him, and departed, leaving him half dead.
.31 And by chance a certain priest was going down that way: and when he saw him, he passed by on the other side.
.32 And in like manner a Levite also, when he came to the place, and saw him, passed by on the other side.
.33 But a certain Samaritan, as he journeyed, came where he was: and when he saw him, he was moved with compassion,
.34 And came to him, and bound up his wounds, pouring on them oil and wine; and he set him on his own beast, and brought him to an inn, and took care of him.
.35 And on the morrow he took out two pence, and gave them to the host, and said, Take care of him; and whatsoever thou spendest more, I, when I come back again, will repay thee.
.36 Which of these three, thinkest thou, proved neighbour unto him that fell among the robbers?
.37 And he said, He that shewed mercy on him. And Jesus said unto him, Go and do thou likewise.

Into the text   Look closely at verses 34 and 35 of all four versions of this story. Using your notes and your closer reading of these four versions, identify the key differences in language and style between them. (Think about spelling, about vocabulary, about punctuation, etc.)

In three or four paragraphs, write about the relative merits of these different versions of the Bible. This might take the form of a letter to the paper, or a recommendation to the Head of RE at your school.

The hate had started: Indoctrination and propaganda

During the first half of the twentieth century, a number of authors began to be concerned about the way in which the developing mass communications could be used by governments to control how people think. The belief that this was possible was based on some contemporary psychological research which suggested that people's behaviour could be influenced. Much of this work was based on experiments conducted on animals whose behaviour could be altered or 'conditioned'. Indoctrination is based on the same approach. Look again at the definitions on page 105.

Approaching the text

This extract was written in 1932 and is set in an imaginary future where people's role in society and their behaviour is determined before birth and in the first few years of life. In this extract, a group of Alpha students are being shown how low-status children are 'persuaded' to dislike books and flowers. As you read the extract, consider the response that the author intended you, the reader, to have.

Brave New World
Aldous Huxley

'Set out the books,' he said curtly.

In silence the nurses obeyed his command. Between the rose bowls the books were duly set out – a row of nursery quartos opened invitingly each at some gaily coloured image of beast or fish or bird.

'Now bring in the children.'

They hurried out of the room and returned in a minute or two, each pushing a kind of tall dumb-waiter laden, on all its four wire-netted shelves, with eight-month-old babies, all exactly alike (a Bokanovsky Group, it was evident) and all (since their caste was Delta) dressed in khaki.   10

'Put them down on the floor.'

The infants were unloaded.

'Now turn them so that they can see the flowers and books.'

Turned, the babies at once fell silent, then began to crawl towards those clusters of sleek colours, those shapes so gay and brilliant on the white pages. As they approached, the sun came out of a momentary eclipse behind the cloud. The roses flamed up as though with a sudden passion from within; a new and profound significance seemed to suffuse the shining pages of the books. From the ranks of the crawling babies came little squeals of excitement, gurgles and twitterings of pleasure.   20

The Director rubbed his hands. 'Excellent!' he said. 'It might almost have been done on purpose.'

The swiftest crawlers were already at their goal. Small hands reached out uncertainly, touched, grasped, unpetalling the transfigured roses, crumpling the illuminated pages of the books. The Director waited until all were happily busy. Then, 'Watch carefully,' he said. And, lifting his hand, he gave the signal.

The Head Nurse, who was standing by a switchboard at the other end of the room, pressed down a little lever.

There was a violent explosion. Shriller and even shriller, a siren   30
shrieked. Alarm bells maddeningly sounded.

The children started, screamed; their faces were distorted with terror.

'And now,' the Director shouted (for the noise was deafening), 'now we proceed to rub in the lesson with a mild electric shock.'

He waved his hand again, and the Head Nurse pressed a second time. The screaming of the babies suddenly changed its tone. There was something desperate, almost insane, about the sharp spasmodic yelps to which they now gave utterance. Their little bodies twitched and stiffened; their limbs moved jerkily as if to the tug of unseen wires.

'We can electrify that whole strip of floor,' bawled the Director in   40
explanation. 'But that's enough,' he signalled to the nurse.

The explosions ceased, the bells stopped ringing, the shriek of the siren died down from tone to tone into silence. The stiffly twitching bodies relaxed, and what had become the sob and yelp of infant maniacs broadened out once more into a normal howl of ordinary terror.

'Offer them the flowers and the books again.'

The nurses obeyed; but at the approach of the roses, at the mere sight of those gaily-coloured images of pussy and cock-a-doodle-doo and baa-baa black sheep, the infants shrank away in horror; the volume of their howling suddenly increased.   50

'Observe,' said the Director triumphantly, 'observe.'

Books and loud noises, flowers and electric shocks – already in the infant mind these couples were compromisingly linked; and after two hundred repetitions of the same or a similar lesson would be wedded indissolubly. What man has joined, nature is powerless to put asunder.

'They'll grow up with what the psychologists used to call an "instinctive" hatred of books and flowers. Reflexes unalterably conditioned. They'll be safe from books and botany all their lives.' The Director turned to his nurses. 'Take them away again.'

Still yelling, the khaki babies were loaded on to their dumb-   60
waiters and wheeled out, leaving behind them the smell of sour milk and a most welcome silence.

Into the text

1 What do you think is the attitude shown by the adults to the conditioning process?

2 What do you understand from the passage by the phrase 'conditioned reflex'?

3 What do you feel about this passage? Huxley wanted to shock the reader. Does it have this effect on you? Refer to the passage to illustrate your answer.

Approaching the text

This extract, written in 1948, also describes an imaginary future in which, in this case, people's thoughts and ideas are controlled through the use of propaganda. Winston Smith, the 'hero' of the novel is beginning to have reservations about the Party – the Government – and this is something he must keep secret. In this extract, he attends a rally that is designed to focus hostility on an enemy in order to deflect criticism away from the Party itself. As you read it, think about the way in which the group experience of watching the telescreen affects Winston Smith.

1984
George Orwell

The next moment a hideous, grinding screech, as of some monstrous machine running without oil, burst from the big telescreen at the end of the room. It was a noise that set one's teeth on edge and bristled the hair at the back of one's neck. The Hate had started.

As usual, the face of Emmanuel Goldstein, the Enemy of the People, had flashed onto the screen. There were hisses here and there among the audience. The little sandy-haired woman gave a squeak of mingled fear and disgust. Goldstein was the renegade and backslider who once, long ago (how long ago, nobody quite remembered), had been one of the leading figures of the Party, almost on a level with Big Brother himself, and then had engaged in counter-revolutionary activities, had been con-demned to death and had mysteriously escaped and disappeared. The

10

programmes of the Two Minutes Hate varied from day to day, but there was none in which Goldstein was not the principle figure. He was the primal traitor, the earliest defiler of the Party's purity. All subsequent crimes against the Party, all treacheries, acts of sabotage, heresies, deviations, sprang directly out of his teaching. Somewhere or other he was still alive and hatching his conspiracies: perhaps somewhere beyond the sea, under the protection of his foreign paymasters, per- haps even – so it was occasionally rumoured – in some hiding-place in   20 Oceania itself.

Winston's diaphragm was constricted. He could never see the face of Goldstein without a painful mixture of emotions. It was a lean Jewish face, with a great fuzzy aureole of white hair and a small goatee beard – a clever face, and yet somehow inherently despicable, with a kind of senile silliness in the long thin nose near the end of which a pair of spectacles was perched. It resembled the face of a sheep, and the voice, too, had a sheep-like quality. Goldstein was delivering his usual venomous attack upon the doctrines of the party – an attack so exaggerated and perverse that a child should have been able to see   30 through it, and yet just plausible enough to fill one with an alarmed feeling that other people, less level-headed than oneself, might be taken in by it. He was abusing Big Brother, he was denouncing the dictatorship of the Party, he was demanding the immediate conclusion of peace with Eurasia, he was advocating freedom of speech, freedom of the press, freedom of assembly, freedom of thought, he was crying hysterically that the revolution had been betrayed – and all this in rapid polysyllabic speech which was a sort of parody of the habitual style of the orators of the Party, and even contained Newspeak words: more Newspeak words, indeed, than any Party member would normally use in real life.   40 And all the while, lest one should be in any doubt as to the reality which Goldstein's specious claptrap covered, behind his head on the telescreen there marched the endless columns of the Eurasian army – row after row of solid-looking men with expressionless Asiatic faces, who swam up to the surface of the screen and vanished, to be replaced by others exactly similar. The dull rhythmic tramp of the soldiers' boots formed the background to Goldstein's bleating voice.

Before the Hate had proceeded for thirty seconds, uncontrollable exclamations of rage were breaking out from half the people in the room. The self-satisfied sheep-like face on the screen, and the terrifying   50 power of the Eurasian army behind it, were too much to be borne: beside, the sight or even the thought of Goldstein produced fear and anger automatically. He was an object of hatred more constant than either Eurasia or Eastasia, since when Oceania was at war with one of these powers it was generally at peace with the other. But what was strange was that although Goldstein was hated and despised by every- body, although every day and a thousand times a day, on platforms, on the telescreen, in newspapers, in books, his theories were refuted, smashed, ridiculed, held up to the general gaze for the pitiful rubbish that they were – in spite of all this, his influence never seemed to grow   60 less. Always there were fresh dupes waiting to be seduced by him. A day never passed when spies and saboteurs acting under his directions were

not unmasked by the Thought Police. He was the commander of a vast
shadowy army, an underground network of conspirators dedicated to
the overthrow of the State. The Brotherhood, its name was supposed to
be. There were also whispered stories of a terrible book, a compendium
of all the heresies, of which Goldstein was the author and which
circulated clandestinely here and there. It was a book without a title.
People referred to it, if at all, simply as *the Book*. But one knew of such
things only through vague rumours. Neither the Brotherhood nor *the*   70
Book was a subject that any ordinary Party member would mention if
there was a way of avoiding it.

    In its second minute the Hate rose to a frenzy. People were leaping up
and down in their places and shouting at the tops of their voices in an
effort to drown the maddening bleating voice that came from the screen.
The little sandy-haired woman had turned bright pink, and her mouth
was opening and shutting like that of a landed fish. Even O'Brien's heavy
face was flushed. He was sitting very straight in his chair, his powerful
chest swelling and quivering as though he were standing up to the assault
of a wave. The dark-haired girl behind Winston had begun crying out   80
'Swine! Swine! Swine!' and suddenly she picked up a heavy Newspeak
dictionary and flung it at the screen. It struck Goldstein's nose and
bounced off; the voice continued inexorably. In a lucid moment Winston
found he was shouting with the others and kicking his heel violently
against the rung of his chair. The horrible thing about the Two Minutes
Hate was not that one was obliged to act apart, but, on the contrary,
that it was impossible to avoid joining in. Within thirty seconds any
pretence was always unnecessary. A hideous ecstacy of fear and vindic-
tiveness, a desire to kill, to torture, to smash faces in with a sledge-
hammer, seemed to flow through the whole group of people like an   90
electric current, turning one even against one's will into a grimacing,
screaming lunatic. And yet the rage that one felt was an abstract,
undirected emotion which could be switched from one object to another
like the flame of a blow-lamp. Thus, at one moment Winston's hatred
was not turned against Goldstein at all, but, on the contrary, against Big
Brother, the Party and the Thought Police; and at such moments his
heart went out to the lonely, derided heretic on the screen, sole guardian
of truth and sanity in a world of lies. And yet the very next instant he
was at one with the people about him, and all that was said of Goldstein
seemed to be true. At those moments his secret loathing of Big Brother   100
changed into adoration, and Big Brother seemed to tower up, an invin-
cible, fearless protector, standing like a rock against the hordes of
Asia, and Goldstein, in spite of his isolation, his helplessness and the
doubt that hung about his very existence, seemed like some sinister
enchanter, capable by the mere power of his voice of wrecking the
structure of civilisation.

    It was even possible, at moments, to switch one's hatred this way or
that by a voluntary act. Suddenly, by the sort of violent effort with which
one wrenches one's head away from the pillow in a nightmare, Winston
succeeded in transferring his hatred from the face on the screen to the   110
dark-haired girl behind him. (. . .) He hated her because she was young
and pretty and sexless, because he wanted to go to bed with her and

would never do so, because round her sweet supple waist, which seemed to ask you to encircle it with your arm, there was only the odious scarlet sash, aggressive symbol of chastity.

The Hate rose to its climax. The voice of Goldstein had become an actual sheep's bleat, and for an instant the face changed into that of a sheep. Then the sheep-face melted into the figure of a Eurasian soldier who seemed to be advancing, huge and terrible, his sub-machine gun roaring, and seeming to spring out of the surface of the screen, so that 120 some of the people in the front row actually flinched backwards in their seats. But in the same moment, drawing a deep sigh of relief from everybody, the hostile figure melted into the face of Big Brother, black-haired, black-moustachio'd, full of power and mysterious calm, and so vast that it almost filled up the screen. Nobody heard what Big Brother was saying. It was merely a few words of encouragement, the sort of words that are uttered in the din of battle, not distinguishable individually but restoring confidence by the fact of being spoken. Then the face of Big Brother faded away again and instead the three slogans of the Party stood out in bold capitals: 130

WAR IS PEACE
FREEDOM IS SLAVERY
IGNORANCE IS STRENGTH.

But the face of Big Brother seemed to persist for several seconds on the screen, as though the impact that it had made on everyone's eyeballs was too vivid to wear off immediately. The little sandy-haired woman had flung herself forward over the back of the chair in front of her. With a tremulous murmur that sounded like 'My saviour!' she extended her arms towards the screen. Then she buried her face in her hands.

Into the text

1 What do you think Orwell's attitude to this rally is?
2 How does he try to persuade you to share his view?
3 Select words and phrases that have a powerful impact on you.
4 How successful is Orwell in persuading you to share his view?
5 What sense can you make (if any) of the Party slogans? These are particularly striking because they are paradoxical ('**paradox** – self-contradictory or apparently absurd statement.' (Concise Oxford English Dictionary)). Why are they so important to the people at the rally? What purpose do they serve?
6 Apart from party political conferences, mass political rallies are rarely seen in contemporary Britain. There are occasions, however, when large groups of people with shared enthusiasms gather together, for example at a football match or pop concert. At these gatherings, emotions run high and people can be persuaded to behave in a way that they wouldn't do in a much smaller group. What Orwell describes is the crowd acting as one. As he says 'The horrible thing about the Two Minute Hate was not that one was obliged to act

apart, but, that it was impossible to avoid joining in.' (lines 85–7). In the passage, can you find other examples of how Orwell describes the group taking over at the expense of individual action? Look especially at the visual images.

7 **Either:** Imagine that you were at the 'Two Minute Hate'. Describe the experience and your feelings as the emotional temperature rises.

Or: Describe an experience of being in another large excited crowd. Think about the atmosphere and your own thoughts and feelings as your individuality is overwhelmed by the mass emotion.

Out of the text

Orwell and Huxley were writing at a time when techniques for changing people's attitudes were in their infancy. Despite this, they were able to create a nightmare vision of mind-control. In the late twentieth century, advances in Information Technology and mass communication systems (eg cable and satellite TV, computers, fibre optics, etc) potentially offer even greater opportunities for governments to control their populations.

Write an updated version of Orwell or Huxley's vision, bearing in mind these developments.

Speak a speech for me: Convincing language

Approaching the text

The following play was written in 1941 by Bertholt Brecht, a German writer, living and working at the time in America. He left Germany in 1934 to escape persecution by the Nazis. The play retells the story of the rise of Adolf Hitler through the character of Arturo Ui, a minor Chicago gangster who aims to take over the fruit and vegetable business in the city. In this extract, Arturo is attempting to gain a more effective public image. As he says, 'It looks like I'm going to have to say a word or two on certain occasions, especially when I get into politics, so I've decided to take lessons.' (lines 8–10). Brecht's success in making this scene humorous is due partly to the accuracy with which he re-creates Hitler's mannerisms, as the photographs show, turning him into a ridiculous, but nevertheless sinister figure. To appreciate the humour of this scene, you need to visualise the gestures that Arturo practises.

The Resistible Rise of Arturo Ui

Bertholt Brecht

Hotel Mammoth. Ui's suite. Two bodyguards lead a ragged actor to Ui.
In the background, Givola.]

1ST BODYGUARD	It's an actor, boss. Unarmed.
2ND BODYGUARD	He can't afford a rod. He was able to get tight because they pay him to declaim in the saloons when they're tight. But I'm told that he's good. He's one of them classical guys.
UI	Okay. Here's the problem. I've been given to understand that my pronunciation leaves something to be desired. It looks like I'm going to have to say a word or two on certain occasions, especially when I get into politics, so I've decided to take lessons. The gestures too.
THE ACTOR	Very well.
UI	Get the mirror.
	[*A bodyguard comes front stage with a large standing mirror.*]
UI	First the walk. How do you guys walk in the theatre or the opera?
THE ACTOR	I see what you mean. The grand style. Julius Caesar, Hamlet, Romeo – that's Shakespeare. Mr Ui, you've come to the right man. Old Mahonney can teach you the classical manner in ten minutes. Gentlemen, you see before you a tragic figure. Ruined by Shakespeare. An English poet. If it weren't for Shakespeare, I could be on Broadway right now. The tragedy of a character. 'Don't play Shakespeare when you're playing Ibsen, Mahonney! Look at the calendar! This is 1912, sir!' – 'Art knows no calendar, sir!' say I. 'And art is my life.' Alas.
GIVOLA	I think you've got the wrong guy, boss. He's out of date.
UI	We'll see about that. Walk around like they do in Shakespeare.
	[*The actor walks around.*]
UI	Good!
GIVOLA	You can't walk like that in front of cauliflower men. It ain't natural.
UI	What do you mean it ain't natural? Nobody's natural in this day and age. When I walk I want people to know I'm walking.
	[*He copies the actor's gait.*]
THE ACTOR	Head back. [*Ui throws his head back.*] The foot touches the ground toe first. [*Ui's foot touches the ground, toe first.*] Good. Excellent. You have a

10

20

30

40

natural gift. Only the arms. They're not quite right. Stiff. Perhaps if you joined your arms in front of your private parts. [*Ui joins his arms in front of his private parts.*] Not bad. Relaxed but firm. But head back. Good. Just the right gait for your purposes, I believe, Mr Ui. What else do you wish to learn?

UI	How to stand. In front of people.
GIVOLA	Have two big bruisers right behind you and you'll be standing pretty.
UI	That's bunk. When I stand I don't want people looking at the two bozoes behind me. I want them looking at me. Correct me!
	[*He takes a stance, his arms crossed over his chest.*]
THE ACTOR	A possible solution. But common. You don't want to look like a barber, Mr Ui. Fold your arms like this. [*He folds his arms in such a way that the backs of his hands remain visible. His palms are resting on his arms not far from the shoulder.*] A trifling change, but the difference is incalculable. Draw the comparison in the mirror, Mr Ui.
	[*Ui tries out the new position before the mirror.*]
UI	Not bad.

50

GIVOLA	What's all this for, boss? Just for those Fancy-pants in the trust?

60

UI	Hell, no! It's for
	The little people. Why, for instance, do
	You think this Clark makes such a show of
	grandeur?
	Not for his peers. His bank account
	Takes care of them, the same as my big bruisers
	Lend me prestige in certain situations.
	Clark makes a show of grandeur to impress
	The little man. I mean to do the same.

GIVOLA	But some will say it doesn't look inborn.
	Some people stick at that.
UI	I know they do.
	But I'm not trying to convince professors
	And smart-Alecks. My object is the little
	Man's image of his master.
GIVOLA	Don't overdo
	The master, boss. Better the democrat
	The friendly, reassuring type in shirtsleeves.
UI	I've got old Dogsborough for that.
GIVOLA	His image
	Is kind of tarnished, I should say. He's still
	An asset on the books, a venerable
	Antique. But people aren't as eager as they
	Were to exhibit him. They're not so sure He's
	genuine. It's like the family Bible
	Nobody opens any more since, piously
	Turning the yellowed pages with a group
	Of friends, they found a dried-out bedbug. But
	Maybe he's good enough for Cauliflower.

70

80

UI	I decide who's respectable.	90
GIVOLA	Sure thing, boss.	
	There's nothing wrong with Dogsborough. We can	
	Still use him. They haven't even dropped him	
	At City Hall. The crash would be too loud.	
UI	Sitting.	
THE ACTOR	Sitting. Sitting is almost the hardest, Mr Ui. There	
	are men who can walk; there are men who can stand;	
	but find me a man who can sit. Take a chair with a	
	backrest, Mr Ui. But don't lean against it. Hands on	
	thighs, to abdomen, elbows away from the body.	100
	How long can you sit like that, Mr Ui?	
UI	As long as I please.	
THE ACTOR	Then everything's perfect, Mr Ui.	
GIVOLA	You know, boss, when old Dogsborough passes on	
	Giri could take his place. He's got the	
	Popular touch. He plays the funny man	
	And laughs so loud in season that the plaster	
	Comes tumbling from the ceiling. Sometimes,	
	though He does it out of season, as for instance	
	When you step forward as the modest son of	110
	The Bronx you really were and talk about	
	Those seven determined youngsters.	
UI	Then he laughs?	
GIVOLA	The plaster tumbles from the ceiling. Don't	
	Tell him I said so or he'll think I've got	
	It in for him. But maybe you could make	
	Him stop collecting hats.	
UI	What kind of hats?	
GIVOLA	The hats of people he's rubbed out. And running	
	Around with them in public. It's disgusting.	120
UI	Forget it. I would never think of muzzling	
	The ox that treads my corn. I overlook	
	The petty foibles of my underlings.	
	[*To the actor.*]	
	And now to speaking! Speak a speech for me!	
THE ACTOR	Shakespeare. Nothing else. Julius Caesar. The	
	Roman hero. [*He draws a little book from his pocket.*] What do you say to Mark Antony's speech?	
	Over Caesar's body. Against Brutus. The ringleader	
	of Caesar's assassins. A model of demagogy. Very	
	famous. I played Antony in Zenith in 1908. Just	130
	what you need, Mr Ui. [*He takes a stance and recites Mark Antony's speech line for line.*]	
	Friends, Romans, countrymen, lend me your ears! [*Reading from the little book, Ui speaks the lines after him. Now and then the actor corrects him, but in the main Ui keeps his rough staccato delivery.*]	

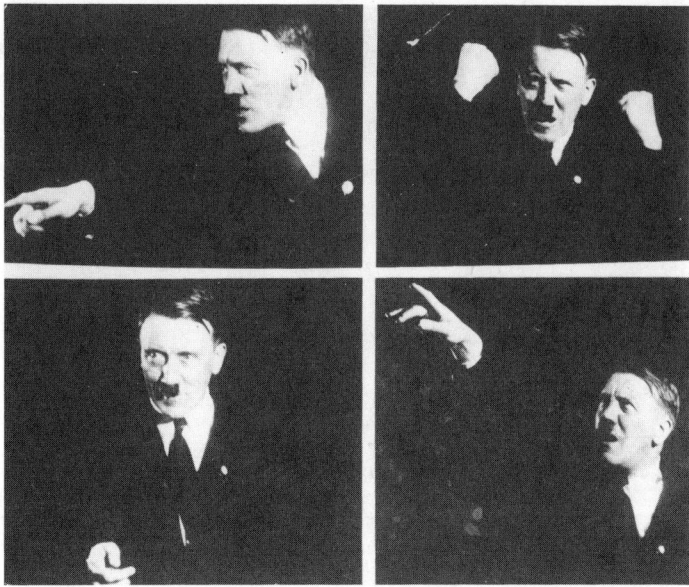

THE ACTOR   I come to bury Caesar, not to praise him.
The evil that men do lives after them;
The good is oft interred with their bones;
So let it be with Caesar. The noble Brutus
Hath told you Caesar was ambitious.
If it were so, it was a grievous fault,
And grievously hath Caesar answer'd it.   140

UI   *[continues by himself]*
Here, under leave of Brutus and the rest –
For Brutus is an honourable man;
So are they all, all honourable men –
Come I to speak in Caesar's funeral.
He was my friend, faithful and just to me;
But Brutus says he was ambitious;
And Brutus is an honourable man.
He hath brought many captives home to Rome,
Whose ransoms did the general coffers fill;
Did this in Caesar seem ambitious?   150
When that the poor have cried, Caesar hath wept;
Ambition should be made of sterner stuff.
Yet Brutus says he was ambitious;
And Brutus is an honourable man.
You all did see that on the Lupercal
I thrice presented him a kingly crown,
Which he did thrice refuse. Was this ambition?
Yet Brutus says he was ambitious;
And sure he is an honourable man.
I speak not to disprove what Brutus spoke,   160
But here I am to speak what I do know.
You all did love him once, not without cause?
What cause withholds you then, to mourn for him?

Into the text

1 Ui has to persuade Givola that his lessons are worth-while. What arguments does he use?

2 Mark Antony's speech from Shakespeare's *Julius Caesar* is regarded as a masterpiece of persuasive language. Julius Caesar has just been murdered by Brutus and his co-conspirators, and Mark Antony seeks to persuade the crowd to give up their support for Brutus and seek vengeance for the death of Caesar instead. If this is so, why does Mark Antony begin his speech with 'I come to bury Caesar, not to praise him.' (line 134)?

3 What is the effect of the repetition of '. . . Brutus says he was ambitious' and '. . . Brutus is an honour-able man'. Do you feel that Mark Antony believes Brutus to be honourable? Do you believe that Caesar was ambitious?

4 How does Mark Antony attempt to present Caesar in a favourable light?

5 Brecht wrote in defence of his play, 'Ui is a par-able play, written in the intention of destroying the usual, dangerous respect for the great killers.' (*Brecht*, R Gray) and 'The great political criminals must be exposed – and particularly exposed to laughter.' (*Brecht*, F Ewen Calder). Does this play 'destroy your respect for great killers'? Does it make you laugh?

6 In this extract there are a variety of persuasion techni-ques used, for example
   • the Actor advises Ui about how to walk and talk
   • Ui persuades Givola of the need for the approach
   • Mark Antony persuades the populace of Rome to avenge Caesar's death
   • Brecht persuades us, the audience, of the dangers of allowing people like Ui to flourish.
   Go back to the text and identify some of these techniques.

Out of the text

Write a dialogue between two characters in which one character tries to persuade the other on a course of action which they might not otherwise choose to do. Remember that the dramatist has dialogue and stage directions available to create character, mood, motives, relationships, etc.

Approaching the text

This play was first performed in 1935 and tells the story of the murder of Archbishop Thomas Becket in Canterbury Cathedral in 1170, by four knights acting on the orders of King Henry II. After the murder, the knights address the audience in order to try and justify their action. As you read the extract, think about the different ways by which the knights try to persuade us of their point of view. The characters are:

First Knight – Sir Reginald Fitz Urse
Second Knight – Sir Hugh de Morville
Third Knight – Baron William de Traci
Fourth Knight – Sir Richard Brito

_____ *Murder in the Cathedral* _____
TS Eliot

FIRST KNIGHT	We beg you to give us your attention for a few moments. We know that you may be disposed to judge unfavourably of our action. You are Englishmen, and therefore you believe in fair play: and when you see one man being set upon by four, then your sympathies are all with the under dog. I respect such feeling, I share them. Nevertheless, I appeal to your sense of honour. You are Englishmen, and therefore will not judge anybody without hearing both sides of the case. That is in accordance with our long estab- 10

lished principle of Trial by Jury. I am not myself
qualified to put our case to you. I am a man of action
and not of words. For that reason I shall do no more
than introduce the other speakers, who, with their
various abilities, and different points of view, will be
able to lay before you the merits of this extremely
complex problem. I shall call upon our eldest member to speak first, my neighbour in the country:
Baron William de Traci.

THIRD KNIGHT   I am afraid I am not anything like such an experi-   20
enced speaker as my old friend Reginald Fitz Urse
would lead you to believe. But there is one thing I
should like to say, and I might as well say it at once.
It is this: in what we have done, and whatever you
may think of it, we have been perfectly disinterested.
[THE OTHER KNIGHTS   Hear! hear!] *We* are not
getting anything out of this. We have much more to
lose than to gain. We are four plain Englishmen who
put our country first. I dare say we didn't make a very
good impression when we came in just now. The fact   30
is that we knew we had taken on a pretty stiff job; I'll
only speak for myself, but I had drunk a good deal –
I am not a drinking man ordinarily – to brace myself
up for it. When you come to the point, it does go
against the grain to kill an Archbishop, especially
when you have been brought up in good Church
traditions. So if we seemed a bit rowdy, you will
understand why it was; and for my part I am awfully
sorry about it. We realise this was our duty, but all
the same we had to work ourselves up to it. And, as   40
I said, *we* are not getting a penny out of this. We
know perfectly well how things will turn out. King
Henry – God bless him – will have to say, for reasons of state, that he never meant this to happen; and
there is going to be an awful row; and at the best
we shall have to spend the rest of our lives abroad.
And even when reasonable people come to see that
the Archbishop *had* to be put out of the way – and
personally I had a tremendous admiration for him –
you must have noticed what a good show he put up   50
at the end – they won't give *us* any glory. No, we
have done for ourselves, there's no mistake about
that. So, as I said at the beginning, please give us at
least the credit for being completely disinterested in
this business. I think that is about all I have to say.

FIRST KNIGHT   I think we will all agree that William de Traci
has spoken well and has made a very important
point. The gist of his argument is this: that we have
been completely disinterested. But our act itself needs   60

more justification than that; and you must hear our
other speakers. I shall next call upon Hugh de Morville, who has made a special study of statecraft and
constitutional law. Sir Hugh de Morville.

SECOND KNIGHT   I should like first to recur to a point that was very
well put by our leader, Reginald Fitz Urse: that you
are Englishmen, and therefore your sympathies are
always with the under dog. It is the English spirit of
fair play. Now the worthy Archbishop, whose good
qualities I very much admired, has throughout been   70
presented as the under dog. But is this really the case?
I am going to appeal not to your emotions but to
your reason. You are hard-headed sensible people,
as I can see, and not to be taken in by emotional
clap-trap. I therefore ask you to to consider soberly:
what were the Archbishop's aims? And what are
King Henry's aims? In the answer to these questions
lies the key to the problem.

The King's aim has been perfectly consistent.
During the reign of the late Queen Matilda and the   80
irruption of the unhappy usurper Stephen, the kingdom was very much divided. Our King saw that the
one thing needful was to restore order: to curb the
excessive powers of local government, which were
usually exercised for selfish and often for seditious
ends, and to reform the legal system. He therefore
intended that Becket, who had proved himself an
extremely able administrator – no one denies that –
should unite the offices of Chancellor and Archbishop. Had Becket concurred with the King's   90
wishes, we should have had an almost ideal State: a
union of spiritual and temporal administration,
under the central government. I knew Becket well, in
various official relations; and I may say that I have
never known a man so well qualified for the highest
rank of the Civil Service. And what happened? The
moment that Becket, at the King's instance, had been
made Archbishop, he resigned the office of Chancellor, he became more priestly than the priests, he
ostentatiously and offensively adopted an ascetic   100
manner of life, he affirmed immediately that there
was a higher order than that which our King, and he
as the King's servant, had for so many years striven
to establish; and that – God knows why – the two
orders were incompatible.

You will agree with me that such interference by
an Archbishop offends the instincts of a people like
ours. So far, I know that I have your approval: I read
it in your faces. It is only with the measures we have

had to adopt, in order to set matters to rights, that 110
you take issue. No one regrets the necessity for violence more than we do. Unhappily, there are times
when violence is the only way in which social justice
can be secured. At another time, you would condemn an Archbishop by vote of Parliament and
execute him formally as a traitor, and no one would
have to bear the burden of being called murderer.
And at a later time still, even such temperate measures as these would become unnecessary. But, if
you have now arrived at a just subordination of the 120
pretensions of the Church to the welfare of the State,
remember that it is we who took the first step. We
have been instrumental in bringing about the state
of affairs that you approve. We have served your
interest; we merit your applause; and if there is any
guilt whatever in the matter, you must share it with
us.

FIRST KNIGHT   Morville has given us a great deal to think about. It
seems to me that he has said almost the last word, for
those who have been able to follow his very subtle 130
reasoning. We have, however, one more speaker,
who has I think another point of view to express. If
there are any who are still unconvinced, I think that
Richard Brito, coming as he does of a family distinguished for its loyalty to the Church, will be able
to convince them. Richard Brito.

FOURTH KNIGHT   The speakers who have preceded me, to say nothing
of our leader, Reginald Fitz Urse, have all spoken
very much to the point. I have nothing to add along
their particular lines of argument. What I have to say 140
may be put in the form of a question: *Who killed the
Archbishop?* As you have been eye-witnesses of this
lamentable scene, you may feel some surprise at my
putting it in this way. But consider the course of
events. I am obliged, very briefly, to go over the
ground traversed by the last speaker. While the late
Archbishop was Chancellor, no one, under the King,
did more to weld the country together, to give it the
unity, the stability, order, tranquillity, and justice
that it so badly needed.   150
  From the moment he became Archbishop, he
completely reversed his policy; he showed himself
to be utterly indifferent to the fate of the country, to
be, in fact, a monster of egotism. This egotism grew
upon him, until it became at last an undoubted
mania. I have unimpeachable evidence to the effect
that before he left France he clearly prophesied, in
the presence of numerous witnesses, that he had not

long to live, and that he would be killed in England. He used every means of provocation; from his con- 160 duct, step by step, there can be no inference except that he had determined upon a death by martyrdom. Even at the last, he could have given us reason: you have seen how he evaded our questions. And when he had deliberately exasperated us beyond human endurance, he could still have easily escaped; he could have kept himself from us long enough to allow our righteous anger to cool. That was just what he did not wish to happen; he insisted, while we were still inflamed with wrath, that the doors should 170 be opened. Need I say more? I think, with these facts before you, you will unhesitatingly render a verdict of Suicide while of Unsound Mind. It is the only charitable verdict you can give, upon one who was, after all, a great man.

FIRST KNIGHT Thank you, Brito, I think that there is no more to be said; and I suggest that you now disperse quietly to your homes. Please be careful not to loiter in groups at street corners, and do nothing that might provoke any public outbreak. 180

Into the text

1 Some public speakers, especially politicians, try to convince us that actions, of which we wouldn't normally approve, are justified because of their benefit to the nation as a whole. Whether we are convinced by their arguments or not depends on their skill in presenting their point of view. In arguing their case, the knights use particular techniques to persuade us of their point of view; eg they appear as reasonable men, they appeal to the intelligence of the audience, they present themselves as ordinary people, they claim to be acting for the benefit of the nation. Find examples of these from the text. What other methods can you identify? Find examples to support your ideas.

2 The knights make these speeches directly to the audience which is invited to judge their actions as if they were twelfth-century onlookers of the event. Imagine you are a member of that audience. Describe how you would explain what happened to someone who hadn't heard the knights' defence but who had been one of Becket's principal supporters.

A case study

The activity that follows will involve you in using different forms of persuasive language, some written and some oral. Some of the time you will be working in groups and sometimes on your own.

Stage 1 – Group work
Your first task is to invent a small, local company of which your group is the Board of Directors. You should decide:
• what your company does (manufacturing, selling, service, etc)
• what it is called
• its address and telephone/fax numbers
• how many employees you have
• what sort of qualifications/experience your workforce has
• the various rates of pay.

Stage 2 – Group work
Your company has recently undergone a period of growth and you need to appoint three new members of staff at various levels. You should now decide:
• the nature of the three vacancies
• the qualifications and experience expected for each vacancy
• the salary you intend to offer.
When you have done that:
• write the job specifications for each post
• write an advertisement for each post to appear in the local newspaper
• design an application form.
Display all your advertisements on a noticeboard.

Stage 3 – Individual work
Invent an imaginary biography for yourself: decide your age, gender, qualifications, experience, marital status. This biography must be someone that you can role-play at a later time. When you have done this, look through all the advertisements for the jobs that have been created and choose two to apply for. (You cannot apply for a job in the company that you have been involved in during stages 1 and 2.) Collect an application form from the companies you wish to apply to and write the letters of application. Put them in an addressed envelope.

Stage 4 – Group work
As the Board of Directors, collect the letters of application and read them all. Select a short-list of two candidates for each job. Write letters inviting them to come for interview. (Remember, you must arrange your own interviews as well.) Allow about ten minutes per interview.

Stage 5 – Group work

Each company will now take it in turns to conduct its interviews. Interview the candidates for each of the three posts. Decide who, if anyone, to appoint. Write letters to each candidate informing them of your decision.

Getting the message across: The business of persuasion

Approaching the text

Advertising is an all-pervasive and powerful influence on our lives. It is impossible to walk down a street, switch on the TV or open a magazine, without being bombarded by advertising messages. But how many of us know about the industry that generates them?

In order to answer this question, the authors interviewed the Managing Director, Phil Nicholson, and Creative Director, Chris Morley, of Quad Advertising and Marketing, a full-service agency based in Preston.

As you read the transcript, make a note of those features which distinguish this as spoken, rather than written, English.

Advertising

ALAN   What would happen if we came along with a product and handed it over to you? Could you take us through the stages which would result in an advert in a newspaper? What kind of stages would you normally go through?

CHRIS   Well, that would depend at what stage you brought the product in. If you'd already decided on a name for it, the identity for it, the packaging design, if you'd done your market research, and you knew who the market was, we could work on it. If you came to me and said 'We've invented this jigglepin, and no-one else has got one of these, it's absolutely wonderful, but we're not really sure how to market it, and we're not really sure what the market is,' what we would do is appoint a market research company to find out if, in fact, there is a demand for it. If it's going to be popular, if it's going to be handy. If you get down to the actual nitty-gritty of naming it, we would check out if any names were previously registered. We would create some suggestions on names, then we'd take it a stage further and look at packaging design. If it's a revolutionary product, there's a lot of use we could make of PR. Very often in the early stages of pushing a product, you can get a lot of coverage with Public Relations.

MIKE   What's the difference between Public Relations and advertising?

CHRIS   Instead of buying advertising space, a PR executive will contact various magazine editors, and say 'I've got a cracking little story here – a smashing little product.' They will write some editorial for it and put it in as a feature. So in essence, you are getting space free.

ALAN   Do you mean that this will not cost the advertiser anything?

CHRIS   Yes, you're not actually paying for the space, although you'll end up paying the PR executive.

ALAN   Could you give us an example?

CHRIS   If what you've got is a particular product, let's say for the central heating market, all the central heating magazines will be interested in running features on it. But if you come with a completely new product in a new area, and assuming we've done market research and they say, 'Right, this product is aimed at thirty-year-old males and its likely to be very popular, because there's a niche in the market – it's needed,' then you have to find out if you're talking to people of ABC lifestyle . . .

MIKE   What do you mean?

CHRIS   . . . if we're talking yuppies, good income, a premium price product, we know who we're talking to. And so we can identify our target, which dictates how you talk to them. If you're talking to intelligent, intellectual people, then you don't treat them like idiots, basically. Don't insult their intelligence. Whereas there's some advertisements where you can get away quite merrily by insulting people's intelligence – some of them don't have any. So it's essential that you identify that first.

ALAN   So you identify the market. What would happen next?

CHRIS   Then we would do a media study.

MIKE   What's a media study?

CHRIS   We would find out what would be the most effective media for the product. Would television be better? Would radio be better? Press advertising? Posters? Which one of these is going to be most effective? Or a combination of them? And if you choose print, ie press advertising, you would then get to the point of saying, 'Exactly what is the circulation of this magazine?' so you can be quite precise about it. Once you've sorted all that out, you get a creative brief which will say 'This product is brand new. It's faster than anybody else's.' That might be its main selling point. 'There's nothing faster than this.' So just tell everybody, 'It's the same price but faster.' Now that may be the single proposition. That would work as an ad, although it would be pretty boring.

ALAN   What do you do then?

CHRIS   The creative staff try to think laterally as opposed to literally for example with visuals, pictures of elephants and rhinos and whatever else! At first glance they appear to have nothing to do with the product at all, but they are ways of using different devices that catch the attention. Once you've done that, you've got to hold their attention and you want the consumers to read the ad and maybe respond to it by sending off a coupon or making a phone call.

MIKE   One of the books that we were reading while doing some research for this interview distinguished in adverts between persuasion and information and it said that there were some adverts that did give information. Is that a secondary purpose? Is the persuasion to buy the most important?

CHRIS   I think it depends. There's two different jobs in advertising. The biggest fault with some advertising is that they try and say too much in one ad. You try and do the persuading and fill in a coupon and get all the benefits across and, by the way, along the bottom they say 'We're a big company, we've been here fifty years, and we've got five service vans.' And it's all too much. It just doesn't work. The basic rule, really, is 'One message, one advertisement.' Though some people say you can make it two.

MIKE   One of the adverts that I like is the full page Epson computer printer advertisements . . .

CHRIS   The long copy ads. They're very very well written. The secret is with good copywriting, they catch you with the headline, then with good copy: if you get people to read the ad from top to bottom, then it works, the copywriting is good. What it does is give you information in a nice way and it makes you respond . . . the thing is, at the end of the advertisement you feel good. And if you feel good you warm to the company. And you warm to the name.

ALAN   I suppose it's about image and status of the company isn't it? You go away thinking Epson must be alright if they produce adverts like this – they must be intelligent, witty and literate people.

CHRIS   Yes, that's right. There's so many ways of doing it. The thing is if they'd have done that ad in a different way and just said 'Our printer is faster than anybody else's, if you want one telephone this number,' you wouldn't have felt any warmth or any affinity with it. You wouldn't have smiled at the end of it.

MIKE   I wonder how that advert would be seen by somebody who is just thinking about buying a computer system. Perhaps a small business needs a computer to help with the account handling or payroll. Would the buyer be looking for something that says 'I am an Epson FX 80. Buy me because I can do this, this, this or this'? Is this an advertising strategy that a company like Epson would also be using?

CHRIS   Yes. They could use different techniques – they may well have below the line advertising – mail shots for example that are not in the vein of entertainment. They're probably more factual. They'd have brochures on the product which are not aimed at being entertaining – factual literature.

MIKE   What about 'below the line' then, could you . . . ?

CHRIS   Well you get above the line and below the line. Above the line advertising is what people call consumer advertising: TV, radio stuff, consumer-orientated products. Below the line advertising, which actually constitutes the biggest part of the advertising world, is trade advertising. Talking direct to the trade. The general public would probably not see it.

MIKE   And that would be primarily informative.

CHRIS   Not always, no. You can get very entertaining, high class advertising below the line. But it's a different target audience. You're talking to different people. For example, if we're trying to sell a gas fire, and we say, 'Isn't this gas fire beautiful? Shouldn't you have one in your living room?' we're talking to the consumer. But if we're talking to wholesalers we could say, 'This gas fire is red hot, people are really going to be very keen on this. Get them on your shelves because the public are going to buy them.' It's a very different message.

ALAN   Your own business, I suppose, covers both? Or do you find that the majority of your . . .

CHRIS   We do cross the line. Some agencies specialize purely in business-to-business.

PHIL   You have two schools of thought. A lot of agencies tend to say that business-to-business advertising is so much easier. We believe however that it is fundamentally more difficult to achieve significant results in business-to-business advertising than it is in talking to the consumer because the consumer can be swayed very very easily.

CHRIS   Inevitably we have to get a more complex message across.

PHIL   Absolutely. The more important aspect of advertising and marketing is the strategy behind it, you know, the promotional programme – that's Chris's area. The client says, 'I've got a problem here. I need to get my products out into the market place, or my services or whatever. I've already got this aspect of the market – I want to develop it and diversify into that area now. How do we do it?' And that's the area where we develop the plan. That's the responsibility of the planning people who are the account handlers – the account executives as we call them.

ALAN   Where does your copy come from? Do you have copywriters? Or do you see that as secondary to the visuals?

PHIL   Copy is fundamental. It is the most important aspect of all that we do. Assuming that you've got an account handler who gets on with the client and is capable of taking the brief and developing a programme with the client, and budgeting properly, the next stage is, 'Well all right, there's the job that we've got to do. Where do we want to get to? How do we get there?' So it comes down to the creativity and that's where the copywriter really comes into his own.

MIKE   What does the copywriter do?

PHIL   A copywriter is not just a person who sits down and writes copy for a brochure, for an ad, for a radio commercial, a voice over. He is the guy who develops the whole creative platform, the concept, right? He has to be a really creative, switched-on guy. He has to be articulate, obviously. He has to have a good command of the English Language, even though he's got his Roget's Thesaurus sitting by the side of him all the time – because you're always struggling and searching for words. But it's the tone of voice in which you talk in the ad which is as important as what you say.

CHRIS   Inevitably, the copywriter tends to be forgotten. The fact is, most creative directors are copywriter-based.

PHIL   What normally happens, and the best way that this industry works is that a good creative copywriter who thinks verbally should work with an art director, who really knows how to put it together to make it look good. Now if you put those two people together: a good creative guy who's got the gift of the gab and the good art director who knows how a thing ought to look, to sell, you put those two people together to work as a team and you've got it.

CHRIS   More often than not the copywriter would pin down the direction that the advertising was going to go. He can then stand back a little bit, after getting the wording exactly right, in exactly the right tone. The art director then will say 'Well, we'll have things this size, this should be red and this should be green, and we'll use this typeface, and we'll have a lot of space and we'll do this that and the other.' Again to make it look good. The best solution is to work as a team.

MIKE   Is there anything that informs the strategies that are successful? Is there a body of knowledge about advertising that you can draw on?

PHIL   Yes. But the fact is, there isn't just one solution to a problem. You could go to ten different advertising agencies or ten different creative people and give them the same brief – and the advertising would be different.

ALAN   How important is the client's contribution to the advertising campaign?

PHIL   You're only as good as your client will allow you to be. If they haven't got their act together then you've got real problems. Because you're being steered down the wrong avenue all the time, or given misleading information. But you're OK if you've got a client that understands the industry, that knows he's got a problem and he doesn't have the skills within his own organisation to solve that problem – the worst thing that any client can do really is to develop his own marketing services department, his own advertising department, because then you're too close to it. It's only because we're dealing with different creative problems on a daily basis that we're able to take an objective and impartial viewpoint.

MIKE   Does that imply that you make any judgements of the product?

PHIL   Oh, it does, you can't help it, you're only human and you have to make judgements of the product and in many cases we will go back to the client and say, 'Look, yeh, we can do that, this and everything else but we think that your product is slightly wrong and you need to revamp that area of it. We think that this will stop people buying it.'

CHRIS We can often be given a direction by a client who will give us a product and say 'This is the fastest one on the market so sell it.' But if you look at this product carefully we can see that it's smaller than anybody else's and that's a better selling point.

PHIL   The other thing is, the client has got to give you firm objectives. He might say that he wants a brochure and the first thing that we may say to him is 'You don't want a brochure at all, brochures can do nothing for you.' He thinks he does because he thinks, 'It's prestigious and if I gave out a load of brochures I will have achieved my objective.' But it may turn out that what he really wants is a direct mail campaign coupled with some public relations activity instead of the 'bought-space' technique – the independent word in the editorial matter is taken far more seriously than any bought-space.

MIKE   Some people have been critical of the language used by advertisers: that advertising can provide a poor model of good written English.

CHRIS I think this is a problem with copywriters . . . if we're talking 'perfect' English, you don't start sentences with this and you don't put a full stop there, if you're talking about all that, those rules in advertising are pretty much out of the window. I could go downstairs and bring you the book up with Saatchi and Saatchi's gold-award winning ads and every English rule in the book is broken . . .

PHIL   We're probably the biggest perpetrators when it comes to rule-breaking – but it works. I mean, at school I was told that you never start a sentence with 'and' but you do. We do. We start a sentence with 'And', we start sentences with 'But', and anything else that works.

Into the text

1 Transcripts can only approximate to the reality of a conversation and, inevitably, this has been edited in order to make the meaning clear. What is missing are such things as tone of voice, laughter, over-talking, pace, pauses, hesitations (er, um, etc). But it nevertheless gives a fair representation of the conversation. From the notes that you have made, what characteristics do you think show this to be spoken rather than written language? What conclusions would you draw about the differences between the two?

2 List the main stages in an advertising campaign from the moment the client arrives with the product to the time when the advertisement appears in public.

3 What do you know to be the differences between the intention and the style of 'above' and 'below the line' advertising?

4 What are the differences between PR and advertising?

5 What is the difference in function between a copy-writer and an art director?

6 Find examples of specialist vocabulary used by the advertising executives in this interview.

7 Find examples from newspapers, magazines, TV and radio advertisements of rule-breaking. Why do advertisers find the need to break the rules in their copy?

8 The Creative Brief on page 149 is a Copy Test given as an exercise to young copywriters employed by Quad Advertising and Marketing. The format is the one used in communicating information from the Account Handler to the Creative Department.

Imagine that you are a copywriter and that this brief has landed on your desk. Explore as many possibilities for an advertising campaign as you can think of and then focus on one or two ideas and prepare them for presentation.

Client Silly Billy Products Ltd	Brand

Requirement
   Client has acquired an endless supply of red boxes. These are
   available in metal or plastic and measure approximately
   12″ × 6″ × 4″. They need to be given a name and a use or
   uses depending on the purchaser

The Target Audience   Everyone and anyone

What are we intending to achieve?
   An advertising campaign, using TV, press and posters, which will
   sell as many boxes as possible.

The single minded proposition   How can you possibly do without one of these boxes.

Substantiation for proposition
   Not only will you find a use for one of these boxes, but you will
   wonder how you ever managed without one.

Mandatory inclusions Address, logo, phone no, fax number etc   Company logo

Desired brand image/tone of voice Sophisticated, contemporary, green etc   A variety depending on the target audience chosen.

Assignments

1 Look again at the sheet that you produced with your group at the beginning of this unit. In the light of your reading and your deeper understanding of how persuasion works, produce another version of this. You can, if you wish, choose a completely new topic and intended audience.

2 During the course of the unit, you have attempted a number of different styles of persuasive writing, sometimes working on your own and sometimes in a group. Look again at this work and choose one piece that you could redraft in the light of your most recent work.

3 Choose two or more of the texts that you have read in this unit. Describe in each case what the author's intentions were, the intended audience and the outcomes that were expected. Comment on how successful you consider the writing to be. Pay close attention to the text, quoting from it to support your argument where appropriate.

4 Look closely at the Greenpeace leaflet on page 150.

   a Answer the following questions:

     • If you were French, why might you object to the statement: 'Greenpeace has: Stopped the French testing nuclear weapons in the atmosphere'?

     • Has Greenpeace stopped radioactive waste being dumped in the Irish Sea? Explain your answer.

     • What exactly are the achievements of Greenpeace as listed in the leaflet?

     • What is the relationship between the photograph and the text in the left-hand column of the leaflet?

     • What do you think is meant by ' . . . peaceful direct action tactics'? What evidence in the leaflet can you find of these tactics?

     • What is intended by the slogan 'Thank God someone's making waves'?

     • Write a letter to Greenpeace explaining either why you intend to join, or why you would choose not to join.

   b Imagine you are a representative of the advertising agency for Greenpeace. Write the presentation that you would make to the Board of Greenpeace describing the principal features of your leaflet, its intended audience, any problems it might cause. Consider features like: text, pictures, layout, print size and style, organisation, use of black and white, the slogan, etc.

G REENPEACE STANDS FOR A SAFE AND NUCLEAR-FREE WORLD · FRESH AIR · CLEAN WATER · THE PROTECTION OF WILDLIFE AND THEIR HABITATS

Greenpeace has: Stopped the French testing nuclear weapons in the atmosphere. ◖G◗ Helped bring an end to commercial whaling. ◖G◗ Prevented baby seals being killed in Newfoundland and the Orkney Isles. ◖G◗ Won an agreement in principle to end radioactive waste

discharges into the Irish Sea. ◖G◗ Won agreements to end the dumping of chemical sludges into the North Sea. ◖G◗ Forced an end to the burning of hazardous wastes in the North Sea. ◖G◗ Blocked proposals to dispose of radioactive wastes at a number of sites within the UK. ◖G◗ Stopped the dumping of radioactive wastes at sea. ◖G◗ Won a review of import procedures of endangered species products into the EEC. ◖G◗ Helped persuade the Government to spend £200m cleaning Britain's beaches and £600m cleaning aerial discharges from coal-fired power stations.

Greenpeace is an international environmental pressure group which maintains complete independence from all political parties anywhere in the world.

G REENPEACE

Against all odds, Greenpeace has brought the plight of the natural world to the attention of caring people. Greenpeace has exposed terrible abuses to the environ-

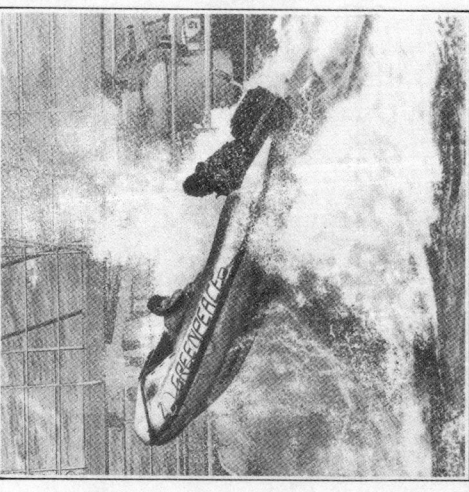

ment, often carried out in remote places or far out to sea.

By using peaceful direct action tactics Greenpeace has invoked the power of public opinion which in turn has forced changes in the law to protect wildlife and to stop the pollution of the natural world.

Aspiration and defeat:
The art of the possible

Contents

Introduction

Human beings have always felt the need to escape the restrictions of environment and circumstance: to better themselves, to explore, to explain and to experiment. Sometimes this is done as a selfish desire for prestige and other times for the good of the wider community. It always involves taking risks and sometimes these aspirations end in defeat and disillusionment.

Some definitions and quotations

In this unit, we are going to explore various forms of risk-taking, both personal and public. Before you recall some of your own experiences, look closely at the following definitions.

Ambition strong desire for success, achievement or distinction; something so desired; goal; aim.

Aspiration strong desire to achieve something, such as success; the aim of such desire.

Defeat to frustrate, frustration; overthrow in contest.

Disillusion to destroy the ideals, illusions, or false ideas of; disenchantment.

Egotism an inflated sense of self-importance or superiority; self-centredness; excessive reference to oneself.

Overreach to defeat or thwart (oneself) by attempting to do or gain too much; to aim for but miss by going too far or attempting too much.

Pipe-dream a fanciful or impossible plan or hope (alluding to dreams produced by smoking an opium pipe).

Utopia any real or imaginary society, place, state, etc, considered to be perfect or ideal.

Cirra, Corneille
Ambition aspires to descend.

Hamlet, William Shakespeare
The very substance of ambition is merely the shadow of a dream. I hold ambition of so airy and light a quality that it is but a shadow's shadow.

Macbeth, William Shakespeare
I have no spur/To prick the sides of my intent, but only/Vaulting ambition, which o'er leaps itself/And falls on the other.

Before you start
1 Part of growing up involves risk-taking. As people progress towards adulthood, they experiment in their behaviour (eg hairstyle), in their relationships (eg challenging authority) and often in doing physical things that adults might regard as foolhardy (eg driving fast motorbikes). Make a list of some occasions where you have taken risks similar to these. Compare your list with others in your group.

2 Choose one of your examples and write about it in detail. To help you develop your ideas, consider the following questions:

    a Were you aware that your behaviour was 'risky'?

    b What did adults think about what you did? Try to recall or reconstruct the words they used.

    c What, if anything, did you learn from what you did?

    d In the light of your experience, would you do it again?

3 As people approach adulthood, different sorts of ambitions and aspirations occupy their minds, eg career, self-fulfilment, travel, marriage, children, making a contribution to society. What, over the next fifteen years, do you hope to achieve, either for yourself or for others? How will you set about achieving it?

You live and learn: A short story

Approaching the text

The following short story, 'Come to Mecca', from the collection of the same name, was first published in 1978. In it, Farrukh Dhondy identifies a range of hopes and ambitions, some personal, some social, some political, all of which are doomed to some extent to be unfulfilled. As you are reading the story, make a note of all those that you can identify.

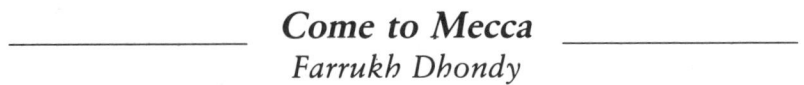

Come to Mecca
Farrukh Dhondy

Whenever Shahid got angry his short cropped hair seemed to stand up off his head, like the feathers on the neck of a fighting cock. He was very angry that day. When the four of us left the factory and reached the street, he said we should go straight to his uncle's house.

'He will deal with the guv'nor,' Shahid said. 'I will show that Rasul. Son of a hired woman. When he comes out of the factory I will see him.'

'We can't make trouble in the street,' I said. 'Guv'nor will call the police. Come on.'

We went to Masterji's house. We all called Shahid's uncle 'Masterji' because back in our village he was the schoolteacher. Shahid didn't want   **10** to waste any more words on us, he walked ahead.

'I don't worry about getting sack. He can keep his bloody job,' one of the others said, 'there's plenty work. My cousin has a factory. I'll ask him job for you too.'

'We're not going to work anywhere,' Shahid said, turning his head. 'We'll fix this guv'nor first. When I say I'll do a thing, I will die but I'll do it, ask Farid.'

Masterji opened the door to us.

'Salaam-aleikum,' we each muttered as he let us in.

'As-aleikum-salaam,' he said, having fun with the greeting.   **20**

Shahid began rattling away in Bengali as soon as we stepped in.

'Wait till you've had a cup of tea. You catching a train?' Masterji said, but as soon as Shahid told him we'd all got the sack and quarrelled with the 'bastard' guv'nor, he changed his tone.

'Sit down, start from the beginning, and don't use such words before your elders.'

Shahid held his tongue between his teeth in a show of repentance and lightly struck both his cheeks with his palm. He told Masterji the story.

We had all been working at 'Nu-Look Fashions'. We'd been there for nearly the whole year now, except when the season was out and there   30
was no work. We left school together, Shahid, myself and four other very close mates. Four of us went with the elder brother of another fellow we knew to Nu-Look and he told the gaffer that he'd brought the four machinists he wanted.

The guv'nor took one look at us and knew that we were straight out of school. But that didn't mean we were inexperienced. All of us had done some tailoring for our fathers or mothers at home. Everyone knows machining in the East End. When you are ten years old you begin to forget about being a pilot on Bangladesh airlines and start thinking of being a cutter or machinist. Of course you usually have to start with   40
just helping out, doing some pressing, fetching Fanta and making tea. This friend of ours told us that there was so much work that this guv'nor would let us start on machines straightaway.

He paid us training wages. After a few weeks we were doing about ten garments a day. He would give us sixty pence for each job we finished, but he wanted us to work faster. The cut cloth was piling up in the corner of the factory and on the guv'nor's desk.

The older workers who sat in the same room were paid sometimes one pound twenty, double what we were getting, but they worked very fast while the Hindi songs played on the cassette all day and the machines hummed with business. 50

The guv'nor would stand beside Shahid's machine and he would say, 'You'll get donkey rates for that, I'll cut you down to fifty pence.' First it was a joke. Then he began saying it every day and it became serious, and he'd get angry if we said we wanted to go home when the others went.

'Even a child can work faster,' the guv'nor would say.

'I'll get my little sister, then,' Shahid would say.

He was not a bad bloke, this guv'nor. He was a white man, but he understood a little Bengali and he joked with us all the time and leave 60 us to go to the toilet when we wanted.

'I don't know what you blokes do in there. Where I come from, a piss doesn't take you half an hour.'

When a man has worked for sixty pence, he doesn't want to work for fifty. One day the gaffer said he'd been fined for not doing the contract on time, we were ruining his business, we were lazy Bengalis, and the old ones only thought of 'taka' (money) and the young ones only thought of 'heta' – a dirty word.

Then he said he'd give us fifty for a garment and no more. He was in a filthy mood. Next morning when he let us in, he stopped the four of 70 us at the door and said,

'Look lads, it's fifty pence a garment from today unless you do more than twenty-five, then it's the old rate.'

We sat at our machines. Shahid said to us he wasn't working for one half penny less, not for this gaffer or for his grandfather.

'You can take your cards and clear off,' the gaffer said, 'you should clean the streets, you can take your time doing that.' At the end of that day he went to the drawer where he kept his ledger, and reaching inside his coat pocket took out his fat wallet and peeled off some notes for the four of us. 80

'That'll be for the last two days,' he said, 'sixty pence a garment. Not from tomorrow, though.'

The next day we turned up to work as usual. Shahid told us to wait near our machines but not to start work. We stood with our arms folded just inside the door of the one-room factory.

'Clear off, lads, I've made other arrangements. If you won't work for new rates there's others as will,' the gaffer said and carried on with his own work, walking round the other machinists and filling his ledgers with scribbles.

For two hours we just stood there. Then the gaffer went out for his 90 sandwich and his beer, which one of us usually went down to the street and fetched for him. Shahid addressed the other workers in Bengali. One of them said they'd taken a cut in rates too and then they all dipped their heads down into their work, ashamed.

Shahid said he was only sixteen years old but he knew liars from truth-tellers. He said they were not men and should wear bangles and sarees and stay at home.

The guv'nor came back with Rasul, an old Bengali with sly eyes whom we all knew. The two of them pushed past us and the guv'nor showed Rasul to Shahid's machine. Rasul sat on the stool. 100

'So you've come to put your foot on my stomach, eh Rasul?' Shahid challenged.

Rasul sheepishly picked up the cloth that Shahid had been working at and started to put it through the machine.

'Don't talk so big when you're only a chit of a boy,' Rasul replied.

'I have more pride in my chin than you have in your white beard. Only orphans work for fifty pence,' Shahid said.

'I work for what I can get. When you have three children you'll stop going to the pub with your money and going with rubbish white girls,' Rasul said, still working away. 110

'Like your mother,' Shahid replied.

'Clear off, that's enough of you,' the guv'nor said.

If I hadn't pulled him out of the factory Shahid would have beaten Rasul there and then.

'I'll see you outside,' he shouted, and Rasul just laughed.

Masterji listened carefully to the story.

'That Rasul is the son of a sow,' Shahid said.

Masterji put on his coat and we went together to the factory for lunch-time. When the other workers came out, Masterji spoke to them. That evening we all met at Masterji's house. He had persuaded three of the 120 older workers to come. Masterji said we had to call a strike at the factory otherwise this guv'nor would get away with murder. We didn't come to this country to be slaves.

'The others won't listen to us,' one of the older workers said. 'You all know what Bengalis are like.'

'Don't talk about Bengalis to me,' Masterji said. 'Don't talk about our countrymen in front of me like that.'

'Look at that Rasul,' Shahid said, 'I'll kill him.'

'You won't kill the disease, you'll kill the germs that cause the disease,' Masterji said. 130

There was a lot of interest in our strike. The next day we went outside the factory with Bengali placards saying, 'PAY US FAIR RATES'.

One by one the other workers decided to join us, especially after a crowd gathered on the pavement and we began shouting. On the second day of the strike the guv'nor called the police because not one person went to work. The police came and then newspapers came. On the third day one of the older workers came to us with Masterji. We were still standing on the pavement and a lot of our friends had come to support us. This man said he had to go back to work. His wife was in hospital and he was heavily in debt. Masterji told us that he had a fair case, we 140 should not stop him going back to work. He should be allowed to go back till the end of the week at least so he could be paid on Friday. Shahid was sulky but he didn't contradict Masterji. On Friday we knew what would happen. The workers would want to get their two days pay for that week. One by one they all went back and began to work. The guv'nor came to the first-floor window of the factory and shouted at us. We didn't reply. By the afternoon there were only the four of us left.

It was that afternoon that Betty and Sylvia came to the door of the factory. We saw these two white girls coming down from Aldgate end, carrying a camera. They stopped and asked us if we were the 'comrades 150 on strike'.

'It's not a strike,' I said. 'We've just stopped working till the guv'nor changes his mind.'

They wrote down everything we told them and then Betty took a photograph of us. We all brushed our hair and they asked us to lift up the placards even though we didn't want to be in the photograph with placards in Bengali. We put our arms round each other's shoulders and stood under the 'Nu-Look' sign. Betty went with the camera and knelt down in the street. All the traffic had to stop as she took her photographs, but she behaved as though she didn't even notice the horns 160 and the shouts from the obstructed cars.

'Cheeky woman,' Shahid said to me in Bengali.

Some days later we were sitting in one of the cafes on Brick Lane drinking tea. All the boys who are out of work hang around the five or six cafes there and drink endless cups of tea and wait to hear of any jobs that might be going. We knew that the season was over and even experienced men couldn't get much work. Betty walked into the cafe and she seemed to recognise us. She came over to our table. At first we didn't recognise her. The day she took the photographs she'd been wearing jeans and a leather jacket and a sweater with a black fist on it. Now she 170 was in dress and her hair looked as though she'd washed it and brushed it just for us.

'I've been looking for you,' she said to Shahid. 'We've written you up magnificently.'

Then she put the pile of newspapers she was holding on to the table and began turning the pages.

Now white girls rarely come into that cafe, and if they come they are with their men. Only rubbish women sit in the cafe all day and go with men who make friends with them and pay them. Bengali girls never come to that kind of place. Some Ugandan people come, and some stylish 180 Punjabi girls, but they are allowed to have boyfriends who bring them. They're decent girls and nobody says anything to them. Betty was a decent girl too, she had a good accent, but like other white girls she didn't know how to behave, where to go and where not to go. She went anywhere she liked and did what she liked and nobody said anything to her.

We didn't want to insult her so we asked her if she would like to have coffee and we told her to sit at a different table from us, because the boys we were with were just staring at her and grinning. They were third-class good-for-nothing rascals, but we were sitting with them because 190 they were telling us how to buy and sell cars for plenty money. Betty motioned to them to push up and sat at our table. There we were in the photograph. The newspaper said 'Workers Fight Blacklegs in

Sweatshops'. Shahid was not sure of what it said so he asked Betty to read it to him.

'No blacks in that factory,' Shahid said to her, 'only Bengalis.'

'It's black *legs*,' Betty explained, 'people who attack workers.'

'If anybody attacks me I will punch them,' Shahid said.

The others in the cafe were now curious and gathered round the newspapers. The papers were passed from hand to hand.   200

We told Betty that the strike was finished and she said that it was a shame.

'I'm not ashamed,' Shahid replied. Then Betty told us that she worked for the newspaper and she started selling the paper to anyone who would buy it for five pence.

'Anyway,' she said to Shahid, 'I'd like to talk to you. We want a whole story on the sweatshop.'

'We don't know much stories, only Bengali stories,' I said.

'About your sweatshops, your factories, Nu-Look.'

Shahid looked puzzled so Betty said, 'We call them sweatshops 210 because the labour is sweated labour.' She was anxious to explain.

'When I sweat I always take bath, not like English people.'

'You've got me wrong. The factories are filthy and dingy, all of this area.'

'My cousin's factory is very clean,' I said.

'You must be joking,' Betty said, 'I've seen some of them.'

'He never jokes with ladies,' Shahid said.

After leaving the cafe that day we went to Shahid's house. Shahid told me not to mention the paper and he screwed it up tight and put it in his shirt because he said that if his father saw it he would say that it was 220 giving Bengalis a bad name. We sat all evening watching telly at Shahid's house. That was the kind of mood that came over us when we were out of work. Sometimes we went to the cinema on Commercial Road and then came back and watched more telly. When we had money we went to the West End.

All the boys told lies about their adventures in the West End. A fellow would be sitting in the cafe and he'd tell us how he'd been to a gambling casino and won fifty pounds on the gaming tables, or how he'd gone to a dance hall in Leicester Square and picked up two beautiful white girls who were really decent girls and they really fancied him because of his 230 hair-style and he could do anything with them whenever he liked. When we were still in school we believed these stories and waited for the day when we could go out, go dancing, get some girl-friends. You live and learn. When Shahid and I went to the West End we had our own fun, but no-one talked to us except to pick a fight. We'd go on the bus and then we'd play the pinball and see some sex films and eat ice-cream and take the last tube back to Aldgate or walk home if it was too late or if all our money was finished, first along the river and then through the echoing stone walls of the City streets.

We were aimless, at least Shahid was aimless until Betty discovered us. 240 Shahid had met her on the street again, he said, and he had made an appointment with her to go to her house with me.

'You're fixed up,' I said, grinning, but he turned savagely on me.

'She's a good girl,' he said, 'she's educated, not like you.'

'Her father will take one look at both of us and kick us down the street.'

'These kind of girls don't have fathers,' he said, thoughtfully.

'Her brothers, then.'

'Just shut your mouth and come with me.'

We went the next day. We sat on the floor in her strange room. She 250
didn't even have a settee, and her bed was just one mattress on the floor,
like a villager. There were hundreds of books all over the place.
Everyone who came to her room sat on the floor on cushions amongst
all the books and tea mugs and papers. Even the light was hanging down
from the ceiling nearly to the floor with a paper bowl on it, and there
were coloured candles which had spread pools of wax on the furniture.

She told us that she was a translator and showed us some Russian
books and French books and Shahid asked her to say something in
French and in Russian, and she said it and we all laughed. When he
asked her what that meant, she said, 'It means "I love you"' and we all 260
laughed again, and she could see that Shahid thought she was saying it
to him, so she said, 'It's the easiest thing to say in any language.'

Then I said it for her in Bengali and Shahid said it in Urdu like they
say it in the pictures and she tried to learn the Urdu.

Whenever we went there, Betty talked about the strike we had been
in, but after the first time there was nothing new to tell her. She told us
that we were not only part of the Bengalis but also we were part of the
working class and we should forget about being Bengalis only. So I said
I'd always be a Bengali and Shahid told me that I didn't understand what
she was trying to say.   270

'Working class are third-class people,' I said. Betty tried to explain
that we had learnt all that from the newspapers who were against
workers.

Betty liked explaining those sorts of things. She would talk very slowly
so we wouldn't have to say, 'pardon'. It seemed to me that Shahid loved
listening to her voice, even though I'm sure he didn't understand half the
things she was saying.

I only went there because Shahid kept wanting to go back. Betty said
we had told her very useful things about Asian life and then she began
telling us about her political party. She was part of a political party and 280
it wasn't secret, anybody could join.

'You are a communist?' Shahid asked.

'Well, I'm a socialist. All workers should be socialists and trade
unionists. It's the only way working people can lift their heads up.
Communism comes after that.'

'Communists are no good,' I said, 'they blow up railway trains in
India.'

'You are ignorant,' Shahid said. 'You know Maulana Bhashani, he's
a communist. Has he ever blown up a train?'

'He's a saint,' I said.   290

'And you are a simpleton. Masterji said he's a communist.'

Betty was very pleased when Shahid agreed to go to the meetings. He
told her that I would come too. She had light grey eyes and Shahid

said that her eyes were like a cats, and she asked us if we thought cats were beautiful.

Shahid said he thought they were very beautiful and they also caught rats.

When she was alone with us Betty talked a lot, but she didn't say much in her group meetings. When we went to the first one with her, it was in a row of houses which had been taken over by people just like hippies. 300 At each meeting there were about a dozen people in the room. A bearded man was their leader. He always spoke second, waiting for someone else to start him off. Shahid asked Betty if he was the president, but she said they didn't need a president, he was only very clever and very active. At the first meeting the leader asked her to tell the meeting about the Nu-Look strike and she told them and we agreed with everything she said. The bearded man talked straight at us and said we had to get into a union if we were going to win. Someone else explained that we could start talking to Bengalis about joining the unions and we should go back to Nu-Look and persuade everybody to join the union. Everyone in the 310 room said that was right and Betty nodded her head and said she should have thought of it first. On the way home Shahid became very sullen and he said that he didn't trust Bengalis, they wouldn't pay any money to join anything. Then he said he didn't trust the man with the beard, the leader. I said I was never going back to Nu-Look even if they paid me a thousand pounds for each coat.

The next time we went to Betty's house the bearded man with the checked trousers was there. Betty didn't chat with us as she usually did and I could see that Shahid was disappointed. Instead, she told us that they were making plans to get all the workers into their party and we 320 must help because we were Bengalis. Then the bearded man started giving us a lecture and walked up and down the room. Shahid didn't want to listen, so he said he had to go to Hessel Street for his mother. Betty said we should listen and after we'd finished the discussion she wanted to do some shopping too. The leader said that we weren't fighting the Nu-Look manager, but we were fighting his whole system. He said the police were on the side of the manager, and the government too, and that even the government of Bangladesh was on the side of the manager.

'Do you like China?' Shahid asked.   330

'We have theoretical disagreement with the Chinese Party,' the man said, impatient at being interrupted.

'So you don't like China? My uncle likes China,' Shahid persisted.

'We disagree with their theory of social imperialism. Look what they did in Chile.'

Shahid didn't know about that, he said, but he added that his uncle had lots of books on China, more books than there were in that room even, but they were all in Bangladesh. If he wanted, Shahid said, his uncle would lend him some books and he could read them and maybe he'd understand a little more. He said this defiantly to the man and the 340 man turned to Betty and said, 'It's useless, I don't know how to reply to that.'

Betty could see that I was uncomfortable because now Shahid was getting angry with the man.

There was a silence and Shahid and I got up to go. Betty walked to the door with us.

'Roger's just a bit impatient,' she said. 'He's brilliant really. You'll get used to him as you start working with us.'

Then she did something she'd not done before. She reached out and held Shahid's hand. She was looking at him and smiling to let him know 350 that she wanted to talk to us too, and to drink coffee and laugh as we usually did, and that she was sorry that it had turned serious with Roger there.

'You have to come to the next meeting,' she said. 'It's really very important. We'll get you organised then. We'll train you to understand all the theory. You must join the group properly, I really want you to.' She winked.

As he walked away, Shahid seemed suddenly happy. He lifted the hand she had held, elegantly to his nose, as though to keep the fragrance of her with him. I didn't say anything. There was nothing to say.　　360

When we were in school together, we had known some rubbish white girls, but we never went to their homes. We'd meet them in the cafes and play Hindi love songs for them on the juke-box, 'Kabhi-Khabi' or any nonsense song of the time and we'd play pinball machines with them and they might let you kiss them once or twice if you could overcome your own shyness. We hadn't known any girls like Betty before.

'Do you like that girl Sylvia, Betty's mate?' Shahid asked me. I didn't like that. It was as though he was trying to make me beg him for favours.

At the next meeting Betty didn't sit with us. She sat next to the leader because she was giving a speech. She got to her feet and talked about 370 fighting the National Front and then something about Jews and about 'Asians'. When she talked to us she said, 'Bengalis', but when she made speeches she said 'Asians'. She abused the National Front for selling newspapers. The rest laughed when she said filthy words. I could see that Shahid admired her for being able to swear in public. He said afterwards that when girls like Betty used filthy language it was all right, it wasn't lowering their family name, it just meant that she had very strong emotions against rubbish people who attacked Asians.

After that meeting he tried to ask her if he could go round to her place, but she said to him that she had to go now, but he should definitely make 380 it a point to come round before the meeting of the group on Saturday. Shahid said that it was a signal. I shouldn't go with him this time. He said she'd asked him to go alone. I understood.

For three days I didn't see Shahid. He was working at a friend's factory, to pick up some quick money. On Saturday the meeting was supposed to start at two o'clock. I didn't want to go. I had gone to be by my brother's side, because Shahid was like a brother to me, but you don't always want to be 'kavab me haddi', the 'bone in the kebab', someone who gets in the way.

I sat in our usual cafe from about ten that morning. About eleven 390 o'clock Shahid came in, his hair looking as though it was flaring out of his head. He was wearing a new suit, blue with pin-stripes, and a new shirt with its huge collar covering the jacket lapels. I could tell from the way his mouth remained slightly opened, his thick lips parted, that things hadn't gone as he had expected. In his right arm he was carrying a whole pack of newspapers.

'Come with me,' he demanded, looking around the cafe to see if anyone else was staring at him.

'You getting married?' the manager asked him, mockingly.

'Why should I, when I get your wife and daughter free?' Shahid said   400
as we walked out.

'What's the rush, where are we going?'

'They gave me these,' he said, thrusting the wad of newspapers at me.

'You've had your picture taken again?'

He was in no mood for mucking about.

'I have to sell them to "Asians",' he said.

'Wasn't she there?'

'She was there. They were all there. She called me before the meeting because she said I was ready to help the group with its work. They gather at her place before Saturday meetings to sell newspapers.'   410

'Where are we going to sell them?'

'Tower Bridge.'

He was angry and walking fast.

'There are none of our people on Tower Bridge, only tourists.'

'Sometimes seagulls,' Shahid replied, tight-lipped.

'Where have you been all these days?' I said trying to get him to talk to me.

'Saving money like a fool,' he said.

We walked on past the Aldgate roundabout and turned down Alie Street.   420

'I asked her to go to Mecca with me,' he said finally.

'So you got somewhere, what're you so furious about?'

'I followed her to the kitchen where she was making coffee for all of them. I said will you come to Mecca with me. She's so stupid, she thought I meant Mecca in Arabia and said she wasn't a Muslim and what did I believe in religion for, because religion was like drugs. So I told her I meant Mecca Dancing, this evening, later tonight. She thought I was messing about.'

'Did she say she'd go with you? Do you want her to be your girl-friend?'   430

Shahid didn't reply. We had reached Tower Bridge. He took the newspapers which I had been holding. The headline said 'Fight Nazi Front'.

We walked down the bridge and when we got to half-way between the two great trunks of the bridge with the water swirling round the curved stone, he threw the whole pile of papers over the grey railing onto the fast water of the high tide.

'What the hell are you doing? Police will catch us for throwing litter about!'

We walked back to the cafe. We drank some coffee and talked to some   440
of our friends about the football fixture between The Welfare Team and Navin Sangh that was to take place on the Vallance Road field that afternoon at two o'clock.

We were lost in our talk when Betty walked into the cafe with Sylvia. She came straight up to us her arms draped with her own pile of newspapers.

'Where's your lot, Shahid?' she asked. 'You can't have got rid of them already!'

Shahid looked up at her, pretending to be very off-hand.

'Oh yeah,' he said, 'I got rid of the lot.'   450

'That's great,' she said, 'fantastic. Now we can really make an impact on blacks. Start with the Asian community.'

She was smiling and she and Sylvia exchanged looks.

'You must have worked very hard and fast,' she said to Shahid.

Shahid pulled out his wallet. He held out a couple of pounds to her.

'I have to pay you off,' he said. 'That's for the papers.'

Into the text

1 List the hopes and ambitions that you have identified for all of the characters. For each one, explain the outcomes, where these are clear. What hopes and ambitions are still left unresolved at the end of the story? What is the likely outcome of these?

2 There are a number of misunderstandings that occur in the story. Go back to the text and identify them. What are the causes of these?

3 You may have noticed that some of the misunderstandings concern the nature of the relationships between the characters, especially Shahid and Betty. Examine their relationship closely. Using evidence from the passage, what tells you that Shahid's expectations of Betty were inaccurate? What was Betty's role, if any, in the misunderstanding?

4 The narrator ('I' — the first person singular) rarely makes his views known. Can you come to any conclusions about his perceptions of these events as they unfold?

5 Why did Shahid throw the newspapers in the Thames? Why did he pretend to Betty that he had sold them? Why does he say 'I have to pay you off' (line 456)?

Out of the text

1 Imagine that Betty finds out that Shahid threw all the papers in the Thames. She later confronts him in the cafe. Write the conversation either from Betty's point of view, or Shahid's.

2 On line 240, the narrator says, 'We were aimless, at least Shahid was aimless until Betty discovered us.' Write about an occasion (real or imaginary) when you developed an enthusiasm for something or somebody (eg a cause, a project, a charismatic person). Describe how you pursued your aim and explain why the outcomes were not what you hoped for.

Too close to the Sun: Myth and fantasy

Approaching the text

In *Metamorphosis*, the collection from which this story is taken, the Latin writer Ovid re-tells the ancient Greek myth of Daedalus and Icarus. Daedalus was a skilled craftsman who had been exiled from Athens. He went to Crete in order to build a labyrinth for King Minos. When the work was complete, Minos refused to let Daedalus and his son Icarus leave because Daedalus knew the secret of the labyrinth.

As you read this story, which is set in a remote time and place, compare the behaviour of Icarus with your experiences of risk-taking that you wrote about in the Introduction to this unit.

Daedalus and Icarus
Ovid

Meanwhile Daedalus, tired of Crete and his long absence from home, was filled with longing for his own country, but he was shut in by the sea. Then he said: 'The king may block my way by land or across the ocean, but the sky, surely, is open, and that is how we shall go. Minos may possess all the rest, but he does not possess the air.' With these words, he set his mind to sciences never explored before, and altered the laws of nature. He laid down a row of feathers, beginning with tiny ones, and gradually increasing their length, so that the edge seemed to slope upwards. In the same way, the pipe which shepherds used to play is built up from reeds, each slightly longer than the last. Then he fastened   10
the feathers together in the middle with a thread, and at the bottom with wax; when he had arranged them in this way, he bent them round in a gentle curve, to look like real birds' wings. His son Icarus stood beside him and, not knowing that the materials he was handling were to endanger his life, laughingly captured the feathers which blew away in the wind, or softened the yellow wax with his thumb, and by his pranks hindered the marvellous work on which his father was engaged.

When Daedalus had put the finishing touches to his invention, he raised himself into the air, balancing his body on his two wings, and there he hovered, moving his feathers up and down. Then he prepared   20
his son to fly too. 'I warn you, Icarus,' he said, 'you must follow a course midway between earth and heaven, in case the sun should scorch your feathers, if you go too high, or the water make them heavy if you are too low. Fly half way between the two. And pay no attention to the stars, to Bootes, or Helice or Orion with his drawn sword: take me as your guide and follow me!'

While he was giving Icarus these instructions on how to fly, Daedalus was at the same time fastening the novel wings on his son's shoulders. As he worked and talked the old man's cheeks were wet with tears, and his fatherly affection made his hands tremble. He kissed his son, whom   30
he was never to kiss again; then, raising himself on his wings, flew in

front, showing anxious concern for his companion, just like a bird who has brought her tender fledgelings out of their nest in the treetops, and launched them into the air. He urged Icarus to follow close, and instructed him in the art that was to be his ruin, moving his own wings and keeping a watchful eye on those of his son behind him. Some fisher, perhaps, plying his quivering rod, some shepherd leaning on his staff, or a peasant bent over his plough handle caught sight of them as they flew past and stood stock still in astonishment, believing that these creatures who could fly through the air must be gods.   40

Now Juno's sacred isle of Samos lay on the left, Delos and Pharos were already behind them, and Lebinthus was on their right hand, along with Calymne, rich in honey, when the boy Icarus began to enjoy the thrill of swooping boldly through the air. Drawn on by his eagerness for the open sky, he left his guide and soared upwards, till he came too close to the blazing sun, and it softened the sweet-smelling wax that bound his wings together. The wax melted. Icarus moved his bare arms up and down, but without their feathers they had no purchase on the air. Even as his lips were crying his father's name, they were swallowed up in the deep blue waters which are called after him. The unhappy father, a   50 father no longer, cried out: 'Icarus!' 'Icarus!' he called. 'Where are you? Where am I to look for you?' As he was still calling 'Icarus' he saw the feathers on the water, and cursed his inventive skill. He laid his son to rest in a tomb, and the land took its name from that of the boy who was buried there.

Into the text

1 What motivated Daedalus to fashion the wings and alter 'the laws of nature' (lines 6–7)?

2 At what point in the story do you realise that Icarus is likely to disobey his father?

3 To what extent do you sympathise with and understand Icarus' behaviour?

4 This is a story about a young **man** who over-reaches himself. Over the centuries, this story has been used to endorse the view that young men are more adventurous, more likely to take chances in order to prove their 'manhood'. Do you agree with the implied belief in this myth that young women are less likely to take these sort of risks?

5 Describe the earth as if you are Icarus flying through the air. Try to include what your five senses experience. Include particularly what is going through your mind as you get more and more ambitious.

6 The flight of Daedalus and Icarus was seen by people on the ground who, Ovid tells us, assumed them to be gods. Imagine you were a witness to the scene. Describe it in your own words.

7 One of the things you may have considered is: Who is responsible for Icarus' death? After all, Daedalus invented the wings. To what extent do you think

Daedalus bears responsibility for what happened? With reference to contemporary examples, to what extent are scientists and inventors responsible for the misuse of discoveries and inventions that were intended to benefit humanity?

Approaching the text

In this story the hero, Aldous Worp, develops a technology for flight in contradiction to the known laws of physics. As you read the story, notice the similarities and differences between it and the story of Daedalus and Icarus.

_ *The Available Data on the Worp Reaction* _
Lion Miller

The earliest confirmed data on Aldous Worp, infant, indicates that, while apparently normal in most physical respects, he was definitely considered by neighbors, playmates, and family as a hopeless idiot. We know, too, that he was a quiet child of extremely sedentary habits. The only sound he was ever heard to utter was a shrill monosyllable, closely akin to the expression 'Whee!' and this only when summoned to meals or, less often, when his enigmatic interest was aroused by an external stimulus, such as an odd-shaped pebble, a stick, or one of his own knuckles.

Suddenly this child abandoned his accustomed inactivity. Shortly   10
after reaching his sixth birthday – the time is unfortunately only approximate – Aldous Worp began a series of exploratory trips to the city dump which was located to the rear of the Worp premises.

After a few of these tours, the lad returned to his home one afternoon dragging a large cogwheel. After lengthy deliberation, he secreted said wheel within an unused chicken coop.

Thus began a project that did not end for nearly twenty years. Young Worp progressed through childhood, boyhood and young manhood, transferring thousands of metal objects, large and small, of nearly every description, from the dump to the coop. Since any sort of formal   20
schooling was apparently beyond his mental capacity, his parents were pleased by the activity that kept Aldous happy and content. Presumably they did not trouble themselves with the esthetic problems involved.

As suddenly as he had begun it, Aldous Worp abandoned his self-imposed task. For nearly a year – again, the time is approximate due to insufficient data – Aldous Worp remained within the confines of the Worp property. When not occupied with such basic bodily needs as eating and sleeping, he moved slowly about his pile of debris with no apparent plan.

One morning he was observed by his father (as we are told by the   30
latter) to be selecting certain objects from the pile and fitting them together.

It should be noted here, I think, that no account of the Worp Reaction can be complete without certain direct quotations from Aldous' father, Lambert Simnel Worp. Concerning the aforementioned framework the elder Worp has said, 'The thing that got me, was every (deleted) piece he picked up fit with some other (deleted) piece. Didn't make no (deleted) difference if it was a (deleted) bedspring or a (deleted) busted egg-beater, if the (deleted) kid stuck it on another (deleted) part, it stayed there.'   40

Concerning usage of tools by Aldous Worp, L.S. Worp has deposed: 'No tools.'

A lengthier addendum is offered us by L.S. Worp in reply to a query which I quote direct: 'How in God's name did he manage to cause separate parts to adhere to each other to make a whole?' (Dr Palmer) A: 'The (deleted) stuff went together, tighter'n a mallard's (deleted), and nobody – but *nobody*, Mister, could get 'em apart.'

It was obviously quite stable, since young Aldous frequently clambered into the maze to add another 'part', without disturbing its equilibrium in the slightest.   50

The foregoing, however sketchy, is all the background we have to the climactic experiment itself. For an exact report of the circumstances attendant upon the one 'controlled' demonstration of the Worp Reaction we are indebted to Major Herbert R. Armstrong, US Army Engineers, and Dr Philip H. Eustace Cross, A. E. C., who were present.

It seems that, at exactly 10:46 A.M., Aldous Worp picked up a very old and very rusty cogwheel . . . the very first object he had retrieved from oblivion on the junk-pile, so long ago when he was but a tad of six. After a moment's hesitation, he climbed up to the top of his jerry-built structure, paused, then lowered himself into its depths. He dis-   60 appeared from the sight of these trained observers for several minutes. (Dr Cross: 4 min., 59 sec. Maj. Armstrong: 5 min, 02 sec.). Finally Aldous reappeared, climbed down and stared fixedly at his creation.

We now quote from the combined reports of Maj. Armstrong and Dr Cross: 'After standing dazed-like for a few minutes, Worp finally came very close to his assembly. There was a rod sticking out with the brass ball of a bed post fastened to it. Aldous Worp gave this a slight tug. What happened then was utterly fantastic. First, we heard a rushing sound, something like a waterfall. This sound grew appreciably louder and, in about fifteen seconds, we saw a purplish glow emanate *beneath* the   70 contraption. Then, the whole congeries of rubbish arose into the air for a height of about three meters and hung there, immobile. The lad Aldous jumped around with every semblance of glee and we distinctly heard him remark 'Whee!' three times. Then he went to one side of the phenomenon, reached down and turned over the rusty wheel of a coffee mill and his "machine" slowly settled to earth.'

There was, of course, considerable excitement. Representatives of the Armed Services, the Press Services, the A. E. C., various Schools for Advanced Studies, *et al* arrived in droves. Communication with Aldous Worp was impossible since the young man had never learned to talk.   80 L.S. Worp, however profane, was an earnest and sincere gentleman, anxious to be of service to his country; but the above quotations from his conversations will indicate how little light he was able to shed on the problem. Efforts to look inside the structure availed little, since the closest and most detailed analysis could elicit no other working hypothesis than 'it's all nothing but a bunch of junk' (Dr Palmer). Further, young Worp obviously resented such investigations.

However, he took great delight in operating his machine and repeatedly demonstrated the "reaction" to all beholders.

The most exhaustive tests, Geiger, electronic, Weisendonk, litmus, *et al* revealed nothing. 90

Finally, the importunities of the press could no longer be denied and early in the afternoon of the second day, telecasters arrived on the scene.

Aldous Worp surveyed them for a moment, then brought his invention back to earth. With a set look on his face, he climbed to its top, clambered down into its bowels and, in due course, reappeared with the ancient cogwheel. This he carefully placed in its original resting place in the chicken coop. Systematically, and in order of installation, he removed each part from his structure and carefully returned it to its original place in the original heap by the chicken coop. 100

Today, the component parts of the whole that was Worp's Reaction are scattered. For, silently ignoring the almost hysterical pleas of the men of science and of the military, Aldous Worp, after dismantling his machine completely and piling all parts in and over the chicken coop, then took upon himself the onerous task of transporting them, one by one, back to their original place in the city dump.

Now, unmoved by an occasional berating by L. S. Worp, silent before an infrequent official interrogation, Aldous Worp sits on a box in the back yard of his ancestral home, gazing serenely out over the city dump. Once in a very great while his eyes light up for a moment and he says 110 'Whee!' very quietly.

Into the text

1 Why is Aldous Worp presented as a 'hopeless idiot' (line 3)? Do you agree with this description?

2 What do you think motivated Worp to build his machine?

3 Why do you think that he dismantles the machine?

4 What do you understand by the last paragraph of the story? If Aldous could speak, instead of 'Whee!', what would he say?

5 This story is written in the style of 'an official report' on the invention. Find some examples of this style. Why do you think the story is told in this way?

6 Unlike Icarus, Aldous Worp for reasons best known to himself, renounces the chance of further flight but also avoids the attendant risks. Compare these two characters, finding similarities and differences between them. Explain which character you prefer, and why.

Power in my hands: Over-reaching

Approaching the text

Many of you will be familiar with Frankenstein's monster, if only from the films which have been made about it. These film versions, only loosely based on the novel by Mary Shelley, rarely represent accurately what the author originally intended. This was to depict the possible consequences of a very ambitious project, to '. . . bestow animation upon lifeless matter . . . (and) renew life where death had apparently devoted the body to corruption.' You will notice that the story is written in the first person, so that we read Dr Frankenstein's 'own' account of these events. As you read the story, consider the reasons why Mary Shelley chose to do this.

The novel was written in 1818 and there are certain words, phrases, references and uses of punctuation which you may find puzzling. Read the extract through quickly to get a flavour of the style and a rough meaning and then re-read it in the light of the subsequent questions.

Frankenstein
Mary Shelley

. . . After days and nights of incredible labour and fatigue, I succeeded in discovering the cause of generation and life; nay, more, I became myself capable of bestowing animation upon lifeless matter.

The astonishment which I had at first experienced on this discovery soon gave place to delight and rapture. After so much time spent in painful labour, to arrive at once at the summit of my desires was the most gratifying consummation of my toils. But this discovery was so great and overwhelming that all the steps by which I had been progressively led to it were obliterated, and I beheld only the result. What had been the study and desire of the wisest men since the creation of the world was now within my grasp. Not that, like a magic scene, it all opened upon me at once: the information I had obtained was of a nature rather to direct my endeavours so soon as I should point them towards the object of my search than to exhibit that object already accomplished. I was like the Arabian who had been buried with the dead and found a passage to life, aided only by one glimmering and seemingly ineffectual light.

I see by your eagerness and the wonder and hope which your eyes express, my friend, that you expect to be informed of the secret with which I am acquainted; that cannot be; listen patiently until the end of my story, and you will easily perceive why I am reserved upon that subject. I will not lead you on, unguarded and ardent as I then was, to your destruction and infallible misery. Learn from me, if not by my precepts, at least by my example, how dangerous is the acquirement of knowledge and how much happier that man is who believes his native town to be the world, than he who aspires to become greater than his

10

20

nature will allow.

When I found so astonishing a power placed within my hands, I
hesitated a long time concerning the manner in which I should employ
it. Although I possessed the capacity of bestowing animation, yet to   30
prepare a frame for the reception of it, with all its intricacies of fibres,
muscles, and veins, still remained a work of inconceivable difficulty and
labour. I doubted at first whether I should attempt the creation of a
being like myself, or one of simpler organization; but my imagination
was too much exalted by my first success to permit me to doubt of my
ability to give life to an animal as complex and wonderful as man. The
materials at present within my command hardly appeared adequate to
so arduous an undertaking, but I doubted not that I should ultimately
succeed. I prepared myself for a multitude of reverses; my operations
might be incessantly baffled, and at last my work be imperfect: yet when   40
I considered the improvement which everyday takes place in science and
mechanics, I was encouraged to hope my present attempts would at least
lay the foundations of future success. Nor could I consider the magni-
tude and complexity of my plan as any argument of its impractibility.
It was with these feelings that I began the creation of a human being. As
the minuteness of the parts formed a great hindrance to my speed, I
resolved, contrary to my first intention, to make the being of a gigantic
stature; that is to say, about eight feet in height, and proportionably
large. After having formed this determination and having spent some
months in successfully collecting and arranging my materials, I began.   50

No one can conceive the variety of feelings which bore me onwards,
like a hurricane, in the first enthusiasm of success. Life and death
appeared to me ideal bounds, which I should first break through, and
pour a torrent of light into our dark world. A new species would bless
me as its creator and source; many happy and excellent natures would
owe their being to me. No father could claim the gratitude of his child
so completely as I should deserve theirs. Pursuing these reflections, I
thought that if I could bestow animation upon lifeless matter, I might
in process of time (although I now found it impossible) renew life where
death had apparently devoted the body to corruption.   60

These thoughts supported my spirits, while I pursued my undertaking
with unremitting ardour. My cheek had grown pale with study, and my
person had become emaciated with confinement. Sometimes, on the very
brink of certainty I failed; yet I still clung to the hope to which I had
dedicated myself; and the moon gazed on my midnight labours, while,
with unrelaxed and breathless eagerness, I pursued nature to her hiding-
places. Who shall conceive the horrors of my secret toil as I dabbled
among the unhallowed damps of the grave or tortured the living animal
to animate the lifeless clay? My limbs now tremble, and my eyes swim
with the remembrance; but then a resistless and almost frantic impulse   70
urged me forward; I seemed to have lost all soul or sensation but for this
one pursuit. It was indeed but a passing trance, that only made me feel
with renewed acuteness so soon as, the unnatural stimulus ceasing to
operate, I had returned to my old habits. I collected bones from charnel-
houses and disturbed, with profane fingers, the tremendous secrets of
the human frame. In a solitary chamber, or rather cell, at the top of the

house, and separated from all the other apartments by a gallery and staircase, I kept my workshop of filthy creation: my eyeballs were starting from their sockets in attending to the details of my employment. The dissecting room and the slaughter-house furnished many of my   80 materials; and often did my human nature turn with loathing from my occupation, whilst, still urged on by an eagerness which perpetually increased, I brought my work near to a conclusion.

(. . .)

It was on a dreary night of November that I beheld the accomplishment of my toils. With an anxiety that almost amounted to agony, I collected the instruments of life around me, that I might infuse a spark of being into the lifeless thing that lay at my feet. It was already one in the morning; the rain pattered dismally against the panes, and my candle was nearly burnt out, when, by the glimmer of the half-extinguished   90 light, I saw the dull yellow eye of the creature open; it breathed hard, and a convulsive motion agitated its limbs.

How can I describe my emotions at this catastrophe, or how delineate the wretch whom with such infinite pains and care I had endeavoured to form? His limbs were in proportion, and I had selected his features as beautiful. Beautiful! Great God! His yellow skin scarcely covered the work of muscles and arteries beneath; his hair was of a lustrous black, and flowing; his teeth of a pearly whiteness; but these luxuriances only formed a more horrid contrast with his watery eyes, that seemed almost of the same colour as the dun-white sockets in which they were set, his   100 shrivelled complexion and straight black lips.

The different accidents of life are not so changeable as the feelings of human nature. I had worked hard for nearly two years, for the sole purpose of infusing life into an inanimate body. For this I had deprived myself of rest and health. I had desired it with an ardour that far exceeded moderation; but now that I had finished, the beauty of the dream vanished, and breathless horror and disgust filled my heart. Unable to endure the aspect of the being I had created, I rushed out of the room and continued a long time traversing my bedchamber, unable to compose my mind to sleep. At length lassitude succeeded to the tumult   110 I had before endured, and I threw myself on the bed in my clothes, endeavouring to seek a few moments of forgetfulness. But it was in vain; I slept, indeed, but I was disturbed by the wildest dreams. I thought I saw Elizabeth, in the bloom of health, walking in the streets of Ingolstadt. Delighted and surprised, I embraced her, but as I imprinted the first kiss on her lips, they became livid with the hue of death; her features appeared to change, and I thought that I held the corpse of my dead mother in my arms; a shroud enveloped her form, and I saw the grave-worms crawling in the folds of the flannel. I started from my sleep with horror; a cold dew covered my forehead, my teeth chattered, and   120 every limb became convulsed; when, by the dim and yellow light of the moon, as it forced its way through the window shutters, I beheld the

wretch – the miserable monster whom I had created. He held up the curtain of the bed; and his eyes, if eyes they may be called, were fixed on me. His jaws opened, and he muttered some inarticulate sounds, while a grin wrinkled his cheeks. He might have spoken, but I did not hear; one hand was stretched out, seemingly to detain me, but I escaped and rushed downstairs. I took refuge in the courtyard belonging to the house which I inhabited, where I remained during the rest of the night, walking up and down in the greatest agitation, listening attentively, 130 catching and fearing each sound as if it were to announce the approach of the demoniacal corpse to which I had so miserably given life.

Oh! No mortal could support the horror of that countenance. A mummy again endued with animation could not be so hideous as that wretch. I had gazed on him while unfinished; he was ugly then, but when those muscles and joints were rendered capable of motion, it became a thing such as even Dante could not have conceived.

I passed the night wretchedly. Sometimes my pulse beat so quickly and hardly that I felt the palpitation of every artery; at others, I nearly sank to the ground through langour and extreme weakness. Mingled with this 140 horror, I felt the bitterness of disappointment; dreams that had been my food and pleasant rest for so long a space were now become a hell to me; and the change was so rapid, the overthrow so complete!

Morning, dismal and wet, at length dawned and discovered to my sleepless and aching eyes the church of Ingolstadt, its white steeple and clock, which indicated the sixth hour. The porter opened the gates of the court, which had that night been my asylum, and I issued into the streets, pacing them with quick steps, as if I sought to avoid the wretch whom I feared every turning of the street would present to my view. I did not dare return to the apartment which I inhabited, but felt impelled to hurry 150 on, although drenched by the rain which poured from a black and comfortless sky.

Into the text

1 Why do you think Mary Shelley told this story as a first person narrative?

2 What do you think is meant by the following:
   a 'consummation of my toils' (line 7)?
   b 'the study and desire of the wisest men' (line 10)?
   c 'I am reserved upon that subject' (lines 21–2)?
   d 'unremitting ardour' (line 62)?
   e 'I kept my workshop of filthy creation' (line 78)?

3 Find other examples of words and phrases which indicate clearly that this was written in the early part of the nineteenth century. Look closely at the last paragraph and then rewrite it in the language of the late 20th century.

4 Why do you think that Dr Frankenstein was so dismayed when he seemed to have achieved all that he set out to do? Look again at the text beginning 'It was on a dreary night of November that I beheld the accomplishment of my toils . . .' (lines 85–6).

5 Do you think that Frankenstein would have had the same reaction to the monster if it had been beautiful (as for example, in the film *Bride of Frankenstein*)? Use evidence from the text to support your point of view.

Out of the text

The great technological and scientific changes that took place during the 19th century had a curious fascination for writers and thinkers. It was the period which saw the beginning of the modern industrial urban world that we now live in. Dr Frankenstein was very much a man of his time. He wished to extend scientific knowledge but nevertheless, he feared where his discoveries could lead to. Modern scientists have experienced the same anxieties, eg the discovery of nuclear fission which led to the development of atomic weapons.

Using either (or both) 'Daedalus and Icarus' and *Frankenstein* as models of what can arise from invention and exploration, write a modern story depicting the possible dangerous consequences of a new invention or discovery.

Approaching the text

In the fifteenth and sixteenth centuries in Western Europe there was an explosion of growth in scientific activity, exploration and knowledge. Shakespeare and his contemporary playwrights like Christopher Marlowe, explored, in their plays, the consequences of this progress for individuals. This is the same theme taken up by Mary Shelley in *Frankenstein* in the nineteenth century.

In *Dr Faustus*, Christopher Marlowe re-tells the well-known story of a man who sells his soul to the Devil in exchange for super-human powers on Earth for a period of 24 years. Initially, Faustus uses these powers to gain knowledge and understanding of the universe, but ends up frittering away his time on pranks and magic trickery. In the extract that follows, Faustus' time remaining on Earth is running out and he is being shown the inevitable consequences of his original contract: he is going to Hell, described at the beginning of this extract by the Bad Angel.

Even if, on first reading it, you are not sure what Faustus is saying, you can draw some conclusions about his state of mind.

Words which you may be unsure about are explained in the brackets.

Dr Faustus
Christopher Marlowe

[*Hell is discovered*]

BAD ANGEL   Now Faustus, let thine eyes with horror
stare
Into that vast perpetual torture-house.   (hell)
There are the furies tossing damned   (devils)
souls
On burning forks; their bodies boil in
lead;
There are live quarters broiling on the   (dismembered
coals,   5   bodies)
That ne'er can die; this ever burning
chair,
Is for o'er-tortured souls to rest them in;
These, that are fed with sops of flaming
fire,
Were gluttons, and loved only delicates,   (rich food)
And laughed to see the poor starve at
their gates: 10
But yet all these are nothing: thou shalt
see
Ten thousand tortures that more horrid
be.

FAUSTUS   O, I have seen enough to torture me.

BAD ANGEL   Nay, thou must feel them, taste the
                   smart of all: (pain)
             He that loves pleasure, must for plea-
                   sure fall.   15
             And so I will leave thee Faustus, till
                   anon,
             Then wilt thou tumble in confusion.

[*Exit. The clock strikes eleven.*]

FAUSTUS   Ah Faustus,
             Now hast thou but one bare hour to live, 20
             And then thou must be damned
                   perpetually.
             Stand still, you ever-moving spheres of   (stars and
                   heaven,   planets)
             That time may cease, and midnight
                   never come.
             Fair nature's eye, rise, rise again and   (the sun)
                   make
             Perpetual day; or let this hour be but   25
             A year, a month, a week, a natural day,
             That Faustus may repent, and save his
                   soul.
             'O lente, lente currite noctis equi!'   (stay, night
             The stars move still, time runs, the clock   and run not
                   will strike,   thus)
             The devil will come, and Faustus must
                   be damned.   30
             O I'll leap up to my God! Who pulls me
                   down?
             See, see where Christ's blood streams in
                   the firmament!   (heaven, sky)
             One drop would save my soul, half a   (a reference
                   drop. Ah my Christ –   to the
             Rend not my heart for naming him my   Crucifixion:
                   Christ;   Christ dying
             Yet will I call on him: O spare me   to save
                   Lucifer!   35 mankind)
             Where is it now? 'Tis gone, and see
                   where God
             Stretcheth out his arm, and bends his
                   ireful brows:
             Mountains and hills, come, come, and
                   fall on me,
             And hide me from the heavy wrath of
                   God.
             No, no!   40
             Then will I headlong run into the earth:

Earth, gape! O no, it will not harbour
    me.
You stars that reigned at my nativity,   (alluding to
Whose influence hath allotted death and   astrology)
    hell,   (birth)
Now draw up Faustus like a foggy mist   45
Into the entrails of yon labouring cloud,
That when you vomit forth into the air,
My limbs may issue from your smoky
    mouths,
So that my soul may but ascend to
    heaven.
             [*The watch strikes*]
Ah, half the hour is past; 'twill all be past
    anon!   50

O God,
If you wilt not have mercy on my soul,
Yet for Christ's sake, whose blood hath
    ransomed me,
Impose some end to my incessant pain:
Let Faustus live in hell a thousand years,   55
A hundred thousand, and at last be
    saved.
O, no end is limited to damned souls!
Why wert thou not a creature wanting
    soul?
Or why is this immortal that thou hast?
Ah,   Pythagoras' 'metempsychosis' – 60 (a theory that
    were that true,   the human
This soul should fly from me, and I be   soul at the
    changed   death of the
Unto some brutish beast.   body took on
All beasts are happy, for when they die,   some other
Their souls are soon dissolved in   form of life)
    elements;
But mine must live still to be plagued in
    hell.   65
Cursed be the parents that engendered
    me!
No Faustus, curse thyself, curse Lucifer,
That hath deprived thee of the joys of
    heaven.
         [*The clock striketh twelve*]
It strikes, it strikes! Now body turn to
    air,
Or Lucifer will bear thee quick to hell.   70
         [*Thunder and lightning*]
O soul, be changed into little water
    drops,

And fall into the ocean, ne'er be found.

[*Enter the Devils*]

My God, my God! Look not so fierce on
me!

Adders, and serpents, let me breathe
awhile!

Ugly hell gape not! Come not Lucifer;   75

I'll burn my books – ah Mephostophilis!   (Lucifer's
main agent)

Into the text

1 For a full understanding of this play, you have to realise that the Elizabethan audience believed in this literal Hell. What, from the evidence of the extract, do you understand the Elizabethan's vision of hell to be?

2 Time is manipulated in all works of fiction and drama. Pick out references to time in this extract. How is the passage of time recorded? What would Faustus like to happen to time? In what ways would the audience's experience of time differ from that of Faustus during this final speech? (Pay particular attention to the stage directions for lines 19 ff)

3 What evidence can you find in the speech, that Faustus, who desired so much, has been utterly defeated in his aspirations? How do his ambitions change? What stages does he go through, for example, from stopping time (line 23) to being changed into drops of water? (line 71)

4 Below are four quotations from the extract. What do you think Marlowe means in each case?

a *Ah Faustus,*
Now hast thou but one bare hour to live,
And then thou must be damned perpetually. (lines 19–21)

b *Fair nature's eye, rise, rise again and make*
Perpetual day; or let this hour be but
A year, a month, a week, a natural day,
That Faustus may repent, and save his soul. (lines 24–7)

c *. . . see where God*
Stretcheth out his arm, and bends his ireful brows:
Mountains and hills, come, come, and fall on me,
And hide me from the heavy wrath of God. (lines 36–39)

d *My God, my God! Look not so fierce on me!*
Adders, and serpents, let me breathe awhile!
Ugly hell gape not! Come not Lucifer;
I'll burn my books – ah Mephostophilis! (lines 73–6)

Out of the text

The idea of being given the power to do anything recurs throughout literature, from the Bible (Christ in the Wilderness) to pantomime (*Cinderella*). There is, however, always a catch.

Imagine that you have been given unlimited power for 24 hours. You can do whatever you want but, at the end of the day, you have to account for your decisions to someone whose good opinion you value. Describe your day and recall your justifications to your 'confessor'.

Approaching the text

Macbeth, like Faustus, is another man who refused to be bound by the restrictions of the world in which he lived, and dared to break the rules in order to fulfil a personal ambition, in his case, to be King. First performed in 1606, *Macbeth* tells the story of a Scottish Lord who is persuaded by supernatural images to kill his rightful King, Duncan, and ascend the throne himself. It is, therefore, a play about political ambition, unlike the intellectual ambition explored in *Dr Faustus*.

Macbeth is struggling with his conscience in this soliloquy. He wants to kill Duncan but he fears the consequences. The complexity of the speech reflects his indecision and throughout the speech, he conducts an argument with himself. As you are reading the extract, look for reasons why Macbeth feels that he should not kill Duncan.

Macbeth
William Shakespeare

MACBETH	If it were done, when 'tis done, then 'twere well	
	It were done quickly: if the assassination	
	Could trammel up the consequence, and catch	
	With his surcease success; that but this blow	
	Might be the be-all and the end-all – here,	5
	But here, upon this bank and shoal of time, –	
	We'd jump the life to come. – But in these cases,	
	We still have judgement here; that we but teach	
	Bloody instructions, which, being taught, return	
	To plague th'inventor: this even-handed justice	10
	Commends th'ingredients of our poison'd chalice	
	To our own lips. He's here in double trust:	
	First, as I am his kinsman and his subject,	
	Strong both against the deed; then, as his host,	
	Who should against his murtherer shut the door,	15
	Not bear the knife myself. Besides, this Duncan	
	Hath borne his faculties so meek, hath been	
	So clear in his great office, that his virtues	
	Will plead like angels, trumpet-tongu'd, against	
	The deep damnation of his taking-off;	20
	And pity, like a naked new-born babe,	
	Striding the blast, o'er heaven's Cherubim, hors'd	
	Upon the sightless couriers of the air,	
	Shall blow the horrid deed in every eye,	
	That tears shall drown the wind. – I have no spur	25
	To prick the sides of my intent, but only	
	Vaulting ambition, which o'er leaps itself,	
	And falls on th'other –	

[*Enter Lady Macbeth*]

	How now! What news?	
LADY MACBETH	He has almost supp'd. Why have you left the	30
	chamber?	
MACBETH	Hath he ask'd for me?	
LADY MACBETH	Know you not, he has?	
MACBETH	We will proceed no further in this business:	
	He hath honour'd me of late; and I have bought	35
	Golden opinions from all sorts of people,	
	Which would be worn now in their newest gloss,	
	Not cast aside so soon.	
LADY MACBETH	Was the hope drunk,	
	Wherein you dress'd yourself? hath it slept since,	40
	And wakes it now, to look so green and pale	
	At what it did so freely? From this time,	
	Such I account thy love. Art thou afeard	
	To be the same in thine own act and valour,	

	As thou art in desire? Would'st thou have that	45
	Which thou esteem'st the ornament of life,	
	And live a coward in thine own esteem,	
	Letting 'I dare not' wait upon 'I would,'	
	Like the poor cat i' th' adage?	
MACBETH	Pr'ythee, peace.	50
	I dare do all that may become a man;	
	Who dares do more, is none.	

Into the text

1 Because Shakespeare's plays were written a long time ago, in language that is highly poetic and in many ways different from modern English, there are versions of his stories which have been given a more immediate style. The passage below is a paraphrase of Macbeth's speech (lines 1–28).

If I'm going to do it, I'd better get on with it. If killing Duncan was the end of the matter, there would be no problem. If nothing would happen to me now or in the future, I'd kill him. But there are always consequences. We are made to pay for our crimes: the law sees to that. And anyway, the King deserves better, for two reasons: I'm related to him and he is my King! – good reasons for not killing him. What is more, he's a guest in my house and I should do all in my power to protect him. And he's been a good King: he's modest and intelligent. To kill such a man would be seen as a totally despicable act. Everybody would be appalled and saddened by his death. The only thing that's driving me on is ambition, which is in danger of running away with me.

In what ways has this helped you to understand what Macbeth is saying? In what ways does it fall short of the original? Try a similar paraphrase of Lady Macbeth's speech (lines 39 ff).

2 What function does Lady Macbeth serve in this episode?

3 Macbeth talks about his 'Vaulting ambition . . .' for Kingship (line 27) — a position of enormous power. Many people feel an almost irresistible desire to achieve power and prestige and are willing to set aside or compromise their moral principles in order to get what they want. On the evidence of the extract you have just read, what do you think is the real cause of Macbeth's indecision? Does he have moral scruples about committing the murder? Or is it simply that he is afraid of being found out?

The end justifies the means: Politics and investigative journalism

Richard Nixon was the Republican President of the USA from 1968 until he was forced to resign in 1974 because of the Watergate scandal. The Watergate complex was a hotel used by Nixon's opponents in the 1972 election as a campaign headquarters. People acting on instructions from CREEP (Committee to Re-elect the President) broke into Watergate and planted electronic bugging devices to enable them to listen in on the Democrats' election strategy.

Two investigative reporters for the Washington Post, Bob Woodward and Carl Bernstein, followed the story, and their reports contributed to Nixon's downfall. Their first efforts resulted in the book *All the President's Men* which was later filmed, starring Robert Redford and Dustin Hoffman.

Approaching the text
In the following extract from Nixon's *Memoirs*, the ex-President recalls a key period in the development of the crisis. As you read it, consider the extent to which Nixon appears to be accepting responsibility for what occurred.

The Memoirs of Richard Nixon
Richard Nixon

The Presidency 1973
My speech on April 30, 1973, was the first time I formally addressed the American people specifically on Watergate. All that most people understood of the complex situation that had precipitated the speech was that my two closest aides were being accused of participation in the Watergate cover-up, while one of my best friends, my former Attorney General, was being accused of having ordered the break-in and bugging.

No matter how much we protested to the contrary, as soon as Haldeman and Ehrlichman resigned, people assumed it was because they were, at least to some extent, guilty of the charges against them. The spotlight automatically turned next to me: people were waiting for   10
a yes or no answer to the question of whether I was also involved in Watergate. That was what they looked for from my April 30 speech. I made the decision of how I would answer the question less on the basis of logical calculation than on political instinct. I made it without stopping to realize that this speech would be a major turning point and that my answer, once given, would have to see me through whatever lay ahead.

I believe that a totally honest answer would have been neither a simple yes or no.

If I had given the true answer, I would have had to say that without   20 fully realizing the implications of my actions I had become deeply entangled in the complicated mesh of decisions, inactions, misunderstandings, and conflicting motivations that comprised the Watergate cover-up; I would have had to admit that I still did not know the whole story and therefore did not know the full extent of my involvement in it; and I would have had to give the damaging specifics of what I did know while leaving open the possibility that much more might come out later.

I sensed that the inept way we had handled Watergate so far had put us so much on the defensive that there would be no tolerance for such a complicated explanation from me at this late date. And the instincts of twenty-five years in politics told me that I was up against no ordinary opposition. In the second term I had thrown down a gauntlet to Congress, the bureaucracy, the media, and the Washington establishment and challenged them to engage in epic battle. We had already skirmished over the limitations of prerogative and power represented in confirmation of appointments, the impoundment of funds, and the battle of the budget. Now, suddenly, Watergate had exposed a cavernous weakness in my ranks, and I felt that if in this speech I admitted any vulnerabilities, my opponents would savage me with them. I feared that any admissions I made would be used to keep the Watergate issue – and the issue of my behaviour in office – festering during the rest of my term, thereby making it impossible for me to exert presidential leadership.

Given this situation and given this choice – given my belief that these were the stakes – I decided to answer no to the question whether I was also involved in Watergate.

I hoped that, after the agony of the past weeks, a firm statement of my innocence, accompanied by the symbolic cleansing of the administration with the departure of Haldeman, Ehrlichman, and Dean and followed by an active rebuilding with new people along open lines, would convince people that the various Watergate probes could and should be brought to a quick conclusion. I was counting on the polls, which showed that the majority of people, even some of the 40 percent who already thought I knew of the break-in in advance, still agreed with me that the whole thing was 'just politics.' I knew I was good at being President, at the really important things, and I was counting on people to become impatient with Watergate and exert pressure on Congress and the media to move on to something else and get back to the things that mattered. I actually hoped that this speech would at last and once and for all put Watergate behind me as a nagging national issue. I could not have made a more disastrous miscalculation.

In the April 30 speech I gave the impression that I had known nothing at all about the cover-up until my March 21 meeting with Dean. I indicated that once I had learned about it I had acted with dispatch and dispassion to end it. In fact, I had known some of the details of the cover-up before March 21, and when I did become aware of the implications, instead of exerting presidential leadership aimed at uncovering the cover-up, I embarked on an increasingly desperate search for ways to limit the damage to my friends, to my administration, and to myself.

I talked in terms of responsibility and the fact that 'the man at the top must bear the responsibility . . . I accept it.' But that was only an abstraction and people saw through it. Finally, I clung to excuses that I really believed made little difference. In a sense Watergate had grown out of the end-justifies-the-means mentality of the causes of the 1960s. It was also true that if we often made the mistake of acting like an administration under siege, it was because we were an administration under siege. And I believed it was true that if I had not been preoccupied with Vietnam and other policy issues, I might have probed until I sensed the full dimensions of the cover-up and perhaps precipitated action   80 sooner – if not on ethical grounds, at least because I would have recognized that we were marching headlong into a trap with no exits.

But these were still only excuses. They were not an accounting of my role. They were not explanations of how a President of the United States could so incompetently allow himself to get in such a situation. That was what people really wanted to know, and that was what my April 30 speech and all the other public statements I made about Watergate while I was President failed to tell them.

Into the text

1 Why did Nixon feel that he had to address the American people?
2 Why did he feel that his political enemies would try to use Watergate to bring him down?
3 What did Nixon hope would follow from the resignations of Erlichman, Haldeman and Dean?
4 Why did he think he was a good President?
5 What did he consider his errors (if any) to be?

Approaching the text

The interpretation of the same events (described by Nixon in the previous extract) by the investigative reporters Woodward and Bernstein, was somewhat different. What view of the President emerges here? As you read this extract, you may be overwhelmed by the number of people mentioned. All you need to know is that these men are part of the President's team working to save his Presidency.

The Final Days
Bob Woodward and Carl Bernstein

. . . The President would not deal directly with people or events. He preferred papers: memos didn't talk back, didn't push him. Laird had told Buzhardt that he always had the feeling that the President didn't want any one person to have the full picture. No one was ever to be given the entire story. With matters thus arranged, the President could counter any argument by hinting that only he had the necessary facts and background. Nixon's strange methodology made timid ministers, Laird had said. Who would confront a President in the full awareness that he had been dealt out of essential information?

But Buzhardt too was committed now. He would serve and do his best.

'The biggest problem here is credibility,' Haig told him. The President's new team would meet matters head on. They would launch a counter-offensive.

Buzhardt was pleased. Throughout Watergate, he firmly believed, Nixon's mistake had been a failure to move off the defensive, to seize the issues and shake them to death. Buzhardt and Haig wanted finally to get ahead of the problem, meet the current charges, anticipate future ones, answer them all. Right now. The barrage of half-truths and speculation was devastating. The general and the lawyer went to the President.

Haig did the talking. A final and definitive statement that dealt with the major allegations, both direct and implied, should be drafted, he said. It would have to stand for all time. It was essential that the statement be consistent with *anything* that might surface.

The President said he was willing to let them give it a try. This would be the new team's first major effort, but they couldn't do it alone. They needed the members of the old White House team, who might have some information and some influence with the President. That would include Garment – it would be good to have the house liberal in on this – and Nixon's two principal speech writers, Raymond K. Price, Jr., and Patrick J, Buchanan, who were regarded by the President as respectively the heart and the soul of his Administration. Price, a forty-three-year-old Yale graduate who had worked for *Collier's* magazine, *Life*, and the *New York Herald Tribune*, was the idealist and gentle theoretician. Buchanan, thirty-five, a conservative former editorial writer for the *St Louis Globe-Democrat* who had signed up with Nixon in 1966, was the hard political realist, the gut fighter, the resident expert on media manipulation.

Time was short, Buzhardt knew. The Senate Watergate Committee's hearings were scheduled to begin on May 17. Four separate matters had to be met head on – and reasons found to explain the President's actions. A rationale had to be offered for (1) the approval of the Huston plan authorizing illegal intelligence-gathering; (2) the wiretapping of Administration aides and of reporters; (3) the directive to the CIA to keep the FBI from investigating the Mexican money connection as stated in the Walters mem-con; (4) the presence of the Plumbers unit in the White House. E. Howard Hunt, Jr., a former CIA agent, and G. Gordon Liddy, a former FBI agent, both convicted in the Watergate case, had been Plumbers. Their role in the Ellsberg break-in had also to be explained.

The President was not very cooperative, Buzhardt and the others discovered very quickly. He did not wish to sit down with Haig or Buzhardt or anybody else and offer his version of events. He told Buzhardt to draft the best defence he could and bring it back for review. The process was excruciating. Slowly, Buzhardt started piecing something together. Though the President always seemed ready, even eager, to review his lawyer's work, he never volunteered anything to Buzhardt, never offered to tell him what had actually happened. Buzhardt would

bring a set of postulates to him, and the President would respond, 'That's
wrong, try it again.' Hide-and-seek. Buzhardt wanted to wrap up the   60
wiretaps, the Plumbers and the Walters mem-cons in a national-security
blanket. Approval of the Huston plan would be acknowledged and
would be cast as a response to a wave of violence, arson and bombing
in the cities and on the campuses in 1970.

Into the text

1 List the criticisms that Woodward and Bernstein made
   of the President's conduct of the affair.
2 Which version of these events do you consider to be
   the most convincing? Why?
3 What is the effect of the direct speech, 'The biggest
   problem here is credibility' (line 12)? Do you think
   Woodward and Bernstein made this up?
4 The two extracts are written in very different styles.
   Identify some of the differences. Look at vocabulary, sentence length, paragraphing, use of jargon,
   etc). How do you account for them?

Assignments

1 The following two poems are about men who are so dissatisfied with their
lives that they have set themselves apart. We can assume that both men have
failed to achieve something. As you read the poems identify yourself with
an observer of the events as they unfold.

The Centre of Attention
Daniel Hoffman

As grit swirled in the wind the word spreads.
On pavement approaching the bridge a crowd
Springs up like mushrooms.
They are hushed at first, intently

Looking. At the top of the pylon   5
The target of their gaze leans toward them.
The sky sobs
With the sirens of disaster crews

Careening toward the crowd with nets,
Ladders, resuscitation gear, their First   10
Aid attendants antiseptic in white duck.
The police, strapped into their holsters,

Exert themselves in crowd-control. They can't
Control the situation.
Atop the pylon there's a man who threatens   15
Violence. He shouts, 'I'm gonna jump –'

And from the river of upturned faces
– Construction workers pausing in their construction work,
Shoppers diverted from their shopping
The idlers revelling in this diversion   20

In the vacuity of their day – arises
A chorus of cries – 'Jump!
Jump!' and 'No –
Come down! Come down!' Maybe, if he can hear them,

They seem to be saying 'Jump down!' The truth is,   25
The crowd cannot make up its mind.
This is a tough decision. The man beside me
Reaches into his lunch box and lets him have it,

'Jump!' before he bites his sandwich,
While next to him a young blonde clutches   30
Her handbag to her breasts and moans
'Don't Don't Don't' so very softly

You'd think she was afraid of being heard.
The will of the people is divided.
Up there he hasn't made his mind up either.   35
He has climbed and climbed on spikes imbedded in the pylon

To get where he has arrived at.
Is he sure now that this is where he was going?
He looks down one way into the river.
He looks down the other way into the people.   40

He seems to be looking for something
Or for somebody in particular.
Is there anyone here who is that person
Or who can give him what it is that he needs?

From the back of a fire truck a ladder teeters.   45
Inching along, up, up up up up, a policeman
Holds on with one hand, sliding it on ahead of him.
In the other, outstretched, a pack of cigarettes.

Soon the man will decide between
The creature comfort of one more smoke   50
And surcease from being a creature.
Meanwhile the crowd calls 'Jump!' and calls 'Come down!'

Now, his cassock billowing in the bulges of Death's black flag,
A priest creeps up the ladder too.
What will the priest and the policeman together   55
Persuade the man to do?

He has turned his back to them.
He has turned away from everyone.
His solitariness is nearly complete.
He is alone with his decision.   60

No one on the ground or halfway into the sky can know
The hugeness of the emptiness that surrounds him.
All of his senses are orphans.
His ribs are cold andirons.

Does he regret his rejection of furtive pills,   65
Of closet noose or engine idling in closed garage?
A body will plummet through shrieking air,
The audience dumb with horror, the spattered street . . .

The world he has left is as small as toys at his feet.
Where he stands, though nearer the sun, the wind is chill.   70
He clutches his arms – a caress, or is he trying
Merely to warm himself with his arms?

The people below, their necks are beginning to ache.
They are getting impatient for this diversion
To come to some conclusion. The priest   75
Inches further narrowly up the ladder.

The centre of everybody's attention
For some reason has lit up a butt. He sits down.
He looks down on the people gathered, and sprinkles
Some of his ashes upon them.   80

Before he is half way down.
The crowd is half-dispersed.
It was his aloneness that clutched them together.
They were spellbound by his despair

And now each rung brings him nearer,   85
Nearer to their condition
Which is not sufficiently interesting
To detain them from business of idleness either,

Or is too close to a despair
They do not dare   90
Exhibit before a crowd
Or admit to themselves they share.

Now the police are taking notes
On clipboards, filling the forms.
He looks round as though searching for what he came down for.   95
Traffic flows over the bridge.

_____ *Death on a Live Wire* _____
Michael Baldwin

Treading a field I saw afar
A laughing fellow climbing the cage
That held the grinning tensions of wire,
Alone, and no girl gave him courage.

Up he climbed on the diamond struts,   5
Diamond cut diamond, till he stood
With the insulators brooding like owls
And all their live wisdom, if he would.

I called to him climbing and asked him to say
What thrust him into the singeing sky: 10
The one word he told me the wind took away,
So I shouted again, but the wind passed me by

And the gust of his answer tore at his coat
And stuck him stark on the lightning's bough;
Humanity screeched in his manacled throat   15
And he cracked with flame like a figure of straw

Turning, burning, he dangled black,
A hot sun swallowing at his fork
And shaking embers out of his back,
Planting his shadow of fear in the chalk.   20

Oh then he danced an incredible dance
With soot in his sockets, hanging at heels;
Uprooted mandrakes screamed in his loins,
His legs thrashed and lashed like electric eels;

For now he embraced the talent of iron,   25
The white-hot ore that comes from the hill,
The Word out of which the electrons run,
The snake in the rod and the miracle;

And as he embraced it the girders turned black,
Fused metal wept and great tears ran down,   30
Till his fingers like snails at last came unstuck
And he fell through the cage of the sun.

Into the text

1 a What significance do these events have for the onlookers?

b In what ways are the two men similar? In what ways do they contrast?

c Both poems find some merit in the actions of the men. What is it about the way in which the poets tell their stories that makes us think of them as 'heroic'?

d The American artist Andy Warhol said that everyone in the future would have fifteen minutes of fame. In both of these poems the central characters achieve that fame but without telling their stories. Both poems describe the events from the point of view of the onlookers. What are the central characters themselves thinking and feeling? By reference to the poems, describe what is going through their minds.

e Choose one of the characters and describe the circumstances which brought him to this crisis.

2 Choosing two or more extracts in this unit that you found particularly interesting, either because of the events themselves or because of the way in which the events were recounted, show to what extent the writers have been successful in describing the failure of human ambition.

3 Choose a famous historical or contemporary character who impresses you. Find out what you can about him/her and write about the way in which your character achieves certain things and fails in other respects.

4 At the beginning of the unit, we asked you what you hoped to achieve in years to come either for yourself or others. Now imagine you are 70 years old: reflect on your life, your successes and failures, and identify those things which you would still like to achieve.

Stability and change: Variations on a theme

Contents

Introduction

We live in a time of continual change in all areas of our experience. This is a consequence of living in an industrial and technological society. This has not always been the case, however. Two hundred years ago, for instance, the circumstances in which most people lived would have remained stable through their lifetimes; the only changes that they would have experienced would have been personal – births, marriages and deaths.

Now, however, in addition to these personal events, we have to live with changes in the wider society around us, for example:
- **political:** the success of 'green' politics showing the extent of concern for the environment
- **medical:** the successful treatment of diseases that were once considered to be terminal
- **scientific:** developments in space exploration, orbiting space-stations, crewed flights to Mars
- **economic:** the increasing power and influence of multi-national companies, 'the new colonialism'
- **education:** the increase in the number of literate people
- **communications:** satellites, FAX machines, fast travel.

Change has always affected individual lives and societies but in the late twentieth century, change has become a way of life. This might be thought to be exciting, but many people long for stability, for security and for certainty.

The following are comments made by a variety of writers about the essential paradox (see **Glossary** on page 234) that change implies. Read them carefully and identify the contradiction that the writer is highlighting.

Comments and quotations

'There is a certain relief in change, even though it be from bad to worse.' (Washington Irving)

'Change is not made without inconvenience, even from worse to better.' (Richard Hooker)

'The release of atom power has changed everything except our way of thinking, and thus we are being driven unarmed towards a catastrophe . . . The solution of this problem lies in the heart of humankind.' (Albert Einstein)

'Change is inevitable. In a progressive country, change is constant.' (Benjamin Disraeli)

'Plus ça change, plus c'est la même chose – The more things change, the more they are the same.' (Alphonse Karr)

'The substitution of the proletarian for the bourgeois state is impossible without a violent revolution.' (Lenin)

Into the text

Choose three of four of the quotations listed above and record incidents or events from your own experience or knowledge which demonstrate the truth of the statement.

Nazis don't have to be Germans: A short story

Approaching the text

This story, taken from the collection *Forties' Child*, is based on an event from the author's childhood in the 1940s.

It is set on VE Day, which marked the end of World War II in Europe: a day on which there were widespread celebrations throughout Britain.

As you read the story, make a note of things that, on this special day, suggest change, and things which are likely to remain the same.

White Hot
Tom Wakefield

Other people had knocked on the door and asked her if she were coming out. 'In a minute, in a minute, I'll be out in a minute,' she had replied pleasantly. I watched her. She was making no attempt to move from her position near the fire. She was too near and her legs had become mottled by the heat. She seemed unaware of this. All the rest of the street were out, all the children, all the mothers. I didn't want to go to the VE party

unless my mother was there singing and wearing a paper hat like all the
other mums. I required her presence at the festivities; if she were not
there, then I couldn't anticipate the enjoyment. We had almost won the
war. It was nearly over. We were expected to sing and dance. A party,   10
a street party was in progress and my mother was sitting crouched over
the fire.

I didn't ask her to come out but she knew well enough why I chose
to sit and sulk and read comics in the corner. She picked up the poker
and thrust it deep into the fire. This was a habit of hers. I would like to
think that it was based on economics because when the end of the poker
was white-hot with heat she would hold it close to her face and light a
cigarette with it. Matches were saved in this way. However, sometimes
she just withdrew the poker and let it cool without lighting a cigarette.
From time to time, I would peer over the edge of my comic, waiting for   20
some movement from her. The poker was still in its place, one end
wedged deeply in the embers of the coal, the handle sticking out
somewhere near her shins.

All the other women in our row of houses liked my mother. She never
gossiped. Queenie and Amelia would have gladly died for her. I couldn't
understand their loyalty. I was not able to recognise either illness or
integrity. Both Queenie and Amelia were out with the other women,
singing and dancing and being happy. The two women had popped in
and not cajoled my mother.

'If you feel like it then Esther,' was all that they had said in the way of   30
persuasion.

My mother looked up from the fire. I pretended that I was unaware
of the fact that she was looking in my direction. I held the comic up and
covered my face from her gaze. I could never fool her, not in the same
way as I could my dad on occasions.

'I'm not stopping you from going. The party has started,' she used her
flat voice. I punished her by not answering and merely turned over
another page of the comic.

'What are you sulking about?' she asked.

'Same as you, I'm being the same as you.' I snapped at her; to my   40
surprise she did not reply. She picked up a newspaper that lay at her feet,
she only seemed interested in looking at one page. She would look at this
page and then place it back on the floor again, only to glance at it again
a few minutes later. That's all she was doing, looking at that page, then
staring into the fire.

If she were in this preoccupied state, I would often try to dispose of
it by drawing her attention to something I had read in a book, or even
tell her the content of the play I had listened to on radio's *Saturday Night
Theatre*, she liked hearing me tell these modern fables. Sometimes I
would ginger up the plot a bit by adding some on. In her present mood   50
I felt no sympathy for her, merely irritation. When I felt like this, I
usually resorted to provocation. Anger I found more palatable than the
silence. She would shout when provoked and call me a little 'snipe',
which, I suppose, is what I was. She reached for her knitting.

'You're not going to knit, are you? We've all got too many pullovers.
You use the wrong colours anyway, the Fair Isle pullover you did last

time is bumpy where the patterns are; it doesn't fit in the right places.'

'Don't wear it then.'

'I won't. I won't wear it. "Did your mam knit that Tommy?"' I mimicked a neighbour. 'Yes, my clever, non-talking mam did it. All on her own – four needles, ever so difficult.'

I tried to sting some action into her, but my taunting had a reverse effect. She put the knitting back in its place and spoke into the air. She didn't sound angry. 'She's a nice woman, Mrs Millington.' My acting had been good, my mother had detected whom I was impersonating. Her bland response made me furious. I screwed my comic into a ball and hurled it on to the fire. She was forced to back away a little as the flames rose.

'I won't order it next week now. I won't order them for you ever again. You can just read books. Books without pictures, it's no loss seeing how clever you are.' She was angry now, but her voice she kept low.

'I'll show you some bloody pictures. Just sit where you are; don't you dare move or you'll get a crack on the head.' She meant it. I sat still, quiet, defiant. 'There, stuff your eyes into that lot and don't forget what you've seen. And if you have bad dreams so much the better – because that's the only way you'll ever remember what this has all been about. People are going to forget; people forget everything with time.' She thrust the newspaper on to my lap.

On a closer scrutiny, it wasn't a daily paper at all; it was bits of pages from three or four papers, the *Herald*, the *Express*, the *News Chronicle*, the *Mail*, they were all represented. Stranger still, some of them were dated 1944. Today was 8 May 1945. It was VE Day. Outside in the street, tables had been dragged out to spell out the letters in a weird geometry, the celebrations had commenced, people were singing and whooping with delight. We could hear them. And here I was with my mother expecting me to look at some papers that were dated 1944. I tried to resist looking at them.

But the first two pictures on one of the papers drew my attention – horror always arouses curiosity. One of the photographs showed a man curled like a coloured snake and ensnared between sections of barbed wire. His head hung down, so that his feet pointed into the air. The barbs on the wire held him in this splayed, petrified position. He wore striped clothing and there was a star printed on his arm.

'Has he been shot mam?' I was already chastened.

'No, you can read what it says; the wire is electrified. He's dead. Electrocuted.'

'What, what did he want to jump on the barbed wire for?' I couldn't see the sense in his action. She answered me as if I were an adult. I deserved it, I had goaded her into it.

'If you had been inside a Nazi Concentration Camp, you might have felt happier ending up on the barbed wire than being part of what was going on inside. I would have done.'

'You wouldn't have thrown yourself on the wire!'

'Yes, I think I could – but you never know. There are other pictures,' she waved her hand.

The next one was one I could identify with. In all pictures or films of the war, it was usually our men or women fighting and winning or losing and dying bravely. These pictures were different. Children had never been shot in any films that I had seen. But there on the same page as the man impaled on the barbed wire was a photograph of a boy. He was 110 holding up his hands, he was wearing clothes like mine, he had a cap like me and he didn't look at all different from me, his face even resembled mine. He looked very frightened.

'They're going to shoot him. He's dead now,' she said.

'Germans?' I asked.

'Nazis, Nazis,' she spat out the words. 'Nazis don't have to be Germans, they can be anybody, their feelings are rotten.'

The last photograph was enough, I looked at it and closed the paper. At first, I thought it must have been the inside of an old slave ship – there were people lying on bunk beds, some half naked, all pathetically thin 120 and emaciated, you couldn't tell whether or not they were dead or alive.

'Are they men or women?' even their sexuality seemed to have disappeared and I had not thought this possible, but I couldn't distinguish
the differences in gender although I knew what points to look for. These
people were shrunken, the parts that might have given some clue were
indistinguishable and all their heads were shaved.

'Both. They're men and women, or they were at some time. They were
just like us; that's what the Nazis have done to them. It's not only
soldiers who have gone under in this bloody war yer know.' She buried
her head in her hands. I wanted to put my arms around her. Comfort   130
her, kiss her neck or lick her ear. But she had never shown me physical
affection and would not have appreciated me expressing any towards
her. She didn't like to be touched by me. Yet I wanted to touch her. I
couldn't reach her suffering but I had glimpsed some of the depths of
it – thanks to the horrible photographs. It dawned then, it entered my
head then, that my mother was clever, she thought about things but had
no one to talk to about them. Her injuries were buried within her. I had
discovered a nest with eggs in.

'Never mind mam, we've beaten the Nazis now. Germany is
conquered, our armies have won.' I spoke in a conciliatory, patriotic   140
manner. I had forgotten the party, the noise outside was still going on
but my concern was for her. She took little solace from my general and
popular observation.

'You don't think that Nazis will ever go away, just like that,' she
snapped her fingers. 'They're still there; there's some in all countries.
There are Nazis in this country, they'll be back. People forget, I've told
you once, people forget. They'll start their bloody marching all over
again. I know it; you'll see, mark my words. People forget, they
shouldn't, but they do.'

I passed the papers back to her and sat next to her, cross-legged on   150
the rug. I got as close to her as possible without touching her. We both
looked into the fire. There was a tap on the window pane. Amelia's face
looked in on us, she smiled at us, beckoned us to come out. My mother
waved, smiled and nodded.

'I'll stop in with you if you like mam. Or if you want – I'll go out on
my own.' These words brought tears to her face, she did not wish me
to see her cry and quickly brushed the drops away with the back of her
hand. She leapt up as though I'd jabbed her with a pin in her bum.

'Come on, it's party time. I'll take me pinafore off and go out in me
pyjamas. That'll give them a laugh. I'll wear your dad's cap and you can   160
wear my best one; the one with feathers in it. Put it on back-to-front and
you'll look like Robin Hood.' She had already begun to change and had
fetched in the hat before I could wholeheartedly respond to the change
in mood. Her histrionics were powerful when turned on. I had the hat,
it was precious.

'They might get broken, the feathers might . . .'

'Oh, bugger the feathers; out we go for a "Knees up Mother Brown",'
she cried.

She jammed the hat on my head and turned me around and pushed
me so that I could see myself in the sideboard mirror. We both looked   170
funny and I began to laugh. She went to leave. I called her back.

'The poker, it's still in the fire. You've left it sticking in the fire.'

For a few seconds she lost her false verve and éclat, she bent down to the grate and removed the iron from the fire and placed it carefully in the hearth. Then we both left to join the festivities.

The poker remained in the hearth still white-hot. In the meantime we danced, and sang, and ate, and laughed. When we returned the poker had cooled and it was necessary for her to heat it up in order to light a cigarette.

Into the text

1 'I required her presence at the festivities; if she were not there, then I couldn't anticipate the enjoyment.' (lines 8–9). Why is this so important to the boy? What does it tell us about the changing relationship between him and his mother?

2 'I screwed my comic into a ball and hurled it on to the fire.' (lines 66–7). Why does he get angry with his mother? What is her immediate reaction? Why is the boy surprised by this?

3 The boy says, 'These pictures were different.' (line 108). Pictures are a key element in the story. He has seen pictures of the war before; he has read his comics. Why do these pictures make such a strong impression on him?

4 'Nazis don't have to be Germans, they can be anybody, their feelings are rotten.' (lines 116–17). Why, on this day of celebration, is the Mother so down-hearted? What, precisely, does she fear when the future should look bright?

5 How does the boy comfort his mother towards the end of the story? What does this tell us about the way he has changed? How does she respond? Is her response deep? Find some words that suggest that she is only pretending to have shaken off her mood.

6 Why do you think the mother was so popular with other women who lived in the street?

7 There are no men in this story. Why not?

8 In what way is the boy's relationship with his father different to that with his mother? Find evidence from the text to support your answer.

9 Do you agree with the mother when she repeatedly says, 'People forget'? How much do you know about the horrors of the Concentration Camps of World War II? Do you agree that 'They'll start their bloody marching all over again.' (lines 147–8). Can you think of examples?

10 Why do you think the story is called *White Hot*?

The changing nature of language

What language do you think this is?

wæs he se mon in weoruldhade geseted oð pa tide pe he wæs gelyfdre ylde; ond næfre nænig leoð geleornode . . .

This is, in fact, ninth-century English, or more precisely, Anglo-Saxon. Although at first glance it does look completely different to us, modern English can be traced back to it.

All languages are constantly changing and English is no exception to this. It has changed in vocabulary, sentence structure, pronunciation, spelling, word endings. New words have been added, old ones have disappeared or have changed their meanings.

When we read old written English the words we often have to be most careful about are not those which we don't recognise (we have got to look those up anyway), but those which we think we do. This is well-illustrated by the best-known of the earliest dictionaries in English which was compiled by Samuel Johnson in the eighteenth century. Below are a list of words and their meanings taken from Johnson's *Dictionary*. However, the words and definitions have been jumbled up. Look at them closely and try to match the words with their eighteenth-century meanings. There are enough similarities of meaning to get them all correct.

acoustics	as much food as one's hand can hold
bad	vulgar, mean, common
chicken	the age from fourteen to twenty-eight
dam	inability to sleep
evil	splendid, magnificent, grand
fireman	medicines to help learning
gob	sick
heater	a term for a young girl
imp	a human mother
jogger	malady, disease
lunch	a man of violent passions
modern	a small quantity
nocent	an iron made hot and put into a box-iron, to smooth and plait linen
ouch	a son
pompous	one who moves heavily and slowly
ruth	guilty, criminal
snivel	an ornament of gold or jewels
teen	mercy, pity, tenderness
vegetable	snot, the running of the nose
watching	any thing that has growth
youth	sorrow, grief

Ignoring 'nocent', write a short definition of each of the words in the left-hand column that would show its modern usage.

'Johnson's *Dictionary*, a booksellers' project, was what its age demanded – a standard and standardizing dictionary . . .'. So wrote Professors J Sledd and G Kolb about the work. The intention was to 'fix' the English Language; to have a standard against which writers could be judged. This was a preoccupation during the eighteenth century. Jonathan Swift, author of *Gulliver's Travels* thought that language change was synonymous with corruption and he was concerned that, as a writer, nobody would be able to understand his writing in the following generation if so many changes were allowed to take place. He wrote a letter to The Earl of Oxford, Lord Treasurer, in 1714:

> 'I do here, in the name of all the learned and polite persons of the nation complain to your Lordship as first minister, that our language is extremely imperfect; that its daily improvements are by no means in proportion to its daily corruptions; that the pretenders to polish and refine it have chiefly multiplied abuses and absurdities; and that in many instances it offends against every part of grammar. (. . .) What I have most at heart is that some method should be thought on for ascertaining and fixing our language for ever, after such alterations are made in it as shall be thought requisite. For I am of opinion, it is better a language should not be wholly perfect, than that it should be perpetually changing.'

Language change continues to be of concern at the present time. Consider, for instance, the words of Prince Charles, in a speech made in 1989. Here the Prince was registering his dismay at what he sees as the way in which English has become corrupted by slang, colloquialism and incorrect usage. In order to make his point, he offers a 'modern' version of a famous speech from Shakespeare's *Hamlet*.

How the Prince of Denmark put it

To be, or not to be – that is the question;
Whether 'tis nobler in the mind to suffer
The slings and arrows of outrageous fortune,
Or to take arms against a sea of troubles,
And by opposing end them? To die, to sleep –
No more; and by a sleep to say we end
The heartache and the thousand natural shocks
That flesh is heir to. 'Tis a consummation
Devoutly to be wish'd. To die, to sleep;
To sleep: perchance to dream, there's the rub;
For in that sleep of death what dreams may come,
When we have shuffled off this mortal coil,
Must give us pause.
(*Hamlet* Act III, Scene i)

How the Prince of Wales put it

Well, frankly, the problem as I see it
At this moment in time is whether I
Should just lie down under all this hassle
And let them walk all over me,
Or, whether I should just say: 'OK,
I get the message', and do myself in,
I mean, let's face it, I'm in a no-win
Situation, and quite honestly,
I'm so stuffed up to here with the whole
Stupid mess that, I can tell you, I've just
Got a good mind to take the quick way out.
That's the bottom line. The only problem is:
What happens if I find that when I've bumped
Myself off there's some kind of a, you know,
All that mystical stuff about when you die,
You might find you're still – know what I mean?

Into the text

Look closely at the language of *How the Prince of Wales put it*. Identify the words and phrases that you recognise as being in current use. Explain what they mean. Are there any that you don't recognise? What do you think they might mean? Can you think of other examples of common speech that some people take objection to?

Approaching the text

Many people consider that 'modernisms' show how language has lost its once high standards. But, it is interesting to see that this view is not shared by Dr Johnson, in his Preface to the *Dictionary*. As you read it, try to identify the main points of his argument.

_____ *Dictionary of the English Language* _____
Samuel Johnson

'Of the event of this work, for which, having laboured it with so much application, I cannot but have some degree of parental fondness, it is natural to form conjectures. Those who have been persuaded to think well of my design, require that it should fix our language, and put a stop to those alterations which time and chance have hitherto been suffered to make in it without opposition. With this consequence I will confess that I flattered myself for a while; but now begin to fear that I have indulged expectation which neither reason nor experience can justify. When we see men grow old and die at a certain time one after another, from century to century, we laugh at the elixir that promises to prolong life to a thousand years; and with equal justice may the lexicographer be derided, who being able to produce no example of a nation that has

10

preserved their words and phrases from mutability, shall imagine that his dictionary can embalm his language, and secure it from corruption and decay, that it is in his power to change sublunary nature, or clear the world at once from folly, vanity, and affectation.

With this hope, however, academies have been instituted, to guard the avenues of their languages, to retain fugitives, and repulse intruders; but their vigilance and activity have hitherto been vain; sounds are too volatile and subtle for legal restraints; to enchain syllables, and to lash   20
the wind, are equally the undertakings of pride, unwilling to measure its desires by its strength. (. . .)

Total and sudden transformations of a language seldom happen; conquests and migrations are now very rare; but there are other causes of change, which, though slow in their operation, and invisible in their progress, are perhaps as much superior to human resistance, as the revolutions of the sky, or intumescence of the tide. Commerce, however necessary, however lucrative, as it depraves the manners, corrupts the language; they that have frequent intercourse with strangers, to who they endeavour to accommodate themselves, must in time learn a   30
mingled dialect, like the jargon which serves the traffickers on the Mediterranean and Indian coasts. This will not always be confined to the exchange, the warehouse, or the port, but will be communicated by degrees to other ranks of the people, and be at last incorporated with the current speech.

There are likewise internal causes equally forcible. The language most likely to continue long without alteration, would be that of a nation raised a little, and but a little, above barbarity, secluded from strangers, and totally employed in procuring the conveniences of life; either without books, or, like some of the Mahometan countries, with   40
very few: men thus busied and unlearned, having only such words as common use requires, would perhaps long continue to express the same notions by the same signs. (. . .) Those who have much leisure to think, will always be enlarging the stock of ideas, and every increase of knowledge, whether real or fancied, will produce new words, or combinations of words. When the mind is unchained from necessity, it will range after convenience; when it is left at large in the fields of speculation, it will shift opinion; as any custom is disused, the words that expressed it must perish with it; as any opinion grows popular, it will innovate speech in the same proportion as it alters practice.'   50

Into the text

1 What was Johnson's hope when he set about compiling his Dictionary? Why was he subsequently disappointed?
2 What factors does he identify as bringing about changes in a language?
3 In the end, does he think that a fixed language is desirable?

Approaching the text

A twentieth-century linguist shows similar recognition that language, by its very nature, cannot be fixed.

The English Language
David Crystal

Of course, not everyone likes the rate at which English vocabulary continues to expand. There is often an antagonistic reaction to new words. Computer jargon has its adherents, but it also has its critics. Old rural dialect words may be admired, but the new words from urban dialects are often reviled. The latest slang is occasionally thought of as vivid and exciting, but more often it is condemned as imprecise and sloppy. The news that fresh varieties of English are developing around the world, bringing large numbers of new words, is seen by some as a good thing, adding still further to the expressive potential of the language; but many people shake their heads, and mutter about the   10
language going downhill. (. . .)

People take vocabulary very personally, and will readily admit to having 'pet hates' about the way other people use words. Vocabulary – and especially change in vocabulary – is one of the most controversial issues in the field of language study. Some people are simply against language change on principle. Others, more sensibly, become worried only when they perceive a usage to be developing which seems to remove a useful distinction in meaning, or to add an ambiguity. (. . .)

It's difficult to say whether this kind of criticism can halt a change in meaning or use. The history of the language shows how thousands of   20
words have altered their meaning over time, or added new meanings. The vocabulary now is not what it was in Shakespeare's day, and Shakespeare's vocabulary wasn't the same as Chaucer's. In Anglo-Saxon, *meat* meant 'food'; today, it means a certain type of food. (. . .) *Notorious* once meant 'widely-known'; today it means 'widely and unfavourably known'. Similarly, *pretty* once meant 'ingenious' ('a pretty plot'), a *villain* was a farm labourer, *naughty* meant 'worth noting', and a *publican* was a public servant.

People do not object to these changes in meaning today, or even notice them, because the new uses have been with·us for a very long time.   30
Objections are only made to words that are currently in the process of change. (. . .)

Do such objections do any good? It is difficult to know whether they can raise public consciousness sufficiently to influence the course of language change. The processes that govern change seem too complex and deeply rooted in society for the voices of a few individuals to have much effect.

Into the text

1 After reading David Crystal's views, what can you find there which **a** supports Dr Johnson's argument? and **b** questions the position adopted by Prince Charles?

2 David Crystal identifies a number of sources for new words and new meanings (eg computer jargon). Below are 24 words and phrases which have come into the language since the 1960s. For each, write a

brief dictionary entry, identifying its meaning and if possible, its source:

- AIDS
- bimbo
- bit
- burnt out
- cd
- chip
- decoder
- designer clothes
- dish
- feedback
- glasnost
- k
- mindset
- mouse
- prioritize
- street-wise
- take it on board
- turbo
- user-friendly
- yuppy.

Also give a modern definition of the words from Crystal's article:

- naughty
- publican
- pretty
- villain.

On a darkling plain: Poetic language

Stability and change has always been a major preoccupation of poets. This takes many forms. At its simplest, poets write about the transitory nature of living things. They also reflect on social and historical change. The very act of writing a poem is an attempt to arrest the processes of time and change. The poems that follow deal with these themes.

Approaching the text

'The Darkling Thrush' was written at the very end of the nineteenth century and reflects the doubts and anxieties that many of us may feel as we approach 'significant' dates. (Think about how you will feel on 31 December, 1999!) As you read the poem, think about the mood and attitude of the poet.

The Darkling Thrush
Thomas Hardy

I leant upon a coppice gate
  When Frost was spectre-gray,
And Winter's dregs made desolate
  The weakening eye of day.
The tangled bine-stems scored the sky   5
  Like strings of broken lyres,
And all mankind that haunted nigh
  Had sought their household fires.

The land's sharp features seemed to be
    The Century's corpse outleant,   10
His crypt the cloudy canopy,
    The wind his death-lament.
The ancient pulse of germ and birth
    Was shrunken hard and dry,
And every spirit upon earth   15
    Seemed fervourless as I.

At once a voice arose among
    The bleak twigs overhead
In a full-hearted evensong
    Of joy illimited;   20
An aged thrush, frail, gaunt, and small,
    In blast-beruffled plume,
Had chosen thus to fling his soul
    Upon the growing gloom.

So little cause for carolings   25
    Of such ecstatic sound
Was written on terrestrial things
    Afar or nigh around,
That I could think there trembled through
    His happy good-night air   30
Some blessed Hope, whereof he knew
    And I was unaware.

Into the text

1 In the first two stanzas, Hardy introduces us to his state of mind by reference to what he sees around him and the particular moment in the calendar. Identify as many elements as you can which create and sustain the pessimistic tone.

2 Although the thrush appears to be part of the scene (in what ways?) it surprises Hardy. How does its behaviour contrast with Hardy's mood?

3 In the final stanza, Hardy is left puzzled, provoking the reader to ask what it means. What conclusions do you draw from the event?

Approaching the text

Matthew Arnold wrote 'Dover Beach' in 1867. The poem reflects on the problems of living through a period of great social and cultural change.

The nineteenth century saw major developments in many areas of life such as industry, technology and science, but this was accompanied by a loss of older beliefs and traditions – especially religious faith. Arnold specifically refers to the retreat of the 'sea of faith' and sees human lives to be now surrounded by doubt and uncertainty. As you read the poem, try to identify any consolations that Arnold turns to in this confusing and pessimistic world.

Dover Beach
Matthew Arnold

The sea is calm tonight.
The tide is full, the moon lies fair
Upon the straits; on the French coast, the light
Gleams, and is gone; the cliffs of England stand,
Glimmering and vast, out in the tranquil bay.   5
Come to the window, sweet is the night air!
Only, from the long line of spray
Where the ebb meets the moon-blanch'd sand,
Listen! You hear the grating roar
Of pebbles which the waves suck back, and fling,   10
At their return, up the high strand,
Begin, and cease, and then again begin,
With tremulous cadence slow, and bring
The eternal note of sadness in.

Sophocles long ago   15
Heard it on the Ægean, and it brought
Into his mind the turbid ebb and flow
Of human misery; we
Find also in the sound a thought,
Hearing it by this distant northern sea.   20

The Sea of Faith
Was once, too, at the full, and round earth's shore
Lay like the folds of a bright girdle furl'd;
But now I only hear
Its melancholy, long, withdrawing roar,   25
Retreating to the breath
Of the night-wind down the vast edges drear
And naked shingles of the world.

Ah, love, let us be true
To one another! for the world, which seems   30
To lie before us like a land of dreams,
So various, so beautiful, so new,
Hath really neither joy, nor love, nor light,
Nor certitude, nor peace, nor help for pain;
And we are here as on a darkling plain   35
Swept with confused alarms of struggle and flight,
Where ignorant armies clash by night.

Into the text

1 Look closely at the first six lines. How would you describe the mood here? Which words would you choose to justify your assessment?

2 At what point in the first stanza does the mood change? What words suggest that the poet's perception of the scene has changed?

3 Like Sophocles, Arnold uses the sea as a metaphor but in this case to illustrate the decline of ideals or principles and a loss of faith in the nineteenth century. How does Arnold develop the metaphor of the sea to allow him to contrast the past with the uncertainties of the present?

4 The final stanza sums up the paradox of the Victorian age: great material progress but a spiritual wasteland. Which two phrases highlight this paradox?

Approaching the text

Unlike 'Dover Beach', 'To Autumn' takes a much more optimistic view of change: that it is necessary; that decay is a reality of life which we have to come to accept. But this is balanced by a perception of another reality: that nature is cyclical; that it renews itself; that if Summer must end and give way to Autumn, there will be another Spring to follow it. As you read the poem, consider the ways in which Keats persuades us to think that it is fitting and appropriate for Autumn to end.

To Autumn
John Keats

Season of mists and mellow fruitfulness,
  Close bosom-friend of the maturing sun;
Conspiring with him how to load and bless
  With fruit the vines that round the thatch-eves run;
To bend with apples the moss'd cottage-trees,   5
  And fill all fruit with ripeness to the core;
    To swell the gourd, and plump the hazel shells
  With a sweet kernel; to set budding more,
And still more, later flowers for the bees,
Until they think warm days will never cease,   10
  For summer has o'er – brimmed their clammy cells.

Who hath not seen thee oft amid thy store?
  Sometimes whoever seeks abroad may find
Thee sitting careless on a granary floor,
  Thy hair soft-lifted by the winnowing wind;   15
Or on a half-reaped furrow sound asleep,
  Drowsed with the fume of poppies, while thy hook
    Spares the next swath and all its twined flowers:
And sometimes like a gleaner thou dost keep
  Steady thy laden head across a brook;   20
  Or by a cider-press, with patient look,
    Thou watchest the last oozings hours by hours.

Where are the songs of Spring? Ay, where are they?
  Think not of them, thou hast thy music too, –
While barred clouds bloom the soft-dying day,   25
  And touch the stubble-plains with rosy hue;
Then in a wailful choir the small gnats mourn
  Among the river sallows, borne aloft
    Or sinking as the light wind lives or dies;
And full-grown lambs loud bleat from hilly bourn,   30
  Hedge-crickets sing; and now with treble soft
  The red-breast whistles from a garden-croft:
    And gathering swallows twitter in the skies.

Into the text

1 In the first stanza, how many examples can you find that reveal Keats' view that Summer has reached maturity?

2 Keats personifies both Summer and Autumn. Concentrate on the figure of Autumn. What qualities does Keats give to Autumn? What do you think happens to 'her' (is it a woman?) in the final stanza?

3 What evidence can you find for renewal and optimism in the final stanza?

Approaching the text

In 'Spring', Hopkins draws on a variety of resources of language in order to create a sense of the vitality and freshness of Spring and his own personal excitement about it. The poem also reflects his own belief that the joys of Spring cannot last. Hopkins, a Jesuit priest, believed that Spring recalled the innocence of the Garden of Eden, now lost. Hopkins believed that faith in Christ was a way of recovering that state. As you read the poem, identify the poetic techniques that Hopkins employs.

Spring

Gerald Manley Hopkins

Nothing is so beautiful as spring –
    When weeds, in wheels, shoot long and lovely and lush;
    Thrush's eggs look little low heavens, and thrush
Through the echoing timber does so rinse and wring
The ear, it strikes like lightnings to hear him sing;   5
    The glassy peartree leaves and blooms, they brush
    The descending blue; that blue is all in a rush
With richness; the racing lambs too have fair their fling.

What is all this juice and all this joy?
    A strain of the earth's sweet being in the beginning   10
        In Eden garden. – Have, get, before it cloy,
    Before it cloud, Christ, lord, and sour with sinning,
Innocent mind and Mayday in girl and boy,
    Most, O maid's child, thy choice and worthy the winning.

Into the text

1 List the features of Spring that Hopkins refers to. What do they have in common?

2 In order to create a sense of the vitality and energy of Spring, Hopkins employs alliteration, assonance, rhyme (including internal rhyme) and repetition. Identify some of these features and comment on their effectiveness.

3 What evidence can you find that Hopkins knows that Spring will decay?

Approaching the text

Shelley often used his poetry to deflate or attack powerful rulers. In this poem, the traveller recounts finding the remains of the statue of Ozymandias, a tyrant whose empire has passed into history. As you read the poem, try and get a notion of the character of the King.

Ozymandias
Percy Bysshe Shelley

I met a traveller from an antique land
Who said: "Two vast and trunkless legs of stone
Stand in the desert. Near them, on the sand,
Half sunk, a shattered visage lies, whose frown,
And wrinkled lip, and sneer of cold command,   5
Tell that its sculptor well those passions read
Which yet survive, stamped on these lifeless things,
The hand that mocked them, and the heart that fed:
And on the pedestal these words appear:
'My name is Ozymandias, King of Kings: 10
Look on my works, ye Mighty, and despair!'
Nothing beside remains. Round the decay
Of that colossal wreck, boundless and bare
The lone and level sands stretch far away."

Into the text

1 What do you think Shelley's attitude towards Ozymandias is?
2 Beside the poet, there are three 'voices' in this poem. Who are they?
3 What is the effect of the words on the pedestal? How does their meaning in the context of the poem differ from that intended by Ozymandias?
4 What message does the poem contain?

Approaching the text

In the Elizabethan period, wealthy aristocrats sometimes paid poets to sing their praises in verse. In this sonnet, unlike the other poems you have read in this section, Shakespeare suggests that the poem itself will resist time and change by conferring immortality on the patron. As you read the poem, consider what aspects of change are identified by Shakespeare.

Sonnet 55

William Shakespeare

Not marble, nor the gilded monuments
Of princes shall outlive this pow'rful rhyme;
But you shall shine more bright in these contents
Than unswept stone, besmear'd with sluttish time.
When wasteful war shall statues overturn,   5
And broils root out the work of masonry,
Nor Mars his sword nor war's quick fire shall burn
The living record of your memory.
'Gainst death and all-oblivious emnity
Shall you pace forth; your praise shall still find room,   10
Even in the eyes of all posterity
That wear this world out to the ending doom.
    So, till the judgment that your self arise,
    You live in this, and dwell in lovers' eyes.

Into the text

1 The poet suggests that his lines about the patron will outlast any statue of him. What would statues be at risk from that the poem is not?

2 How does Shakespeare convince you that the sonnet will last for ever?

3 What impression do you get of the patron from the poem?

4 What do you think is meant by the following:
   . . . besmear'd with sluttish time (line 4)
   . . . all-oblivious emnity (line 9)
   . . . the eyes of all posterity (line 11).

Stepping out: A playscript

Approaching the text

The play from which the following extract is taken tells the story of a disaffected fifth-year pupil who 'kidnaps' three teachers in a store room. In the extract he is exploring his school experiences with his teachers and constructing a possible future for himself as he anticipates leaving school. As you read it, consider the extent to which you share the boy's feelings about his schooling.

Gotcha
Barrie Keefe

KID   What's after today for me . . . anyhow . . . I've been here, getting prepared for today for . . . five years. The great day. Stepping out into the wide wide world, an' that. One of . . . how many kids here? Twelve hundred, eh. What's going to happen to this one here – [*He points at himself.*] – after today? Hmmm? Mmmm? Fifty years of working life is . . . all spread out in front of me . . . they say when you drown, in the last seconds before you go under, the whole of your life passes before your eyes . . . Well, this morning as we all stood there in the assembly, and the choir sang them hymns and the brass band   10 blowed on their bugles and those clever bastards chanted out their bit of rhyme in Latin, an' that . . . and the mayor made his speech, so proud, so proud . . . and we all said them prayers to God Almighty . . . and we watched all them clever kids getting their prizes . . . clapping, clapping . . . going to university . . . clapping clapping . . . playing cricket for England. Boys in Pakistan . . . clapping clapping . . . well, me life didn't pass in front of me eyes . . . but me future did. A great mist of nothing . . . [*Silence. He lights a cigarette. Looks out of the window.*]

(. . .)

KID   (. . .) First day here . . . lined up in front of you, all hundreds of us – the new kids. Lined up in the playground . . . all of us   20 in lines and you wandering along, eyes flickering over us . . . deciding who's doing what, who's going where. Flick of the eyes . . . he's got a nice jacket. Clean trousers and a starched handkerchief . . . GCSEs for him. Like Farty says, you see the no-hopers . . . relegate them. Out of the way.
[*He takes a long drag on his cigarette.*]
Listen to your chat, speech-day – mayor there . . . talking. About how proud he is of this school, this everso terrific comprehensive school . . . the big, big, school . . . everyone all together . . . all chances, hundreds of subjects, something for everyone, put out your hand and take what you want – But . . .   30 watched your eyes . . . not even looking at the poor sod of a mayor. 'Humour him,' your eyes said. 'Humour him. Dreamer!'
[*He sighs. Pause.*]
Now . . . found out . . . I was right. Comprehensive! [*He spits.*] Me brother, me brother wow, what he said about it when I come here! Chance for you, kiddo, he said to me. Secondary school he went to. No hope. Chucked in there. Factory fodder, but this comprehensive! Paradise. So different he said . . . and he supposed to know. Knows the mayor, delivered his leaflets for him at elections, me brother did. Knew all about what was gonna happen in this new school. This is your big chance, kiddo, he   40 says . . .
[*Pause.*]
Got it wrong. Just the same. Only bigger. Anything you want here, they said. Yeah. If you're clever, if you're bright, big hope . . . glittering prizes! Just the same, as it was for me brother . . . just . . . the same. Only bigger. Achievement . . . successes . . . only way it's judged . . . all them GCSEs, all them A levels, all them clever bastards going to university. What a clever headmaster, what a smashing lot a teachers, what a great school. What a fantastic school – What about us? Who don't do GCSEs? What about me, eh? How good is this?   50
[*He throws the report on the floor. Stamps on it. Stands breathing deeply.*]

HEAD   It is . . . never easy to build a perfect world . . . a new Jerusalem in Rainham . . . It's a gradual process, slow steps . . . making a net of tighter mesh . . . it takes time.

KID   Time, I do not have. Only . . . one life.

HEAD   Even so, every opportunity has been afforded to you here. If you have some grievance –

KID   You don't even know me name!

(. . .)

KID   I said, brain surgeon –
HEAD   A doctor first –
KID   I dunno about that.   60
HEAD   I think, the best way –
KID   All right then, I'll take your advice.
HEAD   Good. Doctor, then specialise.
KID   On brains.
HEAD   Quite.
KID   So, it's possible?
HEAD   Probable.
KID   Even though, I never did no exams here, no GCSEs or –
HEAD   O, I think qualifications are somewhat overrated, you know –
KID   Yerr, here – have a fag.   70
HEAD   One thinks of Shakespeare . . . Churchill . . . men who
       achieved, succeeded without the advantage of . . . GCSEs.
       [*He laughs, the kid laughs.*]
KID   Churchill eh.
HEAD   Not a success at school. Nor Milton nor Van Gogh nor –
KID   Andy Fairwheather-Low?
HEAD   Proves my point. Great shortage of brain surgeons.
KID   Specially ones without any GCSEs.
HEAD   Always in demand. Excellent career prospects.
KID   Great.
HEAD   But, have to work hard.   80
KID   Some people'd say – what you're telling me, all a dream. A load
       of crap to keep me quiet.
HEAD   Ah –
KID   But you wouldn't lie to me, would you – wouldn't tell the kids
       here – the ones who ain't no good at nothing – you wouldn't
       raise their hopes would you when you didn't mean what you was
       saying.
HEAD   Certainly not. Dreams materialise here . . . if you work hard,
       study hard, apply yourself – application and –
KID   Be a brain surgeon.   90
HEAD   You shall be a brain surgeon if that is what you want.
KID   And play for West Ham.
       [*Pause.*]
       Striker.

Into the text

1 Why does the kid think the school has failed him? How
   does the Headmaster try to answer his criticisms? Use
   evidence from the text to support your answer.
2 What expectations had the brother raised for the kid
   before he started at the comprehensive school?
3 The kid throws his report on to the floor and stamps on
   it. What do you think it said? From reading the extract,
   could you write an alternative report showing what is
   'good' about the kid?

4 *Gotcha* has a serious intention but presents much of its message through humour. Do you find this extract humorous? Can you identify what you find humorous? Does the humour detract from or enhance the play's message?

Assignments

1 The following poem is about the dreams that people have of a life different from their own.

The Heroines
Penny Windsor

We are the terraced women
piled row upon row on the sagging, slipping hillsides of our lives.
We tug reluctant children up slanting streets
the pushchair wheels wedging in the ruts.
Breathless and bad-tempered we shift the Tesco carrier-bags from hand   5
    to hand
and stop to watch the town.

The hilltops creep away like children playing games.

Our other children shriek against the schoolyard rails –
    'There's Mandy's mum, John's mum, Dave's mum, Kate's   10
    mum, Ceri's mother, Tracey's mummy.'
We wave with hands scarred by groceries and too much washing-up
catching echoes as we pass of old wild games.

After lunch, more bread and butter, tea,
we dress in blue and white and pink and white checked overalls   15
and do the house and scrub the porch and sweep the street
and clean all the little terraces
up and down and up and down and up and down the hill.

Later, before the end-of-school bell rings,
all the babies are asleep   20
Mandy's mum joins Ceri's mum across the street
running to avoid the rain
and Dave's mum and John's mum – the others too – stop by for tea
and briefly we are wild women
girls with secrets, travellers, engineers, courtesans, and stars of   25
    fiction, films
plotting our escape like jail-birds
terraced, Tescoed prisoners rising from the household dust like heroines.

a What does the woman in the poem resent about her present existence?

b What do you think the poet means by

'. . . the terraced women' (line 1)

'. . . hands scarred by groceries' (line 5)

'Tescoed prisoners . . .' (line 28)?

c How do you think 'the terraced women' become 'like heroines'?

d What is the connection between 'the old wild games' (line 13) and the 'wild women' (line 24)?

e The poem may be seen as being about unfulfilled potential: there is more to the women than the outward circumstances of their lives suggest. Do you think that they would be more fulfilled in their fantasy roles?

2 The following extract is taken from *Tess of the d'Urbervilles* by Thomas Hardy, first published in 1891. Hardy often wrote about the changes taking place in rural England in the nineteenth century and how they affected the lives of the people who lived there. Among the changes was the introduction of steam-powered agricultural machinery which replaced the old labour-intensive methods. This extract describes an occasion when a steam-thresher arrives at a farm where Tess has been working.

The Red Tyrant
Thomas Hardy

It is the threshing of the last wheat-rick at Flintcomb-Ash Farm. The dawn of the March morning is singularly inexpressive, and there is nothing to show where the eastern horizon lies. Against the twilight rises the trapezoidal top of the stack, which has stood forlornly here through the washing and bleaching of the wintry weather.

When Izz Huett and Tess arrived at the scene of operations only a rustling denoted that others had preceded them; to which, as the light increased, there were presently added the silhouettes of two men on the summit. They were busily 'unhaling' the rick, that is, stripping off the thatch before beginning to throw down the sheaves; and while this was   10
in progress Izz and Tess, with the other women-workers, in their whitey-brown pinners, stood waiting and shivering, Farmer Groby having insisted upon their being on the spot thus early to get the job over if possible by the end of the day. Close under the eaves of the stack, and as yet barely visible, was the red tyrant that the women had come to serve – a timber-framed construction, with straps and wheels appertaining – the threshing-machine which, whilst it was going, kept up a despotic demand upon the endurance of their muscles and nerves.

A little way off there was another indistinct figure; this one black, with a sustained hiss that spoke of strength very much in reserve. The long   20
chimney running up beside an ash-tree, and the warmth which radiated from the spot, explained without the necessity of much daylight that here was the engine which was to act as the *primum mobile* of this little world. By the engine stood a dark motionless being, a sooty and grimy embodiment of tallness, in a sort of trance, with a heap of coals by his

side: it was the engineman. The isolation of his manner and colour lent
him the appearance of a creature from Tophet, who had strayed into the
pellucid smokelessness of this region of yellow grain and pale soil, with
which he had nothing in common, to amaze and to discompose its
aborigines.   30

What he looked he felt. He was in the agricultural world, but not of
it. He served fire and smoke; these denizens of the fields served
vegetation, weather, frost, and sun. He travelled with his engine from
farm to farm, from county to county, for as yet the steam-threshing
machine was itinerant in this part of Wessex. He spoke in a strange
northern accent; his thoughts being turned inwards upon himself, his eye
on his iron charge, hardly perceiving the scenes around him, and caring
for them not at all: holding only strictly necessary intercourse with the
natives, as if some ancient doom compelled him to wander here against
his will in the service of his Plutonic master. The long strap which ran   40
from the driving-wheel of his engine to the red thresher under the rick
was the sole tie-line between agriculture and him.

While they uncovered the sheaves he stood apathetic beside his
portable repository of force, round whose hot blackness the morning air
quivered. He had nothing to do with the preparatory labour. His fire
was waiting incandescent, his steam was at high pressure, in a few
seconds he could make the long strap move at an invisible velocity.
Beyond its extent the environment might be corn, straw, or chaos; it was
all the same to him. If any of the autochthonous idlers asked him what
he called himself, he replied shortly, 'An engineer'.   50

The rick was unhaled by full daylight; the men then took their places,
the women mounted, and the work began. Farmer Groby – or, as they
called him, 'he – had arrived ere this, and by his orders Tess was placed
on the platform of the machine, close to the man who fed it, her business
being to untie every sheaf of corn handed on to her by Izz Huett, who
stood next, but on the rick; so that the feeder could seize it and spread
it over the revolving drum, which whisked out every grain in one
moment.

They were soon in full progress, after a preparatory hitch or two,
which rejoiced the hearts of those who hated machinery. The work sped   60
on till breakfast-time, when the thresher was stopped for half an hour;
and on starting again after the meal the whole supplementary strength
of the farm was thrown into the labour of constructing the straw-rick,
which began to grow beside the stack of corn. A hasty lunch was eaten
as they stood, without leaving their positions, and then another couple
of hours brought them near to dinner-time; the inexorable wheels
continuing to spin, and the penetrating hum of the thresher to thrill to
the very marrow all who were near the revolving wire-cage.

The old men on the rising straw-rick talked of the past days when they
had been accustomed to thresh with flails on the oaken barn-floor; when   70
everything, even to winnowing, was effected by hand-labour, which, to
their thinking, though slow, produced better results. Those, too, on the
corn-rick talked a little; but the perspiring ones at the machine, including
Tess, could not lighten their duties by the exchange of many words.
It was the ceaselessness of the work which tried her so severely, and

began to make her wish that she had never come to Flintcomb-Ash. The women on the corn-rick – Marian, who was one of them, in particular – could stop to drink ale or cold tea from the flagon now and then, or to exchange a few gossiping remarks while they wiped their faces or cleared the fragments of straw and husk from their clothing; but   80 for Tess there was no respite; for, as the drum never stopped, the man who fed it could not stop, and she, who had to supply the man with untied sheaves, could not stop either, unless Marian changed places with her, which she sometimes did for half an hour in spite of Groby's objection that she was too slow-handed for a feeder.

a What do you think is meant by the following phrases:
  - 'The dawn of the March morning is singularly inexpressive . . .' (lines 1–2)
  - '. . . the threshing machine . . . kept up a despotic demand . . .' (lines 17–18)
  - 'He was in the agricultural world, but not of it.' (lines 31–2)
  - '. . . he stood apathetic beside his portable repository of force . . .' (lines 43–4)?

b There are some words in the passage that even a Victorian readership would have found difficult. Look at the list below. In each case, make a guess at an approximate meaning and then check the accuracy of your guesses in a dictionary.
  - trapezoidal
  - Tophet
  - denizens
  - autochthonous
  - *primum mobile*
  - pellucid
  - Plutonic.

c How does Hardy present the contrast between the past and present? From the evidence of the passage, what do you think is his view of the changes that have taken place?

d Hardy describes the working day in a couple of paragraphs, and at no time does he tell us directly how his heroine feels about working on the machine. Write a description, from Tess' point of view, of her working day, from the time of her arrival in the field until dinner-time. Base your account on the evidence in the passage and make it clear how Tess feels about her experiences.

3 Given the apparent inevitability of change, and the possibility of change being for the better, or for the worse, identify three or four features of modern life that you would like to see change for the better. In each case, describe the current situation and then the changes that you would like to see, and what you can do to help bring them about.

Reference Section

Contents

Introduction

The following pages offer some definitions and some approaches to help you to become an active reader, and some guidelines for some of the writing tasks and assignments. While this section will not meet all of your needs, it will provide you with a starting point in some particular areas where students often need some preliminary explanation or advice.

Students are often intimidated by poetry. The section 'On reading a poem' is designed to help you through the process of understanding a poet's ideas.

'On writing' assumes that you will have practised the skills which lead to effective writing in the earlier years of your education. The questions raised here will help you build on these and take more responsibility for your own written work – its purposes, audience, structure, etc – as you tackle the assignments in the units.

Playwriting is a specialised form of literary creativity and the section 'On writing a play' has been written by practising playwrights and offers preliminary guidance.

The wider reading list is included to give you access to books that you may not know, but which you can read in order to meet the independent reading requirements of the National Curriculum and your GCSE course.

Finally, we have included glossaries of both literary and language terms: in this section you can check any terms that you don't understand. The National Curriculum in English requires that you can use and understand the terms found here.

On reading a poem

As you study the different units in this book, you are asked to read and comment upon a number of poems. The ideas that follow will give you some help in reading poetry, and particularly in reading those poems which you come across for the first time.

Some hints

1 Read the poem through once – perhaps aloud – to get a feel for it. Don't worry about detailed meaning at this stage. Then read it through carefully at least twice more.

2 Note down any words or phrases that you find difficult to understand. Look at the context of any words or phrases that you don't understand. Does the context help you to work out the meaning? Discuss your problems in your group and attempt to clarify the meanings. If in doubt, ask your teacher.

3 Try to identify the tone of the poem. Poems can vary a great deal in their tone. Consider these examples:

> Forgive me for making you weep,
> I should have murdered you,
> I should have dragged out your soul
> and battered you with it.
>
> (Nina Cassian)

The first line suggests an apologetic tone but the other three lines make it clear that the tone of this poem is violent anger.
What do you think is the tone in this extract?

What shall we do with the drunken poet?
> Thinking of you on a waterbed
> Feeling
> Seasick with jealousy.
>
> (Adrian Henri)

or this?

> Woman much missed, how you call to me, call to me,
> Saying that now you are not as you were
> When you had changed from the one who was all to me
> But as at first, when our day was fair.
>
> (Thomas Hardy)

You may come across other tones: thoughtful, optimistic, excited, urgent, pleading, fulfilled, etc.
4 Look for the poet's use of imagery, eg metaphor and simile. These are used to make the writing more powerful; to make the reader use his/her imagination to recreate the 'picture' the writer had.
To remind you, a **simile** uses the words 'like' or 'as', eg
  'My love is like a red, red rose . . .'
A **metaphor** sees one thing in terms of something else, eg
  'He locked me in: his love – a prison.'
Consider the use of imagery in the following poem:

Catching up on Sleep
Roger McGough

i go to bed early
to catch up on my sleep

      but my sleep
is a slippery customer
it bobs and weaves   5
    and leaves
me exhausted. It
side steps my clumsy tackles
with ease. Bed
raggled I drag   10
myself to my knees

The sheep are countless
I pretend to snore
yearn for chloroform
or a sock on the jaw   15
body sweats heart beats
there is Panic in the Sheets
until
as dawn slopes up the stairs
to set me free   20
unawares
sleep catches up on me

5 What is the structure and the form of the poem? Poems can vary a great deal. Some are very regular:

Sonnet 18
William Shakespeare

Shall I compare thee to a summer's day?
Thou art more lovely and more temperate.
Rough winds do shake the darling buds of May,
And summer's lease hath all too short a date:
Sometimes too hot the eye of heaven shines,   5
And often is his gold complexion dimm'd;
And every fair from fair some time declines,
By chance, or nature's changing course, untrimm'd;
But thy eternal summer shall not fade,
Nor lose possession of that fair thou ow'st.   10
Nor shall Death brag thou wand'rest in his shade,
When in eternal lines to time thou grow'st.
   So long as men can breathe or eyes can see,
   So long lives this, and this gives life to thee.

Note:
- all sonnets have 14 lines
- there is a regular rhyme scheme
- all the lines are of the same metrical length: each line has five 'beats'
- the final two lines (a rhyming couplet)) complete the 'argument' of the poem.

Some poems, however, appear to be quite irregular:

> At 3 am
> the room contains no sound
> except the ticking of the clock
> which has begun to panic
> like an insect, trapped   5
> in an enormous box.
>
> Books lie open on the carpet
>
> Somewhere else
> you're sleeping
> and beside you there's a woman   10
> who is crying quietly
> so you won't wake.
>
> (Wendy Cope)

Note:
- there is no rhyme scheme
- the lines are of irregular length
- the title is part of the poem
- even though not as regular as the sonnet, it still has a shape.

6 Finally, ask yourself the questions, 'Do I like this poem?' If so, why? If not, why not?

Try out these simple six steps on this poem:

The Combat
Edwin Muir

> It was not meant for human eyes
> That combat on the shabby patch
> Of clods and trampled turf that lies
> Somewhere beneath the sodden skies
> For eye of toad or adder to catch.   5
>
> And having seen it I accuse
> The crested animal in his pride,
> Arrayed in all the royal hues
> Which hide the claws he well can use
> To tear the heart out of the side.   10

Body of leopard, eagle's head
And wetted beak, and lion's mane,
And frost grey hedge of feathers spread
Behind – he seemed of all things bred.
I shall not see his like again.   15

As for his enemy, there came in
A soft round beast as brown as clay;
All rent and patched his wretched skin;
A battered bag he might have been,
Some old used thing to throw away.   20

Yet he awaited face to face
The furious beast and the swift attack.
Soon over and done. That was no place
Or time for chivalry or for grace.
The fury had him on his back.   25

And two small paws like hands flew out
To right and left as the tree stood by.
One would have said beyond a doubt
This was the very end of the bout,
But that the creature would not die.   30

For ere the death-stroke he was gone,
Writhed, whirled, huddled into his den,
Safe somehow there. The fight was done,
And he had lost who had all but won.
But oh his deadly fury then.   35

A while the place lay blank, forlorn,
Drowsing as in relief from pain.
The cricket chirped, the grating thorn
Stirred, and a little sound was born.
The champions took their posts again.   40

And all began. The stealthy paw
Slashed out and in. Could nothing save
These rags and tatters from the claw?
Nothing. And yet I never saw
A beast so helpless and so brave.   45

And now, while the trees stand watching, still
The unequal battle rages there.
The killing beast that cannot kill
Swells and swells in his fury till
You'd almost think it was despair.   50

On writing

Writers very rarely produce a final version of their work at the first sitting. For instance, the previous sentence went through two versions before we were satisfied with it. Many of the writers represented in this collection will have spent a great deal of time reworking their material until they (and their editors) were happy with it.

You will have been introduced to draft/redraft techniques in the earlier years of schooling and it becomes particularly important as you begin your examination course.

There are certain things that all writers need to think about when putting pen to paper:

- purpose
- audience
- product
- effectiveness
- format
- technique.

Purpose

The question to ask yourself is 'Why am I writing this?'. It may be to record your thinking; to organise your ideas; to remember what you've said in discussion; to inform; to persuade; to recount; to entertain. You need to be clear about your purpose because this will determine the kind of writing you do.

Audience

Who is going to read it? You? Your friends? Your teacher? Your teacher *as examiner*? A stranger? You need to have some idea about your audience as this will affect the style of your writing – its appearance, use of vocabulary, sentence structure, paragraphing, formality.

Product

Writing can be: notes which can be thrown away; something that expects an answer; something that will appear in an examination folder; something that you will keep; a poem; something you use as a basis for discussion; something sent as a message. Knowing what the piece of writing will eventually look like will affect how it is written.

Effectiveness

An effective piece of writing is one where the writer had something to say in such a way that a desirable response would be evoked in a reader. It should also appear as a product that did justice to its importance. In other words, a successful combination of purpose, audience and product.

Format

The format of a piece of writing needs to be consistent with all the above. It could appear as: jottings, notes, typescript, word-processor print-out, letters, entry in a journal, draft manuscript, book, newspaper, magazine, etc.

Technique
How are writing skills developed? By experimenting, talking about writing, responding to your own and others' writing, knowing about techniques and strategies for planning, revising and editing. Central to this is drafting and redrafting.

On writing a play

Some guidelines from Raw Cotton Theatre Company, Blackburn.

Here are a few things to think about before you begin writing short plays, and to refer back to as you are writing.

Dialogue
The basis of drama, as opposed to poetry or prose, is dialogue – two or more people talking to each other. Dialogue should be set out as follows:

JOHN   Sorry to hear about your Dad.
NASEEM   I know. Mum's taken it very hard. I don't know what to do about her.
[She puts her head in her hands. John goes to comfort her.]
JOHN   He's bound to get better, bound to.
NASEEM   He's only 39.
JOHN   That's not old.

Notice the use of **stage direction**. You can also use **monologue** as part of the style of your play. A monologue is where a character speaks directly to the audience and doesn't talk to any other character.

As dialogue is usually built around how people actually speak – do just that. Use your own dialect, unless you want to make a point by having a character who speaks Standard English, or another variety of English. It is important to listen to the way people speak.

Characters
Think about the characters you want to build your play around. These might be young people, similar to yourselves; they may be parents or they might be old people with long memories. Think about the jobs they do: plumbers, bakers, doctors, teachers. Once you have found your characters, you can think about how they interact – how they talk to each other – mothers with daughters, fathers with sons, doctors with patients, etc.

Situation

Where are you going to set your play? If it is to be centred around the family, it is very likely to take place in a living room, with perhaps a few scenes elsewhere – the kitchen, the garden, etc. Think of other places where people might meet – a pub, a café, a doctor's surgery, at the bus-stop, in a car. The place might make a difference to what people might say.

Structure

Through the structure of your play, and its development, you tell your story. Each scene must have a beginning, a middle and an end.

Theme

Writing a play is a chance to say something important, something that you really care about. Your theme might be something that affects us all – love, death, the family; it might be an issue that concerns you alone. Even a serious theme can be written with humour and this is often the best way to get your message across.

Preparation

If your play (or part of it) is set in a hospital or a police station, for example, go to those places, meet the people who work there, ask questions about their jobs. Before you start to write, think carefully about what you want to say. When you start to write, don't hurry to tell the story. Think what people say to avoid saying what they mean. Importantly, re-read your work frequently. Ask yourself questions like: 'Do people speak like this?'; 'Would you say it that way?'; 'Is there another way of saying the same thing?', etc. Be prepared to rewrite it in the light of our own and others' thoughts.

Finally, **read other plays**. You can learn a lot by looking at the work of other writers.

Wider reading list

Val Randall

The National Curriculum in English requires pupils to 'Show involvement and independent choice over a range of genres' and the list that follows is designed to encourage you towards texts that you can read on your own, in addition to the ones that you will read in class.

In each case, there is some information about the book that will help you to choose something that is of possible interest to you. While some of the books may not be available in school, you can always request them from public libraries or bookshops.

When you read the texts, keep a record of what you have read, and brief notes about what you liked or disliked about them. Enthusiastic readers of books öften share their enthusiasm with friends. Be prepared to listen to other people's recommendations and also to recommend books that you have read and enjoyed.

Love and hate

Melusine, a Mystery, Lynn Reid Banks (Hamish Hamilton, ISBN 0 241 12548 0)
Roger and his family occupy a Vendée chateau for a gîte holiday. Melusine, the chatelain's daughter, is woman by day, snake by night and a victim of her father's sexual abuse. Myth references abound and Reid Banks weaves a skilful contrast between the two families which emphasises the horror of Melusine's treatment by her father.

The Woods at the End of Autumn Street, Lois Lowry (Collins, ISBN 0 00 673054 X)
Six-year-old Elizabeth is the narrator of a story set in white, middle-class America during World War II. She tells of her growing relationship with Charles, the son of their negro cook and his brutal murder focuses the racism with which the book is concerned.

Kiss, Linda Hoy (Walker Teens, ISBN 0 7445 1336 7)
Julian Christopher refuses his parents' wealth and joins the Radical Christian Fellowship, allowing him to explore his developing faith and sexuality but placing him under state surveillance. Insecure and vulnerable, he is exploited by James, his homosexual surveillance officer with whom he becomes unwittingly involved.

Annie on my Mind, Nancy Garden (Virago, ISBN 0 86068 271 4)
Liza and Annie fall in love – they appear total opposites and have very different backgrounds and lifestyles, but they are in love. Their developing relationship is chronicled and explored until one dreadful day when their love is put on trial by school, parents and society.

The Secret Line, William Corbett (Walker Teens, ISBN 0 7445 1314 6)
Jo Carson is mixed race, at ease with neither black nor white. The reappearance of her childhood friend, Mit, leads to fantastic journeys on the mysterious Secret Line – a secret section of the Underground. Here she must come to terms with Straker, the vicious thug who menaces her, and with love – love for Mit and, most importantly, for herself.

Belief and conflict

Salt on the Snow, Rukshana Smith (Bodley Head, ISBN 0 370 31203 1)
Julie is re-taking 'A' levels and joins a Volunteer Agency, finding herself tutoring Rashmi, a middle-aged and helpless woman who is being exploited by her brother. Julie's racist family, her own relationship with Rashmi's nephew Kijay, and Rashmi's impoverished immigrant status, raise questions which the reader must resolve.

Frankie's Story, Catherine Sefton (Hamish Hamilton, ISBN 0 241 12206 6)
In present-day Northern Ireland, tough, no-good Frankie, struggling to cope with her father's departure to live with another woman, innocently and absent-mindedly witnesses an IRA/Army incident and is branded a traitor. Frankie is lively and intelligent to those who know her and the novel gives a bleak insight into how such teenagers cope with the Northern Ireland situation.

Up the Attic Stairs, Angela Bull (Virago, ISBN 0 85381 060 6)
Suffragette history unfolds around fashion student Gabriel Klavir as she explores a family attic for antique clothes. Her discoveries stimulate an awareness and understanding of her own relationships and place in society. Bull quietly – and rightly – insists that it is the past which gives us our understanding of the present.

The Devil in Vienna, Doris Orgel (Simon and Schuster, ISBN 0 671 69953 9)
Inge Domerwald, an Austrian Jew, tells of her family's ordeal during the German invasion of Austria in 1938. This is a personal story, telling of relationships fractured by the occupation and of changes in the basic components of life – school, work, leisure.

The Fire of the Kings, Julian Atterton (E J Arnold, ISBN 0 560 55009 X)
Set in seventh-century Britain, this book tells the story of the warring kingdoms of Bernicia and Deira. Edwin and his cousins Henc, Lilla and Osric struggle to maintain peace and in Edwin's case, to rule with strength and fairness in the face of treachery and feuds.

Truths and persuasion
The Last April Dancers, Jean Thesman (Pan, ISBN 0 330 30693 6)
Cath is sixteen. Her long-term friendship with Cameron is beginning to
develop into love but tensions at home cloud the excitement and promise of
her immediate future. Her mother is a perfectionist and her father's state of
mind is deteriorating rapidly. When her father commits suicide, Cath simply
wants to hide but is persuaded back into acceptance of all that life brings
through her trust in Cameron.

The Moves Make the Man, Bruce Brooks (Pan, ISBN 0 330 30236 1)
Jerome Fox is the first black student in Wilmington's biggest white
school and a highly talented basketball player, unruffled by anything he
encounters – until he meets Bix Rivers. Bix is disturbed, unable to realise his
own potential. Jerome is the catalyst, ready to help him to make his move.

Wise Child, Monica Furlong (Gollancz, ISBN 0 575 04046 7)
Wise Child is abandoned by her parents and taken in by Juniper – branded
a witch by the local community. Juniper is, in fact, a healer and Wise Child
becomes her apprentice and close friend but is drawn irresistibly by her
ruthless mother's attempts to reclaim her by sorcery.

On Summer Light, Zibby O'Neil (Collins, ISBN 000 672 7972)
Kate Brewer is the daughter of a famous artist but wants 'her own field
to plough'. The Brewer household revolves around her father and she
is determined to reject this. Instead, through a study of literature, she
reappraises her opposition of him and comes to a better understanding of
him and of herself. A sensitive and delicate exploration of realities through
a subtle layering of experience.

Fade, Robert Cormier (Gollancz, ISBN 0 575 04402 0)
Paul Moreaux discovers he can fade, become invisible. He also discovers
that this is as much a curse as a gift. Years later he becomes a famous writer
and discovers that his nephew has inherited his 'gift'. Can he help? Can he
warn? Will he be believed? The structure of the novel reflects the chro-
nological progression through Moreaux's life but he twists the readers'
expectations in a variety of ways.

Ambition and defeat
Waiting for the Rain, Sheila Gordon (Collins, ISBN 0 00 673389 1)
Frikkie and Tengo have been friends since childhood – but this is South
Africa and Frikkie is white, Tengo black. Tengo has ambitions – education,
self-improvement – but soon senses that white political domination makes
this impossible. Civil unrest divides Tengo and Frikkie and the goals that
each strove for suddenly seem devalued.

Rainbow in the Gutter, Rukshana Smith (Bodley Head, ISBN 0 370 30526 4)
Philip Browne is a black artist – his sister a journalist on a radical newspaper. He tells their story from childhood to maturity, detailing with clarity and restraint the tragedies which befall his family. White society destroyed ambitions, trust and its own integrity.

Dark Toys and Consumer Goods, Lawrence Staig (Macmillan, ISBN 0 333 47561 5)
Staig shows us a futuristic world in these eight short stories, each dedicated to consumerism. Protagonists are metaphorically or literally consumed by the objects of their desires – a dire warning for a world too concerned with the outward show of wealth and the superficial pleasures gained from spending it.

The Fat Girl, Marilyn Sachs (Oxford University Press, ISBN 0 19 271534 8)
Ellen de Luca is fat, unhappy and friendless. Jeff Lyons is revolted by her, then obsessed as he realises she hero-worships him and he can take complete control of her life. When Ellen loses weight Jeff becomes superfluous and Ellen realises how her ambitions have been manipulated by his desire to dominate.

The Ash-Blonde Witch, Kenneth Lillington (Faber, ISBN 0 571 14625 2)
Sophie Margaret Oakroyd, traveller from a sophisticated technological world arrives in the simple community of Urstwile. Her powers get her mistaken as a witch, her skill convinces the people of Urstwile she is a magician. However, Sophie herself is changed by this world of superstition and magic which she has been ordered to observe.

Stability and change
The Day I Shot my Dad, John Branfield (Gollancz, ISBN 0 575 04486 1)
This collection of short stories looks at teenagers finding their independence from adults or adjusting their preconceived ideas about their elders. Boyhood memories, reminiscences of an elderly man, imitation of parents – the scope is wide and the writing interesting and relevant.

The Map of Nowhere, Gillian Cross (Oxford University Press, ISBN 0 19 271583 6)
The title encapsulates the message of this book – each individual must work out his/her own maps for existence and have the strength to do what is right and not be swayed by the opinions of others. Nick's friendship with Joseph and Ruth revolves around playing fantasy games, but he fails to realise that he has been used by his brother, Terry, to provide information for the burglary of the shop which Joseph's parents own.

Blitzcat, Robert Westall (Macmillan, ISBN 0 333 47498 8)
A cat searches for his master in the war-torn England of 1940. This provides a fascinating comment on the social history of the period and a real immediacy in descriptions of such tragedies as the bombing of the city of Coventry. The story skilfully avoids sentiment and provides a rich backdrop of varied and colourful characters.

Nell's Quilt, Susan Ferris (Virago, ISBN 0 86068 087 8)
Nell's diary reveals a familiar dilemma – she is intelligent and ambitious, hoping for a college education, fascinated by her grandmother's role in the suffragette movement. The demands of the New England farming community in which she lives prove impossible to resist, however, and she commits herself to a marriage which will be financially useful to her family. She resolves to control her own body in the way she wished to control the environment and, absorbed in her wedding-quilt making, she begins to sink towards starvation and death.

Where Nobody Sees, James Watson (Collins, ISBN 0 00 672986 X)
Luke has always lived in Wynster Bridge and regarded Furmiston Forest as inviolate, safe and constant as a haven for his beloved badgers. The discovery of a camp deep in the wood leads to a struggle to prevent the nuclear waste secretly stored there being buried in the area. Violence, lies and political manoeuvring await Luke as, with unsuspected allies, he seeks to make the truth heard.

Glossary of literary terms

Alliteration repetition of initial consonants in a line of poetry, eg 'In a summer season, when soft was the sun,' (*Piers Plowman*, William Langland).

Archaism using an out-of-date style of speech, form of words or syntax, eg Mary Shelley's *Frankenstein* (see page 169).

Assonance repetition of vowel sounds in a line of poetry, eg 'The moan of doves in immemorial elms,/And a murmering of innumerable bees.' (*The Princess*, Alfred, Lord Tennyson).

Audience the receivers and responders of a text whether in print, on the stage, or on film. The writer needs to be aware of the intended audience and the audience in turn needs to actively engage with what is seen or read.

Autobiography an account of a person's life written by him/herself. Often writers draw on autobiographical material as the basis for their fictionalised accounts, eg 'White Hot', Tom Wakefield (page 193).

Ballad originally a song intended to accompany a dance, usually a narrative poem written in four-line stanzas.

Biography at its most simple, an account of a person's life written by another party. Biographies, however, are much more than simple histories: they are selective and more important, they interpret and have a point of view towards their subjects.

Characterisation the creation of characters in a literary work and the techniques that make characters credible and clear such as their actions, speech, thoughts, appearance, etc.

Comedy generally applied to Drama, usually humorous, and with a 'happy' ending, eg *Twelfth Night*, William Shakespeare.

Couplet two consecutive lines of verse which rhyme, eg 'Had we but world enough and time,/This coyness Lady were no crime.' ('To His Coy Mistress', Andrew Marvell – see page 38).

Diction the choice of words a poet makes to create a particular effect or tone.

Fable a poem or story in which animals often take the place of humans. The purpose of a fable is usually to teach a moral or to make satirical comments on human society, eg Aesop's *Fables*, Orwell's *Animal Farm*.

Genre a term that is used to distinguish between forms of writing (viz poetry, prose, drama); and within forms of writing (viz science fiction, theatre of the absurd, etc).

Haiku a three-line poem of Japanese origin. Strictly the poem should contain seventeen syllables in lines of five, seven and five syllables.

Imagery figures of comparison (metaphors, similes, personification, etc), see the section 'On reading a poem' on page 220.

Irony a form of words in which the intended meaning is the opposite of that expressed by the words used, eg in *Gotcha*! by Barrie Keefe on page 212.

Limerick a poem of five lines, rhyming *aabba*, usually humorous in intent.

Literary writing that shows an awareness of style, use of vocabulary, imagery, etc.

Lyric originally a song but can also mean a short poem which expresses the poet's feelings and ideas.

Metaphor a comparison implied or stated between two usually unconnected objects, see the section 'On reading a poem' on page 220.

Mood the overall emotional effect or feeling of the poem; the impression that the reader is left with when s/he has read it carefully.

Myth a legendary or traditional story, usually one concerning a super-human being and dealing with events that have no natural explanation, eg 'Daedalus and Icarus' by Ovid on page 164.

Onomatopoeia a word that sounds like the object or action being described.

Parable a story with a hidden meaning designed to teach a particular message, eg *The Parable of the Good Samaritan* on page 116.

Paradox a statement which appears contradictory but when considered, contains a great deal of truth, eg 'Cowards die many times before their death.' (*Julius Caesar*, William Shakespeare.)

Personification a type of metaphor, in which inanimate, objects are described in terms of people, eg 'Famine stalked the land'.

Plot the plan, design, scheme or pattern of events in a play, poem or work of fiction; and the organisation of incident and character in such a way as to induce curiosity and suspense in the spectator or reader.

Pun a play on words for humorous effect, eg 'The quality of life depends on the liver'.

Rhetoric an attempt to convince people by using elaborate language either spoken or written, eg Mark Antony's speech in *Julius Caesar* by William Shakespeare on page 132.

Rhyme the effect of two or more words sounding the same, eg Moon/June.

Satire an attempt to ridicule, often with the intention of correcting the defects that are being criticised, eg as in 'The Available Data on the Worp Reaction' by Lion Miller on page 166.

Sarcasm a wounding or cutting remark. The purpose behind the use of sarcasm is to cause pain, whether the criticism is justified or not, eg 'You are a clever boy, Smith' to a careless pupil.

Simile a comparison for the purpose of explanation, allusion or decoration which uses *like* or *as* (see the section 'On reading a poem' on page 220).

Soliloqy a character speaking his/her thoughts aloud when alone, eg in *Dr Faustus* by Christopher Marlowe on page 175.

Sonnet lyric poems consisting of fourteen lines and often ending with a rhyming couplet (see the section 'On reading a poem' on page 220).

Stanza lines of verse which are grouped together to form a pattern which is repeated throughout the poem.

Symbol a simple image or comparison which represents or sums up a much larger idea, eg the Cross as a symbol for Christianity.

Theme a major topic or topics which a work of literature is about, eg the theme of relationships between parents and children in 'My Oedipus Complex' by Frank O'Connor on page 15.

Tone the prevailing feeling or attitude behind a piece of writing, see the section 'On reading a poem' on page 220.

Tragedy a piece of writing which ends badly, often with the downfall and death of the hero, eg *Dr Faustus* by Christopher Marlowe on page 175.

Glossary of language terms

Accent a feature of spoken language, often associated with a part of the country (eg, Geordie (Newcastle), Cockney (London)), or the world (eg American, etc). One particular accent, known as Received Pronunciation (RP), is the spoken language often associated with BBC, Royal Family, Court of Law, Parliament, etc. This accent does not have the same regional base as others.

Acronym a word made from using the initial letters of a scientific invention (RADAR, LASER), an organisation (NATO) or a phrase in common usage (RSVP).

Adjective a word that qualifies a noun or a pronoun, eg a *small* person, he is *small*.

Adverb a word that describes the action of an adjective, verb or another adverb, eg he ran *quickly*, he ran *very quickly*.

Ambiguity a statement that can have two different meetings, eg 'General flies back to Front.'

Clause a distinct part of a sentence that contains a subject and a verb.

Cliché a phrase that has become meaningless because it has been overused, eg 'sick as a parrot' and 'over the Moon'.

Colloquialism language which is particularly informal, more often used in spoken non-standard English, although permissible within speech in writing, eg bloke, feller, geezer.

Conjunction a word used to join clauses within a sentence, eg but, however, and, etc.

Dialect a regional variety of language with its vocabulary and syntax, often spoken in an accent (see **Accent**).

Draft an early, unedited version of a piece of writing.

Euphemism a way of referring to something often thought of as difficult or unpleasant in a discrete way, eg 'He passed away last night.'

Graffiti a very public form of writing, often on walls, railway carriages, bus shelters, etc, with humorous, political or territorial intent, eg 'Sics monthes ago I cudn't spel enginere, now I are wun.', 'Tories Out!', 'Kop Rules OK.'

Grammar a system of rules that governs the use of a language.

Jargon words which belong to a specific sphere of activity (eg computers) often used to mystify the uninvolved, eg 'This hardware has 25 megabyte of RAM on board and the software is menu and mouse driven.'

Loan word a word that has been borrowed from another language, eg bungalow, juggernaut.

Logo a design, sometimes incorporating word or letter shapes, to provide an organisation with an easily recognisable identity.

Noun a word used to denote a person, place or thing, including abstract ideas like 'truth', etc.

Phrase a part of a sentence without a verb.

Preposition a word relating words to each other, eg he sat *at* the table.

Pronoun a word used instead of a noun, eg he, she, it, etc.

Register a form of language appropriate to a particular situation, eg ranging from informal conversation to a form of words in a legal judgement.

Riddle a contrived play on words that provides clues to a concealed meaning – 'Q: What's black and white and red all over? A: A newspaper'.

Sentence a group of words that normally obey the rules of syntax and communicate meaning.

Slang words and phrases that are more informal than colloquialisms. Slang is often identified with particular social or age groups.

Standard English a public and international variety of spoken and written English that conforms to an agreed standard usage. Although, in its spoken form, it can be spoken with regional accents, in its written form it is regionally neutral.

Syntax the way in which words are ordered in a sentence.

Tabloid a newspaper which gives its news in concentrated and easily assimilable form; the popular newspapers (eg *Sun*, *Mirror*) as opposed to the 'qualities' (*Guardian*, *Times*).

Text any written or spoken language presented in any medium.

Verb a word that describes an action, sensation or state of being.

A further reading index

Apart from enabling you to locate quickly major items included in *The Active Reader*, this index will help you to find other stories and poems by many of the writers mentioned or to read the original texts (novels, plays, non-fiction) from which extracts were taken. For the most part, references are to inexpensive (paperback) editions currently in print, and the ISBN number will help a bookshop order the book you want. Occasionally you are referred to an anthology: where this is the case we feel the anthology is interesting in its own right as well as containing other poems by the writer concerned.

Author	Title	Page
Albee, Edward	*Who's Afraid of Virginia Woolf* (1962) Penguin, ISBN 0 14 048061 7	50
Allison, Wm. & Fairley, John	*The Monocled Mutineer* (1979) Quartet, ISBN 0 7043 3287 6	101
Arnold, Matthew	'Dover Beach' (1867) *Poems*, ed. Kenneth Allott (Poetry Library) Penguin, ISBN 0 14 058509 5	206
Auden, W.H.	'The Unknown Citizen' (1939) *Collected Poems* Faber, ISBN 0 571 11396 6	79
Baldwin, Michael	'Death on a Live Wire' *Death on a Live Wire* and *Stepping from a Sixth Storey Window* (1962) Longman	189
Beidler, Martha	'Mohammad Ibrahim Speaks' *The Honey and the Gall: Poems of Married Life* (1967), an anthology, ed. Chad Welsh Macmillan	40
Brecht, Berthold	*The Resistible Rise of Arturo Ui* (1941) Eyre Methuen, ISBN 0 413 47810 6	129
Burns, Jim	'Communiqué to a Child' *The Goldfish Speaks from Beyond the Grave* (1976) The Salamander Imprint, ISBN 0 904632 02 4	90
Cassian, Nina	'A Happening' 'Forgive me for making you weep' *Call Yourself Alive? Love Poems* (1988) Forest Books, ISBN 0 948259 38 8	41 221
Cope, Wendy	'At 3am' 'Lonely Hearts' *Making Cocoa for Kingsley Amis* (1986) Faber, ISBN 0 571 13747 4	223 32

Crystal, David	*The English Language* (1988) Penguin, ISBN 0 14 013532 4	203
Dhondy, Farrukh	'Come to Mecca' *Come to Mecca and Other Stories* (1978) Collins, ISBN 0 00 184134 3	153
Dickens, Charles	*Hard Times* (1854) ed. David Craig (Penguin Classics) Penguin, ISBN 0 14 043042 3	111
Earley, Tom	'Pictures in the Paper' *The Sad Mountain* (1970) Chatto and Windus, ISBN 0 7011 1613	88
Eliot, T.S.	*Murder in the Cathedral* (1935) Faber, ISBN 0 571 06327 6	135
Ghose, Zulfikar	'Geography Lesson' *Jets from Orange* (1967) Macmillan	89
Greene, Graham	'The Destructors' (1954) *Twenty-One Stories* Penguin, ISBN 0 14 003093 X	64
Hardy, Thomas	*Tess of the d'Urbervilles* (1891) ed. David Skilton (Penguin Classics) Penguin, ISBN 0 14 043135 7	216
	'The Darkling Thrush' (1900) 'The Voice' (1912) *Hardy*, ed. David Wright (Poetry Library) Penguin, ISBN 0 14 058538 9	204 221
Henri, Adrian	'In the Midnight Hour' (1967) 'What shall we do with the drunken poet?' (1978) *Collected Poems 1967–85* Allison and Busby, ISBN 0 85031 656 1	35 221
Hoffman, Daniel	'The Centre of Attention' *Poe, Poe, Poe, Poe, Poe, Poe, Poe* (1973) Robson Books, ISBN 0 903895 00 5	186
Holdsworth, Angela	*Out of the Doll's House* (1988) BBC Books, ISBN 0563 20631 4	29

Hopkins, G.M.	'Spring' (1877) *Poems & Prose*, ed. W.H. Gardner Penguin, ISBN 0 14 042015 0	209
Hughes, Ted	'Hill-Stone was Content' *Remains of Elmet* (1979) Faber, ISBN 0 571 11426 1	114
Huxley, Aldous	*Brave New World* (1932) Panther, ISBN 0 586 04434 5	121
Johnson, Linton Kwesi	'Sonny's Lettah' (1980) *News from Babylon: The Chatto Book of Westindian-British Poetry* (1984), an anthology, ed. James Berry Chatto and Windus, ISBN 0 7011 2797 X	47
Johnson, Samuel	*Dictionary of the English Language* (1755) ed. E.L. McAdam & G. Milne Macmillan, ISBN 0 333 32984 8	201
Joyce, James	'Eveline' *Dubliners* (1914) Panther, ISBN 0 586 04476 0	106
Keats, John	'To Autumn' (1818) *Selected Poetry*, ed. John Barnard (Poetry Library) Penguin, ISBN 0 14 058598 2	208
Keefe, Barrie	'Gotcha' (1976) *Gimme Shelter* (1977) Eyre Methuen, ISBN 0 413 38900 6	212
Lawrence, D.H.	*Lady Chatterley's Lover* (1928) Penguin, ISBN 0 14 001484 5	113
Lawrence, D.H.	*The Rainbow* (1915) Penguin, ISBN 0 14 011980 9	45
Leach, Graham	*South Africa* (1987) Methuen, ISBN 0 413 15330 4	81
Lehrer, Tom	'We will all go together when we go' (1958) *Too Many Songs* (1981) Eyre Methuen, ISBN 0 413 48580 3	84
Lessing, Doris	*The Grass is Singing* (1950) Paladin, ISBN 0 586 08924 1	56